INTERMEDIATE
ACCOUNTING

the text of this book is printed
on 100% recycled paper

INTERMEDIATE ACCOUNTING

W. Asquith Howe

Professor of Accounting
School of Business Administration
Temple University

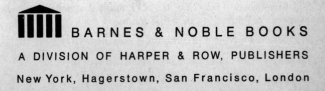
BARNES & NOBLE BOOKS

A DIVISION OF HARPER & ROW, PUBLISHERS

New York, Hagerstown, San Francisco, London

First BARNES & NOBLE BOOKS edition published 1974

ARY OF CONGRESS CATALOG CARD NUMBER: 72–9912

BOOK NUMBER: 06–460143–9

12 11 10 9 8 7 6 5 4 3

Contents

*PART 3: FINANCIAL STATEMENTS AND
THEIR ANALYSES*

Preface

This outline is designed to serve two purposes:

1. It can be used in conjunction with a standard intermediate accounting textbook. It emphasizes the main points normally covered in standard texts and may also enhance the reader's comprehension of the subject by giving a slightly different explanation or presentation. It can serve as a survey of the subject or as a guide for further study in special areas.

2. It provides a brief but comprehensive review for those readers who have had courses in intermediate accounting but who feel the need for a refresher program.

The text material in this outline is brief and to the point. It is accompanied by carefully chosen illustrations. At the end of the text material, there are a few short problems that may be used by the reader to test his comprehension of the material covered. The answers are given so that he may check his work.

The author expresses his appreciation to the American Accounting Association and to the American Institute of Certified Public Accountants, Inc., for their permission to use certain valuable quotations from their literature, lending authenticity to this outline.

INTERMEDIATE ACCOUNTING

CHAPTER 1

Accounting: A Review

Accounting has been variously defined as the "language of business," a "management tool," and an "aid to management."

The American Institute of Certified Public Accountants (AICPA) has defined accounting as follows:

Accounting is the art of recording, classifying, and summarizing in a significant manner and in terms of money, transactions and events which are, in part at least, of a financial character, and interpreting the results thereof.[1]

The American Accounting Association (AAA) has provided the following definition:

Accounting is the process of identifying, measuring, and communicating economic information to permit informed judgments and decisions by users of the information.[2]

Thus, it is evident that accounting embraces the formal design, installation, and operation of a system of accounts in order that business transactions may be properly recorded and reported.

Accounting is basically a service function: that of aiding management and others in making wise decisions and of protecting the firm's assets. Thus, accounting must provide appropriate information in usable form, and it must also provide the means of safeguarding the firm's assets.

The following groups have need of a firm's accounting information:

1. *Accounting Research and Terminology Bulletins,* Final Edition, 1 (1961), p. 9.
2. *A Statement of Basic Accounting Theory* (Evanston, Ill.: American Accounting Association, 1966), p. 1.

1. Management
2. Creditors, actual and prospective
3. Investors, actual and prospective
4. Stockholders
5. Employees, unions
6. Regulatory and taxing authorities

The firm's assets may be safeguarded through the application of internal and external controls based largely on accounting data.

ACCOUNTING PRINCIPLES AND POSTULATES

The primary functions of accounting are to record, classify, summarize, and interpret accounting data in a significant manner. If general reliance is to be placed on such data, it must be accumulated and analyzed in conformity with a body of generally accepted rules. In recent years, teachers and practitioners of accounting, as well as accounting groups, have devoted a great deal of time and effort to developing a practical yet theoretical structure for accounting from diverse and often-conflicting doctrines, definitions, and terminology. This has been made more difficult because of the dynamic nature of business. Because business is changing, the needs of business served by accounting are changing. Therefore, the structure and philosophy of accounting must change in order to satisfy the changing demands of business.

Some accountants hold that there are three basic levels or tiers in accounting: postulates, rules, and principles. Others believe that there are only two levels: postulates (which includes rules) and principles.

Accounting Postulates. *Accounting postulates* are basic assumptions used in developing the system of thought or the philosophy necessary to the establishment of an organized accounting structure. The validity of a postulate is taken for granted or generally admitted as self-evident. It thus serves as a basis for further theoretical development. Postulates are selected for their usefulness in this development.

Accounting postulates are few in number. They or the rules developed from them are the basis on which accounting principles are built. Because accounting is dynamic, it is to be expected that accounting postulates will change over time.

Accounting Rules. *Accounting rules* are held by the majority of accountants to be synonymous with postulates. A smaller group of accountants believes that they are established methods or instructions developed from postulates for solving a particular problem or meeting a given situation. A rule is more objective and admits less discretion on the part of the practitioner than a principle does.

Accounting Principles. *Accounting principles* are the basic body of premises that control accounting theory and practice. They are the general truths and laws developed from postulates and rules. The validity of principles is not self-evident, as is the case with postulates, but depends on the general acceptance by the accounting profession. Accounting principles are not immutable; they may change as the dynamic profession and society dictate.

In order for a person to be able to read and interpret correctly accounting data and the financial statements prepared from such data, he must understand and be familiar with the *generally accepted accounting principles*.

A word of caution: The demarcation between postulates, rules, and principles is not so clear-cut as may be desired. Also, other terms such as *axioms, concepts,* and *conventions* are sometimes used indiscriminately instead of postulates, rules, or principles.

SCOPE OF ACCOUNTING

An effective accounting system is of the utmost importance to management in carrying out its responsibility for successfully planning and controlling the operations of a firm. In order to be most useful to management, such a system must provide not only data for effective planning and control of the firm but also sufficient data for the preparation of correct and informative financial statements. These statements must be prepared according to generally accepted accounting principles and also in a form that will be useful to the various interest groups. The major typical interest groups are management, owners, creditors and potential creditors, employees, and public agencies.

Management requires accounting data in order to evaluate past operations and policies, plan future operations, and protect the assets of the firm adequately.

Owners require reliable accounting data, usually confined to published statements, in order to evaluate properly the performance of management and the quality of their investment.

Creditors and potential creditors rely on financial statements in estimating the amount of risk involved in granting credit to the particular firm.

Employees, often through their unions, rely heavily on the firm's financial statements in determining whether or not they are receiving a fair share of the firm's earnings for their labors.

Various public agencies, such as regulatory and taxing authorities, must rely heavily on a firm's accounting data as a basis for their findings.

Accounting is a profession per se and as such enjoys professional prestige quite comparable with that of medicine, law, and engineering. In addition, accounting is closely related to other areas of business. Individuals involved in finance, banking, production, management, marketing, engineering, and so forth find a knowledge of accounting and its applications very helpful.

As a body of knowledge that is deeply involved in many different business and economic areas, accounting must develop along two lines: (1) In order to satisfy the general needs of business and society, accounting must provide a body of general or survey-type knowledge that is useful to the layman as well as to the practicing accountant. (2) However, because of the complexity of business organizations today, a vast amount of complex and specialized data is needed. It was, therefore, imperative that accounting develop in-depth bodies of knowledge and techniques in specialized areas for the use of the respective specialists. It is true that just as accounting in general cannot operate successfully if it is isolated from other areas of business, so too, a specialized area of accounting cannot operate successfully and efficiently if it is isolated from other areas of accounting. There is, of necessity, some overlapping of specialties. However, a number of specialized areas of accounting are commonly recognized. The groups described in the following paragraphs are typical but not all-inclusive.

Financial Accounting. *Financial accounting*, sometimes referred to as *general accounting,* deals with the overall accounting systems and procedures of the firm or economic unit. This area involves the preparation of the general financial statements, the most common being the income statement and the balance sheet. If the firm is a holding company, the financial accountants are charged with the preparation of appropriate consolidated statements. A primary goal of financial accounting is the determination of the firm's profit.

Cost Accounting. *Cost accounting* involves primarily the determination and control of costs. Because large manufacturing firms incur the largest amount and greatest variety of costs, together with a great need for the proper allocation of such costs, cost accounting has sometimes been referred to erroneously as *manufacturing accounting.* A common brief definition that is in accord with the fact that, in present-day society, costs are incurred in many areas other than manufacturing (even charitable and nonprofit organizations incur costs) is: Cost accounting is the accounting for costs wherever they may be found.

The primary functions of the cost accountant are to accumulate, allocate, and interpret cost data, both *actual* (past) and *anticipated* (budgeted, planned), in the most effective and useful manner. Such data are very valuable to management in controlling current operations and in planning for the future.

Managerial (Management) Accounting. *Managerial accounting,* sometimes referred to as *administrative accounting,* is designed to provide information and control at the various administrative levels. Managerial accounting involves the preparation of a vast variety of reports in terms of money and/or other quantities that are intended primarily for internal use by management, as contrasted with the limited number of general-purpose statements developed by the financial accountants that are intended basically (but not exclusively) for external use.

In managerial accounting, both actual past costs and expected future costs are used as a basis for planning day-by-day operations and for developing future programs. Managerial accounting can be very useful in providing and interpreting data as a basis for the determination of alternate courses of action and policy making.

Tax Accounting. *Tax accounting* involves primarily the timely preparation of the firm's many and varied tax returns. In addition to preparing these records, the tax accountant must be able to advise management of the tax consequences of various proposed business transactions and, if possible, to suggest alternative courses of action that would result in more favorable tax impacts. In order to do this effectively, an individual must be an expert not only in accounting but also in current tax law.

Auditing. Auditing is the specialized area of accounting that deals with examination and review of the accounting records and activities of the firm. Such reviews may be conducted by employees of the firm, known as *internal auditors,* or by independent accountants, referred to also as *independent* or *external auditors.*

Originally, auditing was conceived of as essentially a means of discovering errors and fraud and thus of reducing such occurrences. Today, the audit function is concerned with accounting systems and procedures and their effectiveness, as well as with management policies and procedures.

EXTERNAL AUDITING. *External auditing* is the review or examination conducted by a practicing accountant who, rather than having an employee-employer relationship with the firm, has a professional practitioner-client relationship with the firm. Such audits are usually conducted by a *certified public accountant* (CPA) with the objective of forming an opinion of the fairness of the statements and giving consideration to the consistency of application of generally accepted accounting principles in their preparation. At the conclusion of the audit, the auditor may give an unqualified or a qualified opinion, or he may give a disclaimer, depending on his findings during the audit.

INTERNAL AUDITING. *Internal auditing* is performed by a firm's own employees. It is a staff function, the purpose of which is to appraise and evaluate the firm's records, controls, and operations. Thus, it is one aspect of internal control. The internal audit is relatively independent in that the internal auditors report to an officer of the firm rather than to a person whose functions are subject to audit.

In a *departmental* internal audit, all the varied activities of a particular department are reviewed. In a *functional* internal audit, all the activities of a particular function are reviewed. Departmental lines are ignored, and all or at least several of the firm's departments are involved with respect to the particular function.

Budgeting. *Budgeting* is the preparation of a plan. In accounting, it is common to express such plans in monetary terms. However, it may be desirable to prepare some budgets in units other than money or in money and also other units, such as man-hours, tons, gallons, or yards.

The greatest value of a budget lies in the fact that it is usually a formalized plan of operations; thus, it provides management with an element of control over such operations.

ACCOUNTING AND RELATED ORGANIZATIONS

Accounting is generally considered to be one of the most rapidly expanding professions today. It is to be expected that such a large and expanding profession would create a number of accounting or accounting-related organizations. Those discussed in the following paragraphs are among the most important.

American Accounting Association (AAA). The American Accounting Association was founded in Columbus, Ohio, in 1916, as the American Association of University Instructors in Accounting. The organization was renamed the American Accounting Association in 1936 because of the change in the composition of its membership. Although membership is now open to anyone interested in accounting, professors of accounting make up the vast majority of the membership. Most of the other members are practicing accountants, public or private. There are also some student members. The organization has well over 10,000 members. The annual national meeting is held in late August, usually on a college campus.

The association publishes a quarterly magazine, the *Accounting Review*, as well as monographs on accounting.

American Institute of Certified Public Accountants (AICPA). When the American Institute of Certified Public Accountants was founded in 1887, it was known as the American Association of Public Accountants. The name was changed to the American Institute of Accountants in 1916 and to the present one in 1936. Although membership is restricted to certified public accountants, it exceeds 80,000. The organization publishes a monthly magazine, the *Journal of Accountancy*.

From 1939 to 1959, the group published over fifty *Accounting Research and Terminology Bulletins*. In 1959, the committee on accounting procedure and the committee on terminology was replaced by the Accounting Principles Board (APB) which assumed the responsibilities of the former committees. Since that time, it has conducted a number of research studies and has issued a number of opinions. In 1973 the APB was superseded by the *Financial Accounting Standards Board* (FASB) as the body to establish accounting principles.

Institute of Chartered Accountants. This is the United Kingdom's counterpart to the AICPA.

Financial Executives Institute (FEI). The Controllers' Institute was founded in New York in 1931. In 1962, the name was changed to the Financial Executives Institute. In order to qualify for membership, an individual must be an executive officer carrying out the functions of a controller or treasurer in an eligible firm. A firm must meet minimum size requirements, measured in one or more of several ways, in order to be eligible. Also, a limited number of associate memberships are granted to educators. The group maintains an active research foundation to further the art and science of controllership and treasurership. Its monthly publication is entitled the *Financial Executive*.

National Association of Accountants (NAA). The National Association of Cost Accountants was founded in Buffalo, New York, in 1919. Originally, membership was supposed to be restricted to cost accountants. However, the restrictions were gradually eased until membership was opened to anyone interested in accounting. In line with this change, the name was changed to the National Association of Accountants in 1957. This is the largest accounting association in the United States. Its annual national meeting is held in June. The group publishes a monthly magazine entitled *NAA Management Accounting*.

Securities and Exchange Commission (SEC). The Securities and Exchange Commission, created by the Securities Exchange Act of 1934, administers the federal laws regulating securities for the protection of investors. The commission requires publicly held corporations issuing securities to file a registration statement and prospectus giving detailed financial information about the company. This helps to promote uniform standards and to prevent unfair practices in regulated companies. Thus, even though the commission has not directly participated in the development of accounting principles, it has had great indirect bearing on accounting principles and reporting.

Internal Revenue Service (IRS). Although not an accounting organization, the IRS affects accounting theory and practice to such a degree that it should be considered a related organization. The IRS has the responsibility of collecting federal revenues from a multitude of sources. However, its best-known and largest source is the federal income tax. For many years, the federal income tax has drained off such large amounts of the before-tax profits that the tax laws have had a profound effect on accounting methods and procedures.

PART 1

Assets

Assets may be defined as anything tangible or intangible that is owned and that has monetary value. Any property, property right, or claim owned that has value in terms of money, either at the present time or in the future, is an asset. It should be pointed out, however, that some property (in the broad sense) is not considered an asset, either because it lacks monetary value or because the owner has not assigned a monetary value to it (e.g., goodwill).

The following definition of an asset is provided by the AICPA:

Something represented by a debit balance that is or would be properly carried forward upon a closing of books of account according to the rules or principles of accounting (provided such debit balance is not in effect a negative balance applicable to a liability) on the basis that it represents either a property right or value acquired, or an expenditure made which has created a property right or is properly applicable to the future. Thus, plant, accounts receivable, inventory, and a deferred charge are all assets in balance-sheet classification.[1]

The usual major groupings of assets are:

1. Current assets
2. Noncurrent assets
3. Deferred charges

Normally, assets are presented on the balance sheet in the order of liquidity, with the exception of deferred charges, which because of their usual immateriality are presented last.

1. *Accounting Research and Terminology Bulletins,* Final Edition, 1 (1961), p. 13.

CHAPTER 2

Current Assets: Cash and Receivables

Current assets consist of unrestricted cash or other assets that will be converted into cash or used in lieu of cash within the next operating cycle or year, whichever is longer, or assets generally considered current in that particular trade or business.

The AICPA has provided the profession with the following definition of current assets:

For purposes of accounting, the term *current assets* is used to designate cash or other assets or resources commonly identified as those which are reasonably expected to be realized in cash or sold or consumed during the normal operating cycle of the business. The term comprehends in general such resources as (a) cash available for current operations and items which are the equivalent of cash; (b) inventories of merchandise, raw materials, goods in process, finished goods, operating supplies, and ordinary maintenance material and parts; (c) trade discounts, notes and acceptances receivable; (d) receivables from officers, employees, affiliates, and others, if collectible in the ordinary course of business within a year; (e) installment or deferred accounts and notes receivable if they conform generally to normal trade practices and terms within the business; (f) marketable securities representing the investment of cash available for current operations; and (g) prepaid expenses such as insurance, interest, rents, taxes, unused royalties, and operating supplies.[1]

CASH

Cash is generally considered the most liquid of current assets; therefore, it is usually listed first on the left-hand side of the balance sheet.

1. Ibid., p. 20.

Accounting Concept of Cash. This concept is more comprehensive than a mere definition of the term *cash,* and it should be considered separately from cash management.

DEFINITION OF CASH. *Cash* is legal tender, coin and specie, negotiable money orders and checks, demand-deposit balances in banks, and currently, under some conditions, even time deposit balances—any medium of exchange that a bank will accept for deposit. The term *cash* used without a restrictive word or phrase implies that it is immediately available for any ordinary use by the firm and, hence, qualifies as a current asset.

CASH: AN ACCOUNT TITLE. Cash as an account title or as a balance-sheet item implies a lack of restriction on the use of the cash; that is, it is available for current operating needs. Cash that is restricted as to use should be designated and reported separately. Such restricted cash should be reported as a current asset if it is to be used for a current purpose, to liquidate a current liability, or to liquidate a current installment of a long-term liability that is treated as a current liability.

Cash not available for current purposes—such as funds set aside for the retirement of a noncurrent debt or capital stock, for the purchase of long-term assets, or even for the retirement of a current installment of a long-term debt that has not been classified as a current liability—should be classified as a noncurrent asset.

ITEMS IMPROPERLY TREATED AS CASH. Some items often but improperly treated as cash are postage stamps, IOUs or cash-due memos, postdated checks, and checks deposited but returned because of insufficient funds in the debtor's account.

Postage stamps may properly be considered a current asset, but because they do not meet the cash requirement for acceptability by bankers, they cannot correctly be considered as cash.

IOUs, cash-due memos, and advances to employees lack depositability and therefore cannot properly be considered cash. They may be considered current assets if collection is expected within a year; otherwise, they should be considered noncurrent assets.

A postdated check cannot be deposited before the date indicated on the check, and therefore, either should not be recorded at all before this date or should be recorded as a note receivable until it can be deposited. Checks returned by the bank because of insufficient funds can no longer be treated as cash, and the entry crediting the customer or client should be reversed upon the return of such a check.

Cash Management. In recent years, the management of cash has been given increasing consideration. Cash management involves much more than the recording of cash flows in and out. It entails any and all management functions having to do with the control, safeguarding, effective planning, and use of cash. In order to attain these goals, various budgets, analyses, and reports are utilized. It may be said that cash management involves the following major functions:

1. Determination of an effective minimum cash balance
2. Advantageous borrowing practices and procedures
3. Effective investment of temporary or permanent excess cash
4. Acceleration of cash inflows
5. Efficient control and safeguarding of all cash

Cash per se is not a productive asset. Its value lies in what it can do for the firm. Because idle funds produce no revenue, good management dictates that only cash sufficient to pay obligations as they come due be kept on hand (and in the bank). Of course, all discounts should be taken. All excess cash should be invested temporarily. Keeping idle cash at a minimum and yet always having sufficient cash available to meet daily needs is a constant, important management problem. In order to solve this problem, management needs as much information as promptly as possible regarding the amounts and the timing of expected cash receipts and disbursements.

INTERNAL CONTROL OF CASH. Control of cash includes the control of the use of cash, the verification of cash balances, and the timely discovery and rectification of errors and misapplications of cash. Because cash is difficult to identify, easy to conceal and has universal appeal, it is the most difficult asset to control.

Basic to an internal-control program are the promotion of efficiency in operations, increased accuracy in record keeping, timely correction of errors, and prevention and early detection of fraud. In applying such a program to the control of cash, consideration must be given to the following functions:

1. Adequate accounting for cash received
2. Adequate accounting for cash disbursed
3. Adequate protection of cash balances against unauthorized or improper withdrawal

The separation of duties and responsibilities is an essential feature of any internal-control system. In order to control cash effectively, the responsibility for the physical handling of the cash should be assigned to the treasurer, and the responsibility for recording and accounting for cash should be assigned to the controller or chief accountant.

Although the system of internal control of cash must be adapted to the needs of the particular firm, the following specific steps are considered essential in most systems:

1. Immediate recording of cash.
2. Daily intact depositing of receipts.
3. Making all disbursements by check, including the replenishment of petty cash and other imprest funds (any special-purpose funds that must be restored periodically to a predetermined level) by checks drawn against the general cash account.
4. Making minor cash disbursements only from imprest funds.
5. Signing checks only when supported by documented evidence that the disbursement is proper. In order to prevent duplicate payment, an indication of payment should be placed on the document when payment is made.
6. Separating the responsibility of the function of handling the cash from that of recording the cash. If the firm is large enough to afford an internal auditor, this third person or group should make surprise audits of the cash and the cash records.

DAILY CASH REPORT. A *daily cash report* is indispensable in forecasting cash receipts, disbursements, and balances. The format for such a report is not standardized; it is tailored to meet the conditions and needs of the particular firm involved.

The following simple form of a daily cash report is self-explanatory:

THE DO RITE COMPANY

DAILY CASH REPORT
JUNE 16, 1973

Balance from previous report		
First National Bank		$ 1,000
First State Bank		1,500
Cash on hand		500
Total		$ 3,000
Collections		
Cash sales	$10,000	
Accounts receivable	8,000	
Short-term loans	1,000	
Other	2,000	
Total collections		21,000
Total available cash		$24,000
Disbursements		
Accounts payable	$ 9,000	
Loan repayments	5,000	
Payroll	4,000	
Other	1,000	
Total disbursements		19,000
Balance, end of day		
First National Bank	$ 2,000	
First State Bank	1,500	
Cash on hand	1,500	
Total balance		$ 5,000

BANK RECONCILIATION. The balance at the end of the month as shown on a depositor's bank statement and as shown in the depositor's records rarely agree. The amount reported on the depositor's balance sheet as cash in bank should be the amount arrived at after adjustments have been made for correcting the errors made by the depositor as well as for the time lag in receiving data from the bank. Usually, because of the communication delays between the two parties, neither the balance reported on the bank statement nor the preliminary balance developed by the depositor will show the correct balance.

There are four general reasons, in addition to errors, for the differences between the unadjusted balances reported by the bank and by the depositor.

1. Items already charged (added) by the depositor but not yet credited (added) by the bank; for example, a deposit recorded at the end of the month by the depositor but not recorded by the bank until the next month

2. Items already credited (deducted) by the depositor but not yet charged (deducted) by the bank; for example, checks drawn and issued by the depositor but which have not yet cleared the bank

3. Items already credited (added) by the bank but not yet charged (added) by the depositor; for example, the collection by the bank of a note or draft for the depositor without notification to the depositor until the presentation of the bank statement

4. Items already charged (deducted) by the bank but not yet credited (deducted) by the depositor; for example, a bank service charge of which the depositor is not informed until the receipt of the bank statement

An example of a bank reconciliation statement follows:

THE JONES COMPANY
BANK RECONCILIATION—FIRST NATIONAL BANK
DECEMBER 31, 1973

Balance per bank statement, December 31, 1973		$10,545.65
Add		
Deposit in transit, December 31	$1,345.00	
James Co. check to Jones Co. in error	500.00	1,845.00
		$12,390.65
Deduct		
Outstanding checks		
No. 1145	$ 300.30	
No. 1163	125.50	
No. 1221	200.00	625.80
Corrected (bank) balance		$11,764.85
Balance per books, December 31, 1973		$ 6,947.10
Add		
Proceeds of Brown Co. draft collected by bank	$5,000.75	
Check on Green Co. for $96 recorded as a deposit for $69	27.00	5,027.75
		$11,974.85
Deduct		
Bank service charge	$ 10.00	
Williams Co. check returned because of insufficient funds	200.00	210.00
Corrected (book) balance		$11,764.85

The following entries would be required on the Jones Company's books to correct its cash balances:

Cash	$5,000.75	
Drafts receivable—Brown Co.		$5,000.75
Cash	27.00	
Accounts receivable—Green Co.		27.00
Bank service charges	10.00	
Cash		10.00
Accounts receivable—Williams Co.	200.00	
Cash		200.00

It should be observed that no entries showing additions or deductions from the bank balance are required in order to arrive at the corrected (bank) balance.

BANK OVERDRAFT. A *bank overdraft* is the amount a depositor owes a bank because the bank has honored the depositor's checks for amounts in excess of his deposits. In effect, an overdraft creates an involuntary non-interest-bearing loan by the bank on the initiation of the depositor. It constitutes a current liability of the bank's patron and should be reported as such on his financial statements. The overdraft at one bank cannot properly be offset against the debit balances in other banks in order to report only the net debit balance of bank accounts. However, if a depositor has two or more unrestricted accounts with one bank and he has overdrawn one of them while there is a greater debit balance in the other, he may exercise the *right of offset* and report a net debit balance.

KITING. *Kiting* is the act of drawing an unrecorded check on one bank, followed shortly by an unrecorded deposit, usually in the form of another unrecorded check drawn on another bank; thus, the time it takes checks to clear the banks is utilized to conceal a cash shortage, an overdraft, or unauthorized "borrowing." The process may be repeated a number of times, involving different banks. Each such maneuver affords the kiter several days' use of another's money before the shortage is detected or before a final covering deposit is made. This practice cannot occur in situations in which banks disallow withdrawals against uncollected deposits.

RECEIVABLES

The term *receivables* may be applied in a broad sense to all claims one party has against other parties. In accounting, the term is usually applied in the narrow sense to only those claims that are expected to be settled with money in the ordinary course of business.

Receivables may be separated into two classifications:

1. *Accounts receivable:* those claims for which no formal written evidence of the claim signed by the debtor exists

2. *Notes receivable, bills of exchange,* and *trade acceptances receivable:* those claims for which a formal written promise or order to pay a sum certain in money signed by the debtor exists

Technically notes receivable, bills of exchange, and trade acceptances receivable differ, but it is not unusual to group them under the general heading notes receivable.

Although it would be appropriate to refer to claims arising from the sale of goods or services to customers as "accounts receivable—trade" or "notes receivable—trade," through custom it has become acceptable accounting practice to exclude by implication from accounts receivable and notes receivable any claims of material amounts not arising from the sale of goods or services in the ordinary course of business. Accounts or notes originating from other transactions should be given appropriate descriptive account titles. Thus, the sale of merchandise on account to an officer of the firm may be included in accounts receivable; whereas a cash advance to the officer should be included in a special account such as advanced to officers.

Claims arising from the sale of merchandise or services are considered current if it is expected that they will be collected within the operating cycle, even though the operating cycle is longer than a year. Other receivables should be classified as current or noncurrent strictly according to the *one-year rule.* Thus, receivables originating from installment sales may be classed as current assets, although the collection of a given installment contract may extend over three or four years. However, if the amount of such contracts is material, some indication of the maturity of the claims should be provided in the financial statements. Thus, an advance to an officer would be considered current only if it is expected that it will be collected within one year; otherwise, it should be classified as noncurrent.

Accounts Receivable. An *account receivable* is the amount owed to a firm or person by another firm or person (the debtor), generally on an open account, and usually limited to claims arising from the sales of goods or services in the ordinary course of business. The title "accounts receivable" may also be applied in the general ledger to the control account for the subsidiary ledger for such receivables.

A receivable for the sale of merchandise should be recognized when the title to the goods passes. Thus, when goods are shipped on approval (title remaining with the seller) or on consignment, the goods are still considered part of the potential seller's inventory, and only a memorandum entry is made until the title actually passes.

A receivable for services rendered to a customer, client, or patient should be recognized at the time the service is rendered. Certain receivables may be accrued as rent or interest earned but not yet received.

VALUATION OF ACCOUNTS RECEIVABLE. Theoretically, receivables, whether open accounts or notes, should be carried at their net realizable value. However, for practical reasons, certain adjustments involving small amounts are omitted in the valuation procedure.

In valuing the total accounts receivable, deductions may be made for the following:

1. Uncollectible accounts
2. Freight-out and possible freight-in on returns
3. Returns and allowances
4. Cash discounts
5. Discount to present value

Deductions for uncollectible accounts are made frequently. Deductions for freight, returns and allowances, and cash discounts are made infrequently. Theoretically, it is correct to discount the expected amount to be collected in the future in order to establish the present value of the receivable to be reported; however, because of the small amount involved, it is rarely done, if ever.

The chief problem in valuing accounts receivable is the establishment of the time at which the loss on an uncollectible account should be recognized. The estimated loss may be provided for (recognized) at the time the sale is made; this is referred to as the *allowance method*. Or the recognition of the loss (actually sustained) may be deferred until the account is determined to be uncollectible; this is referred to as the *direct write-off method*.

Allowance Method. Most large firms use the allowance method because although it has the disadvantage of requiring estimates of future losses, the timing of the recognition of the loss is much better than it is by the direct write-off method. The loss, although estimated, is matched against the revenue of the period in which the loss occurred. It should be pointed out here that there is general agreement among accountants that a loss on sales on account is incurred when the sale is made rather than at some future time when the receivable is determined to be uncollectible.

When the allowance method of recognizing losses is used, periodic adjustments are made in anticipation of future actual losses (write-offs). This entry would result in a charge to loss on bad debts and a credit to allowance for loss on bad debts for an estimated amount of loss. Then, when a specific account is determined to be uncollectible, the following entry (which will not affect income) would be made:

Allowance for loss on bad debts	XX	
Accounts receivable (John Doe)		XX

If the account written off by an entry such as the one just shown is collected later within the same period as the write-off, or if the amount involved is small, the collection may be recorded by reversing the write-off entry, followed by an entry charging cash. The recovery of a substantial amount subsequent to the period of the write-off would require the following entries:

Accounts receivable (John Doe)	XX	
Accounts written off in prior periods		XX
Cash	XX	
Accounts receivable (John Doe)		XX

Direct Write-off Method. The direct write-off method has the advantage of simplicity and exactness, in that no adjustment or allowance is made for a reduction in the value of a receivable until the specific receivable is known to have lost value. At this time, a simple journal entry is made debiting loss on bad debts, and crediting accounts receivable for the amount of the determined loss. In the event the written-off account is collected later, the entry recording the write-off is reversed.

The direct write-off method has a serious disadvantage: poor timing in the recognition of the loss. Good accounting theory dictates that revenues and expenses (or losses) be matched as closely as possible period by period. Under the direct write-off method, this is not likely to be accomplished because often a sale on account is made in one period and the loss is not determined until some future period.

BAD DEBT ADJUSTMENT BASED ON SALES. Accounts receivable are generated by sales on account. Therefore, it follows that the loss due to uncollectible accounts results from sales on account. A relationship as a percentage of sales may be established between expected loss (based on past experience and modified by an evaluation of current conditions) and account sales. The percentage applied to the amount of sales on account for the period yields the amount that should be charged to bad debt expense and credited to the allowance for bad debts. Since a loss on bad debts cannot result from cash sales, it is logical that the percentage used in calculating the loss be developed from and applied to sales on account only. However, if the ratio of account sales to total sales remains fairly constant period after period, essentially the same results may be obtained by using total sales instead of sales on account only. For example, if total sales are divided equally between account sales and cash sales, the estimated loss will be the same whether the loss is calculated at 2 percent of total sales or 4 percent of account sales.

BAD DEBT ADJUSTMENT BASED ON RECEIVABLES. Bad debt adjustments based on receivables may be developed by either of two common methods:

1. Raising the balance in the allowance for bad debts account to an amount established by aging the accounts receivable

2. Raising the balance in the allowance for bad debts to a given percentage of accounts receivable

The adjustment based on sales emphasizes the determination of a loss, whereas the adjustment based on accounts receivable emphasizes the valuation of an asset.

Aging Accounts Receivable. An effective way of determining the adequacy of the allowance for bad debts is to age the accounts receivable. Even though it may be agreed that the loss actually occurred when the sale was made, there is a close correlation between the length of time an account is past due and its collectibility. Under the *aging method,* a schedule should be prepared on which all accounts receivable are analyzed according to due date. The following schedule is typical:

AMES COMPANY

ANALYSIS OF ACCOUNTS RECEIVABLE
DECEMBER 31, 1973

| Customer | Total | Not Due | Days Past Due | | | | | |
			0–30	31–60	61–90	91–180	181–365	Over 365
Ace	$1,000	$ 500	$200	$300				
Barker	2,000	500	500		$1,000			
Cantor	500					$500		
Day	500						$100	$400
Engel	1,500	1,500						
Total	$5,500	$2,500	$700	$300	$1,000	$500	$100	$400
Uncollectible rate		0	1%	2%	4%	5%	10%	50%
Uncollectible amount	$ 288		$ 7	$ 6	$ 40	$ 25	$ 10	$200

Based on the aging of the accounts receivable of the Ames Company, the balance in the allowance account after adjustment should be $288. Therefore, if the preadjustment balance is $40, the adjusting entry should be as follows:

| Loss on bad debts | $248 | |
| Allowance for loss on bad debts | | $248 |

Percentage of Accounts Receivable. Calculating the amount of uncollectibles on the balance of the accounts receivable is intended to accomplish the same results as aging the receivables. However, this method lacks the accuracy of the aging method in that it uses an average rate of uncollectibility rather than a series of rates applicable to a series of balances arrayed according to age. Calculating the uncollectibles on the balance of the accounts receivable is based on the assumption that a certain portion of the accounts will be uncollectible without much regard to age.

Proper Balance in the Allowance Account. The adjusted balance in the allowance for loss from bad debts account should be such that when it is deducted from the balance of accounts receivable, the result will closely approximate the realizable value of the accounts receivable. If the balance of the allowance for loss of bad debts account is too large, the asset accounts receivable—net is understated, the expense loss on bad debts is overstated, and the rate of charge-off is too high. If the balance in the allowance account is too low, the opposite is true.

Usually, when a substantial adjustment to the allowance account is required, it is because of an accumulation of errors over several accounting periods. For example, if it is determined that the allowance account is too large by $5,000, of which $4,000 is due to an overstatement of expenses in prior periods, the adjusting entry would be as follows:

Allowance for loss on bad debts	$5,000	
Loss on bad debts		$5,000

As a practical matter, if the balance in the allowance account is not too much out of line when the error is discovered, the correction may be made over the next several periods, simply by adjusting the rate of accumulation; that is, if the amount of the allowance is too large, the rate should be reduced; if the accumulated balance is too small, the rate should be increased. This method is acceptable to the IRS.

USE OF ACCOUNTS RECEIVABLE FOR RAISING IMMEDIATE CASH. Under usual operating procedures, cash for current operations is obtained from the collection of accounts receivable in due course. It is possible to accelerate the conversion of receivables into cash and thus to reduce the amount of working capital required by borrowing against the receivables or by factoring them. Both procedures are forms of hypothecation.

Borrowing against Receivables. Borrowing against receivables may be informal or formal. A firm may negotiate a loan and simply pledge the receivables as collateral. Such an informal arrangement usually requires that as the receivables are collected, the proceeds will be used to retire the loan for which they were pledged as collateral. In a formal arrangement, specific receivables are assigned by the owner (assigner) to the lender (assignee) at the time a note is signed by the assigner. Such an assignment gives the assignee the same rights of collection as those possessed by the assigner. Usually, the assigner assumes and retains the credit risk and collection function; that is, the assignment is made "with recourse." Normally, the creditor is not notified of the assignment, and he continues to make the payments to the assigner. Such assignments are said to be on a *nonnotification* basis.

As the assigner collects the assigned accounts, the checks are endorsed and forwarded to the assignee. The assignee, by arrangement with the bank, either uses a code endorsement or no endorsement on depositing these checks. Thus, the debtors are not aware of the assignment, even when their canceled checks are returned.

Depending upon the assignee's evaluation of the receivables, the assignee may advance from 70 to 95 percent of the gross value of the receivables assigned. Usually, when a particular assigned account becomes very delinquent or uncollectible, the assigner is asked to accept its release and either to provide another account in its stead or to give the assignee a check for the amount of the poor account.

Assigned accounts should be transferred to a separate subsidiary ledger. The general ledger should include an account for accounts receivable—assigned and a contra-account notes payable to assignee.

The following example illustrates an assignment: The Green Sales Company assigned $100,000 of accounts receivable to the Business Finance Company on January 2. The finance company agreed to advance 90 percent of the face value of the accounts, less a 2 percent discount charge. Collections were to be forwarded to the finance company at the end of each month. It was agreed that interest of 1 percent per month would be allowed on the unpaid balance. The sales company collected $50,000 during January and $30,000 during February. The journal entries should be as follows:

Jan. 2	Accounts receivable—assigned	$100,000	
	Accounts receivable		$100,000
	To record the transfer of the accounts to a special subsidiary ledger		
Jan. 2	Cash	88,000	
	Finance charges	2,000	
	Note payable—Business Finance Co.		90,000
	To record issuance of a note for 90% of assigned receivables and receipt of cash		
Jan. 31	Cash	50,000	
	Accounts receivable—assigned		50,000
	To record collections on assigned receivables		
Jan. 31	Note payable—Business Finance Co.	49,100	
	Interest expense	900	
	Cash		50,000
	To record payment of note and monthly interest		
Feb. 28	Cash	30,000	
	Accounts receivable—assigned		30,000
	To record collection on assigned receivables		
Feb. 28	Note payable—Business Finance Co.	29,591	
	Interest expense	409	
	Cash		30,000
	To record payment on note and monthly interest		

The balance sheet as of February 28 should show the following data in the current assets section.

Accounts receivable		$xxxxx
Accounts receivable—assigned	$20,000	
Less: Note payable—Business Finance Co.	11,309	
Equity in assigned receivables		8,691
Total equity in receivables		$xxxxx

Factoring Accounts Receivable. Factoring is a special type of financing whereby a finance company or bank (a *factor*) buys outright, and usually without recourse, accounts receivable for which the finance company or bank pays cash. Generally, factoring is done on a notification basis; that is, the customers whose accounts are sold are notified of the transfer, and they are instructed to pay the factor directly. Under a continuing factoring contract, it is customary for the factor either to check the credit of each debtor before purchasing the account, or the factor assumes the credit-granting function for his client, who then sells on account only to those customers whose credit has been approved by the factor.

The factor performs a number of services for his client for which he receives commissions and interest that often approximate 20 percent of the factored receivables. On the surface, a 20 percent "interest charge" may appear excessive; but when considered in the light of the services rendered, it may be reasonable. A factor may render the following services:

1. Provide cash quickly, making it possible for the client to operate with less working capital
2. Provide the credit-granting function and absorb losses resulting from poor credit risks
3. Provide the collection function
4. Provide the bookkeeping service

Factoring originated, and is frequently used, in the textile industry. Since World War II, it has spread to many other industries.

Other Receivables. Other common forms of receivables are notes receivable, bills of exchange, and acceptances receivable. Notes receivables are promises to pay; whereas bills of exchange are orders to pay. Bills of exchange become acceptances when accepted by the drawee.

NOTES RECEIVABLE. A *note* is defined by the Uniform Negotiable Instruments Act as follows:

A negotiable promissory note within the meaning of this act is an unconditional promise in writing made by one person to another, signed by the maker, engaging to pay on demand or at a fixed or determinable future time a sum certain in money to order or to bearer.

Notes receivable are usually shown in the accounts and on the balance sheet at their face value, regardless of whether they are interest-bearing or non-interest-bearing. Because of the time value of money, a non-interest-bearing note (or one bearing interest at substantially lower than the prevailing rate) will be worth less than its face value before maturity. However, this fact is usually ignored in valuing notes. Notes receivable often are a quicker source of cash than accounts receivable are, because notes receivable are more easily discounted at banks than open accounts are.

Collection of Notes at Maturity. When a note is collected at maturity, the following journal entry is made by the holder:

Cash	xx	
Interest income		xx
Notes receivable		xx

The charge to cash is the total amount of money received, including the principal amount of the note and interest. The credit to notes receivable is the face value of the note. The credit to interest income is applicable only for interest-bearing notes. It represents the amount of interest earned and is the difference between the charge to cash and the credit to notes receivable. In other words, the charge to cash is determined by the sum of interest income and the face value of the note receivable.

Discounting Notes Receivable. A negotiable note may be transferred to another payee by endorsement, either "with recourse," or "without recourse." If a note is endorsed "without recourse," the endorser cannot be required to pay the note in the event that the maker or another endorser fails to pay. If a note is endorsed without the restrictive clause "without recourse," the endorser may be required to pay the note. Because in most cases banks and other institutions or persons accepting notes for discount wish to hold the one presenting a note for discount, along with its maker, liable for its payment, they will not usually discount notes endorsed "without recourse." Anyone who endorses a note other than "without recourse" is contingently liable for its payment, and that contingency should be shown in the records.

Because a discount is computed on the maturity value of the note, there are two steps in the calculation.

1. Calculate the maturity value: Maturity value = face value × rate (interest) × time (original life of the note) + face. (It is obvious that the face value and the maturity value of a non-interest-bearing note are the same.)

2. Calculate the discount: Discount = maturity value × discount rate × time (remaining life of note).

The *proceeds of a note* is the maturity value of the note less the discount charged.

For example, consider a $1,000 sixty day 6 percent note, discounted at 8 percent thirty days after the date of the note.

$$\text{Maturity value} = \$1,000 \times .06 \times \frac{60}{360} + \$1,000 = \$1,010.00$$

$$\text{Discount} = \$1,010 \times .08 \times \frac{30}{360} = \quad 6.73$$

$$\text{Proceeds} = \$1,003.27$$

The endorser of such a note would make the following entry to record the contingent liability and the net interest earned:

Cash	$1,003.27	
Interest earned		$ 3.27
Notes receivable—discounted		1,000.00

The account notes receivable—discounted should be considered as a contra-account to notes receivable. Thus, when the note in the preceding example is paid and the contingent liability is eliminated, the following entry is made:

Notes receivable—discounted	$1,000	
Notes receivable		$1,000

If the maker of a note fails to pay when the note is presented at maturity, the note is said to be *dishonored*.

In the event the endorser is required to pay this same note at maturity, plus interest of $10 and a protest fee of $5, the following entries would be required:

Notes receivable—discounted	$1,000	
Notes receivable		$1,000
Accounts receivable	1,015	
Cash		1,015

Because it is highly possible that a dishonored note is not currently collectible, some accountants suggest that such a note should be listed *not* in accounts receivable but in a special dishonored notes receivable account.

Some other accountants suggest that it is sufficient to indicate the contingent liability on a note receivable discounted by a footnote on the balance sheet or by a note following the account notes receivable on the balance sheet. When a note is discounted, those accountants using this method credit notes receivable instead of notes receivable—discounted and add a note or footnote to the balance sheet indicating the amount of contingent liability. Here is a typical example:

Note: On December 31, 1973, the company was contingently liable on discounted notes in the amount of $1,000.

BILLS OF EXCHANGE. Bills of exchange are considered receivables and are similar to notes receivable. There are technical differences, which are indicated in the following definition from the Uniform Negotiable Instruments Act:

A bill of exchange is an unconditional order in writing addressed by one person to another, signed by the person giving it, requiring the person to whom it is addressed to pay on demand or at a fixed or determinable future time a sum certain in money to order or to bearer.

Such a bill becomes an acceptance when it is accepted in writing by the person against whom it was drawn.

TRADE ACCEPTANCES RECEIVABLE. A *trade acceptance* is an accepted bill of exchange arising from the sale or purchase of merchandise for resale. It is assumed that a trade acceptance will be *self-liquidating* through the resale of the purchased merchandise giving rise to the acceptance.

Bankers usually prefer to discount accepted bills, rather than a customer's own note, because accepted bills are two-name papers; whereas the customer's note may be a single-name paper.

Although there are technical and legal differences between notes and bills of exchange, it is permissible for accounting purposes to include accepted bills with notes unless they represent a substantial amount of money. The accounting treatment is similar to that discussed in "Discounting Notes Receivable."

CHAPTER 3

Current Assets:
Inventory Accounts and Methods

The term *inventory,* or *inventories,* is used to designate the aggregate of goods held for sale "as is" in the ordinary course of business or for use in the normal manufacture of goods for sale. In merchandising firms, both wholesale and retail, it is customary to use a single inventory classification, such as *merchandise inventory* or *merchandise.* In a manufacturing firm, for control purposes, it is customary to use three or four classes of inventories in the accounting records, even though they are generally combined on the balance sheet under one caption, either Inventory or Inventories.

INVENTORY ACCOUNTS

The following inventory accounts are frequently found on the books of a manufacturing firm:

1. Raw materials (materials)
2. Work (or goods) in process
3. Finished goods
4. Supplies (sometimes included in the material inventory and sometimes treated as a prepaid item)

In many firms, inventories constitute a substantial portion of the working capital. It is therefore necessary to maintain close control over both the physical quantities and the amount of the investment. It is important to note that the term *inventory* applies to items owned (rather than merely physically possessed) and to items acquired for resale or for use in producing items for resale. Thus, an inventory may include items bought but not yet received and goods out on consignment, title not having passed to the consignee.

A building under construction by a contractor may be part of his work-in-process inventory, but to the firm buying such a building for use in manufacturing, it is a fixed asset. By the same token, land is generally considered to be a fixed asset, but to the real estate developer, it is stock-in-trade, a current asset, *inventory*.

Raw Materials. *Raw materials* are goods or items acquired by a manufacturer for use in production. They may be obtained directly from natural sources (e.g., various ores that are to be refined) or, more often, from other manufacturers. The finished goods of a preliminary manufacturer may become the raw material of a subsequent manufacturer. For example, cloth represents finished goods to a weaving firm but becomes raw materials when sold to a dressmaker. Often component parts are manufactured and inventoried prior to their assembly into larger parts or units. Such parts may be included either in the raw-materials inventory or in a separate inventory for semifinished parts. The term *raw materials* is frequently used in a narrow sense to apply only to materials that are to be physically incorporated in the manufactured product. This definition excludes items such as lubricating oils and greases and maintenance and cleaning supplies, which are necessary to efficient production but which do not become a part of the manufactured product. Such items are then classified as *factory supplies* or *supplies*.

Work in Process (Goods in Process). *Work in process,* frequently referred to as *goods in process,* consists of items partly processed but requiring further processing before they are ready for sale. Such an inventory includes the following three cost elements: (1) direct materials, (2) direct labor, and (3) manufacturing overhead. It is a relatively simple task to determine the cost of direct material used by examining (and adding together) the requisitions for it. It is also rather easy to determine the direct labor costs by reviewing time tickets, or time cards, and other payroll records. It is quite difficult to establish the amount of manufacturing overhead. *Manufacturing overhead* has been defined as all manufacturing costs other than direct material costs and direct labor costs. Because of the great variety of indirect costs included in this one group, it is difficult to allocate them to the various units of production.

Finished Goods. *Finished goods* are items on which the manufacturing process has been completed and that are therefore ready for sale. Finished goods contain the same three cost elements as work in process. Generally, finished goods should not be confused with *finished parts*, which will reenter the production cycle for further processing or assembly, ultimately to become a unit of finished goods.

Supplies. The term *supplies* is applied to a vast variety of items that normally do not become a part of the finished end product but through their use render essential services and thereby improve the operating efficiency of the firm. All such items may be carried in a single supplies inventory. However, they are sometimes segregated according to the functions to be benefited and, thus, may be separated into specific supplies inventories such as manufacturing, office, packing, delivery, selling, and administrative. Sometimes the manufacturing supplies are included in the raw-materials inventory.

Merchandise. *Merchandise inventory* encompasses any and all items acquired by a firm for resale in essentially the same condition in which they were acquired in the ordinary course of its business. This type of inventory is in contrast with the several inventories—raw materials, work in process, and finished goods—that may be found in a manufacturing firm, where the reason for acquiring the items is not to sell them "as is," but to change them prior to sale.

INVENTORY KEEPING METHODS

There are two generally accepted methods or procedures for accounting for inventories: the periodic- or physical-inventory method and the perpetual-inventory method.

Periodic (or Physical) Inventory. This method is commonly used by sales organizations and by some small manufacturing firms. The actual counting, weighing, or otherwise measuring of the goods on hand is done at the end of each accounting period. Then, in order to develop an inventory value, properly selected unit prices are applied to each group of items. When goods are acquired, the charge is to purchases, rather than to inventory. End-of-period entries are required either to adjust the beginning inventory value to that of the ending inventory or to close the beginning inventory and open an ending inventory. The cost of goods sold is determined by adding the purchases for the period to the beginning inventory and subtracting from this sum the ending inventory. This method has the advantage of simplicity but the disadvantage of poor control. It is sometimes said that this is a method not so much of inventory keeping as of merely inventory taking.

Perpetual Inventory. The *perpetual-inventory method* requires detailed records for each inventory item to be kept in such a manner that there is a continuous and current record of receipts, issues, and resulting balances. These records usually are kept in terms of both physical units and dollar amounts. However, in some cases, the continuing record of receipts, issues, and balances is kept only in terms of physical units, with a monetary value being established for the inventory only at the end of each accounting period. Under this method, periodic taking of physical inventory, the actual counting of items on hand, is usually considered necessary in order to establish the accuracy or inaccuracy of the balance established by the accounting records. Discrepancies between the accounting balance and the actual balance may occur because of errors in recording, shrinkage, loss, theft, and so forth. When a discrepancy is discovered, it is necessary to adjust the book inventory to the actual inventory. Usually, the actual quantity is less than the quantity shown by the accounting records. In such cases, an adjusting entry charging an account such as inventory adjustment and crediting the inventory account should be made for the amount of the difference. If the actual balance exceeds the book balance, then the adjustment account should be credited and the inventory account should be charged for the difference. The balance of the adjustment account should be closed to cost of goods sold; prorated to work in process, finished goods, and cost of goods sold; or closed directly to income and expense.

Most manufacturing firms use the perpetual-inventory method. In fact, it is generally considered to be an essential part of a good cost-accounting system.

This method's major disadvantage is the detail and expense involved in the record keeping. Its major advantage is the good control that it makes possible for a sizable and active investment.

INVENTORY-VALUATION METHODS

The value of the inventory at any given time is the sum of the values assigned to the physical units in the inventory at that time. Inventory valuation depends on two factors: (1) the method of developing and assigning unit values and (2) the assumed flow of goods into and out of the inventory.

The following cost methods are available for valuing inventory:

1. Cost (occasionally referred to as *full cost*)
2. Lower of cost or market
3. Standard cost
4. Marginal costing
5. Basket purchase

COST. When the term *cost* without restriction is used in referring to valuation procedures, full, absorption, total, or conventional cost-accounting methods are implied, rather than marginal, direct, or differential costing methods.

Cost, as defined by the AICPA, is the primary basis for inventory valuation.

The primary basis of accounting for inventories is cost, which has been defined generally as the price paid or consideration given to acquire an asset. As applied to inventories, cost means in principle the sum of the applicable expenditures and charges directly or indirectly incurred in bringing an article to its existing condition and location.[1]

It is easy to state principles for cost determination, but cost allocation is often very difficult, especially in cases of work in process and finished goods, because many costs essential to production cannot be directly identified with the product. Also, some costs that may be identifiable with the product may or may not

1. *Accounting Research and Terminology Bulletins,* Final Edition (1961), p. 28.

be applicable in "bringing an article to its existing condition or location."

Any costs properly incurred in acquiring and preparing goods for sale are inventoriable costs. Theoretically, the net invoice price plus costs of transportation, inspection, receiving, storing, even the cost of operating the purchasing department, and that portion of the general and administrative expenses applicable to the production function should be inventoried. However, for practical reasons, many of these costs are often charged off as period costs, rather than being charged to the inventory by some allocation method.

Transportation costs are particularly troublesome at times. If only one commodity is received in a given shipment, it is a simple matter to allocate the transportation costs proportionately to each identical unit received in the shipment. However, if several different commodities are received in a single shipment, should the transportation cost be allocated on the basis of weight, of cost, or of bulk? In order to avoid this problem, transportation costs are often charged off as period costs.

It is generally considered that place utility has value. Therefore, the cost of freight-in is a proper product (inventory) cost. Furthermore, if goods are sent out on consignment, the transportation cost of getting them to the consignee may be charged to the goods; however, if the goods are not sold but are returned to the consignor, the transportation costs both out and back in should be charged to expense.

The treatment of purchase discounts affects the cost of goods placed in inventory. Formerly, it was customary to cost goods on the basis of their gross invoice price and to treat purchase discounts taken as other (or financial) income. This method is a little illogical in that it results in reporting the discount as income when goods are paid for, rather than deferring the income recognition until the goods are sold. The present preferred treatment is to charge only the net (of discount) invoice cost to the inventory and to treat any discounts not taken as other expense. This procedure is especially appropriate in those industries in which rather-uniform purchase discounts are granted.

LOWER OF COST OR MARKET. The AICPA gives the following brief, informative statement on the *lower-of-cost-or-market method.*

As used in the phrase *lower of cost or market* the term market means replacement cost (by purchase or by reproduction, as the case may be) except that:

(1) Market should not exceed the net realizable value (i.e., estimated selling price in the ordinary course of business less reasonably predictable costs of completion and disposal); and

(2) Market should not be less than net realizable value reduced by an allowance for an approximately normal profit margin.[2]

It is said that the reason for using the lower-of-cost-or-market method is to report more accurately the income for the periods involved. In order to support this position, it must be assumed that the loss occurred at the time of purchase or during the holding period rather than at the time of sale. For example, too much inventory was purchased at too high a price, as evidenced by later conditions. This would be a case of a loss due to poor judgment in acquiring inventory.

The lower of cost or market is more conservative in the year of write-down than the cost method is because when the inventory value is shown at a lower value on the balance sheet, then the net income for the period is reduced by the amount of the decline in inventory value. However, such a write-down will increase profit the following year.

With the emphasis in accounting shifting from the balance sheet to the income statement, it is suggested that a reduction from cost is appropriate only when there is evidence that the utility of the goods is no longer equal to their cost. The overriding principle now is to report fairly the periodic income.

Originally, each item in inventory was valued at cost and at replacement, and the lower value was used. Now the lower of cost or market may be applied to each item, to groups of items, or to the total inventory. This is recommended by the AICPA:

Depending on the character and composition of the inventory, the rule of *cost or market, whichever is lower* may properly be applied either directly to each item or to the total of the inventory (or, in some cases, to the total of the components of each major category). The method should be that which most clearly reflects periodic income.[3]

The three ways of applying the lower-of-cost-or-market method of valuation to an inventory are shown in the following table:

2. Ibid., p. 31.
3. Ibid., p. 32.

| Items | Cost | Market | Lower of Cost or Market Applied to | | |
			Each Item	Major Classes	Total Inventory
Class I					
A	$ 400	$ 300	$ 300		
B	400	500	400		
C	600	700	600		
Total	$1,400	$1,500		$1,400	
Class II					
X	$1,000	$1,200	1,000		
Y	2,000	1,400	1,400		
Z	3,000	2,400	2,400		
Total	$6,000	$5,000		5,000	
Grand Total	$7,400	$6,500	$6,100	$6,400	$6,500

Originally, in applying the lower-of-cost-or-market rule, cost and replacement costs were compared, and the lower value was used without restriction. The effect of the AICPA statement with respect to application of the lower-of-cost-or-market procedures was to set a floor and a ceiling for the amount to be used as the lower-of-cost-or-market value.

The upper limit (ceiling) is applied to prevent carrying goods forward at a value in excess of net realizable value and thus charging a future period with a previously incurred loss. The lower limit (floor) is applied to make a reasonable profit on the sale of goods carried forward from prior periods by valuing them at net realizable value, less a normal profit. These limitations are illustrated in the following example:

| | Cases | | | | |
	1	2	3	4	5
Cost	$10	$10	$10	$10	$10
Replacement value	$ 8	$ 9	$ 6	$ 9	$12
Ceiling—estimated selling price, less cost to complete and sell	9	8	8	12	13
Floor—estimated selling price, less cost to complete and sell and normal profit	7	7	7	11	11
Value to use—lower of cost or market	8	8	7	10	10

In case 1, the replacement value is used because it is lower than cost and falls within the ceiling and floor limits.

In case 2, the ceiling value is used because although replacement value is less than cost, it exceeds the ceiling value.

In case 3, the floor value is used because replacement value is less than cost and is also less than the prescribed floor value.

In case 4, the cost value is used because although the replacement value is less than cost, the allowed range for lower of cost or market is greater than cost.

In case 5, cost is used because both the replacement value and the allowed range for the lower of cost or market are above cost.

In connection with the application of the lower-of-cost-or-market method of valuing inventory, it must be remembered that goods were initially recorded at cost and that now some adjustment is necessary to reduce that valuation. Consideration must be given to the presentation of the results on the statements. There are two distinct factors involved: (1) the cost of the goods sold during the period and of those still on hand at the end of the period, and (2) the loss sustained because of the decreased utility or value of the goods sold as well as those still on hand.

There are three generally accepted methods of recording such write-downs:

1. The ending inventory is recorded at or adjusted to (in the case of a perpetual inventory) the lower value, and the resulting loss is combined with or buried in the cost-of-goods-sold amount for the period.

2. The ending inventory is recorded at or adjusted to the lower value, and the amount of loss occasioned by the write-down is recorded separately.

3. An inventory allowance account is used so that the cost of and losses on all inventories may be reported separately.

The following example illustrates these three methods:

Date of Inventory	Cost	Market
December 31, 1971	$100,000	$100,000
December 31, 1972	75,000	70,000
December 31, 1973	50,000	40,000

Entries if periodic inventory is used   *Entries if perpetual inventory is used*

METHOD 1

1972	Income and expense	$100,000		Cost of goods sold	$ 5,000	
	Inventory		$100,000	Inventory		$ 5,000
	Inventory	70,000				
	Income and expense		70,000			
1973	Income and expense	70,000		Cost of goods sold	10,000	
	Inventory		70,000	Inventory		10,000
	Inventory	40,000				
	Income and expense		40,000			

METHOD 2

1972	Income and expense	$100,000		Inventory write-down	$ 5,000	
	Inventory		$100,000	Inventory		$ 5,000
	Inventory	70,000				
	Inventory write-down	5,000				
	Income and expense		75,000			
1973	Income and expense	70,000		Inventory write-down	10,000	
	Inventory		70,000	Inventory		10,000
	Inventory	40,000				
	Inventory write-down	10,000				
	Income and expense		50,000			

METHOD 3

1972	Income and expense	$100,000		Inventory write-down	$ 5,000	
	Inventory		$100,000	Inventory allowance		$ 5,000
	Inventory	75,000				
	Inventory write-down	5,000				
	Inventory allowance		5,000			
	Income and expense		75,000			
1973	Income and expense	70,000		Inventory write-down	10,000	
	Inventory allowance	5,000		Inventory allowance		10,000
	Inventory		75,000			
	Inventory	50,000				
	Inventory write-down	10,000				
	Inventory allowance		10,000			
	Income and expense		50,000			

Method 1 is frequently used because of its simplicity; however, it has the disadvantage of burying the loss due to inventory write-down in the cost of goods sold. Methods 2 and 3 are a little more involved but have the advantage of being more accurate and informative, as the following abbreviated income statements show:

	Method 1	Method 2	Method 3
Sales (supplied), 1973	$200,000	$200,000	$200,000
Cost of goods sold			
Beginning inventory	$ 70,000	$ 70,000	$ 75,000
Less: Allowance			5,000
Net	$ 70,000	$ 70,000	$ 70,000
Purchases (supplied)	100,000	100,000	100,000
Total available	$170,000	$170,000	$170,000
Less: Ending inventory	40,000	50,000	50,000
Cost of goods sold	$130,000	$120,000	$120,000
Gross profit	$ 70,000	$ 80,000	$ 80,000
Less: Inventory write-down		10,000	10,000
Gross profit after write-down	$ 70,000	$ 70,000	$ 70,000

STANDARD COST. A *standard-cost system* is a method of valuing production (goods sold as well as goods on hand) at predetermined unit values. It is used exclusively by manufacturing firms. For a full explanation of standard costs, the reader should consult a book on cost accounting. However, an intermediate accounting text would be incomplete if it did not include a brief explanation of such a system. A standard-cost system is useful primarily as an aid to management in evaluating the degree of efficiency in the utilization of material, labor, and plant (overhead) and in fixing responsibility for the various areas of performance. Its greatest value is as a control device, rather than as a means of valuing production. In fact, although it is considered a very useful system for management and internal-reporting purposes, it is not acceptable to the AICPA, the AAA, or the IRS for reports to the public. Therefore, firms that use standard costs for internal-reporting purposes usually adjust the reports to an actual-cost basis for external reporting.

Standard costs are predetermined costs that are expected to show what costs *should* be, as compared with *estimated costs*, which are also predetermined costs but which are expected to indicate what costs *will* be.

Actual costs are recorded as they are incurred, but production is charged with standard costs. Differences, known as *variances*, are isolated and analyzed for control purposes. Ordinarily, in the case of material, a *quantity* variance and a *price* variance are isolated. For labor, a *time* variance and a *rate* variance are usually isolated. But in the case of overhead costs, because of the varying characteristics of such a large group of costs, from two to twenty-nine different variances may be isolated. At the end of the year, the accumulated variances should be closed into work in process, finished goods, and cost of goods sold. If raw material is carried at standard cost, a part of the material price variance should be closed to that inventory.

MARGINAL COSTING. *Marginal costing*, also referred to as *direct costing* or *variable costing*, is distinguished from absorption costing, conventional costing, full costing, or total costing in the assignment of manufacturing overhead. Under conventional costing methods, both fixed and variable overhead costs are charged to the product. Under marginal-costing methods, only variable costs (i.e., direct material, direct labor, and the variable portion of manufacturing overhead) are charged to the product. Therefore, only under marginal costing must fixed and variable overhead be separated. Under marginal costing, variable manufacturing costs are referred to as *controllable costs* and are the only overhead costs charged to the product. Fixed costs are referred to as *period costs* and are charged not to the product but directly against the period in which they accrued.

Marginal revenue is the additional revenue from the sale of an additional unit.

Sales less the marginal cost of goods sold yields the manufacturing margin, which when reduced by the variable selling and administrative expenses, yields the operating (or merchandising) margin. The period costs (all fixed expenses) are deducted from the operating margin to establish the net operating profit. In conventional- or absorption-costing systems, the total cost of goods sold (fixed as well as variable costs) is deducted from sales to determine gross profit.

Marginal costing has the following advantages over conventional costing:

1. It allows better analysis and control of costs.

2. It eliminates the need for arbitrarily allocating fixed costs.

3. It facilitates budgeting.

4. It makes it easier to determine income (marginal) by products, divisions, territories, and so forth.

5. It makes it easier to establish and explain cost-volume-profit relationships.

The disadvantages of marginal costing are:

1. It is not approved (for public reports) by the AICPA, the IRS, or the SEC.

2. It is a short-run approach to costing and pricing. Because of the exclusion of all fixed costs from the inventory, it is likely that in the long run, selling prices will be set lower than they should be.

BASKET PURCHASE. The *basket-purchase method,* sometimes referred to as the *lump-sum-purchase method,* is useful in establishing unit prices when a number of nonidentical units are acquired for a lump sum. Under such conditions, it becomes necessary to allocate the total cost to the various units on some equitable basis. The basis used most frequently is the estimated market value of the various units.

For example, assume that a developer bought a tract of land for $100,000. He planned to subdivide the tract into lots that, because of differences in size and location, could be sold for different prices. After a survey was made, it was determined that there would be 10 first-quality lots which would sell for $6,000 each; 20 second-quality lots, which would sell for $4,000 each; and 20 third-quality lots, which would sell for $3,000 each. The allocation would be made as follows:

Quality	Unit Selling Price	Units	Total Selling Price	Cost (Percent)	Total Cost Price	Unit Cost
1	$6,000	10	$ 60,000	50	$ 30,000	$3,000
2	4,000	20	80,000	50	40,000	2,000
3	3,000	20	60,000	50	30,000	1,500
Total		50	$200,000		$100,000	

Noncost. Inventories are usually calculated on one of the cost bases available. However, for reasons of practicality or necessity, noncost methods are sometimes used. In all the inventory-valuation methods just discussed, cost was used in establishing the value, even though the method of computing cost varied. (For example, in the lower-of-cost-or-market method, cost was used in the calculation, even though it might be ignored in the final valuation of the inventory.) In the methods to be discussed in the following paragraphs, values other than cost are the bases of valuing the inventory. They are often referred to as *estimated* values to differentiate them from cost values.

CASH REALIZABLE VALUE. In some cases, it is appropriate to inventory goods at a net realizable value, that is, the estimated selling price reduced by the estimated costs of conditioning and disposing of goods. The value may be reduced further to allow for a normal profit when sold. This method is especially suitable in cases of obsolete, shopworn, damaged, or repossessed goods.

The loss on such goods should be charged against the revenue of the period in which the loss occurred. Care must be taken to distinguish between these kinds of losses and the extraordinary losses resulting from fire, flood, wind, and so forth, which should be charged off separately as extraneous losses.

Scrap resulting from manufacturing operations is material or a by-product having less value than a by-product in the normal sense but more value than *waste,* which is held to have very little value, if any. Hence, scrap may be considered to be a by-product having exceedingly little value. If it has an insignificant or undeterminable value, it should be assigned no inventory value. If it is determined to have an inventoriable value because it has net realizable value, this amount should be credited against the original material cost of the main product or against the production costs of the period. If scrap valued at net realizable value represents a significant amount, it is appropriate to establish a special inventory account for it.

SELLING PRICE. The *selling-price method* is a special application of the cash-realizable-value method. There is no better or more authoritative statement justifying and explaining the selling-price basis for valuing inventories than the one given by the AICPA:

It is generally recognized that income accrues only at the time of sale, and that gains may not be anticipated by reflecting assets at their current sales prices. For certain articles, however, exceptions are permissible. Inventories of gold and silver, when there is an effective government-controlled market at a fixed monetary value, are ordinarily reflected at selling price. A similar treatment is not uncommon for inventories representing agricultural, mineral, and other products, units of which are interchangeable and have an immediate marketability at quoted prices and for which appropriate costs may be difficult to obtain. Where such inventories are stated at sales prices, they should of course be reduced by expenditures to be incurred in disposal, and the use of such basis should be fully disclosed in the financial statements.[4]

There may now be some question concerning the effectiveness of government control of the price of gold and silver. However, such metals can still be priced at selling price less marketing costs on the grounds that such values are more exactly determinable than the production costs are, which is also the case with other mineral products and with agricultural products.

GROSS PROFIT. The *gross-profit method* is a way of estimating the value of an inventory when some evidence or data are lacking or when taking an inventory in the usual manner is either too time consuming or too expensive. This method is applicable for the following purposes:

1. To obtain an interim inventory, for example, at the end of each month except the last month of the fiscal year
2. To test the validity of inventory figures as established by other means (a method frequently used by auditors to test the accuracy of previously taken inventories)
3. To estimate the value of an inventory that has been destroyed by fire or some other cause and for which the accounting data necessary for its valuation by other methods are also lacking

The accuracy of this method depends to a very great extent on the correctness of the gross-profit percentage used. The gross-profit percentage may be established by averaging the gross profit for several past periods and then adjusting the resulting figure in the light of the current period's conditions.

Five distinct steps are necessary to the calculation of the ending inventory by the gross-profit method:

4. Ibid., p. 34.

1. Calculate sales in the normal manner.

2. Calculate the total cost of goods available for sale in the usual way. This is the sum of the beginning inventory plus goods bought or produced during the period.

3. Calculate the rate of gross profit by dividing the gross profit for one or more periods by the sales for the same period or periods, and adjust the results for current conditions.

4. Calculate the cost of goods sold by multiplying the sales figure by the complement of the gross-profit percentage.

5. Calculate the ending inventory by subtracting the cost of goods sold (as established in step 4) from the cost of goods available for sale (as calculated in step 2).

The following example demonstrates the application of the gross-profit method: The Easy Do Company was able to provide the following data after a fire had completely destroyed its inventory:

Beginning inventory at cost	$ 50,000
Purchases during period	300,000
Net sales during period, at selling price	550,000
Ending inventory destroyed by fire	?

The rate of gross profit was estimated at 40%.

The value of the ending inventory may be estimated as follows:

Beginning inventory at cost		$ 50,000
Purchases		300,000
Goods available for sale		$350,000
Sales	$550,000	
Cost of sales percentage (1.00–.40)	.60	330,000
Estimated ending inventory		$ 20,000

RETAIL. As its name indicates, the *retail method* of inventory valuation is most commonly used by retail establishments. However, it may also be used by wholesalers if appropriate accounting records are kept. Under this method, it is necessary to have records of both the cost and the selling prices of the beginning inventory, as well as records of purchases during the period, together with all changes in the selling prices.

This method is especially suited to retail stores in which goods received are marked at selling price only. Inventories are initially valued at selling prices and later reduced to cost (or lower of cost or market) by applying a percentage that represents the relationship of cost and selling price of goods available for sale to the selling price of the ending inventory. Briefly, it is a method of inventory valuation under which cost (or lower of cost or market) is determined by applying the cost–selling-price ratio to an inventory reported at selling price.

The advantages of the retail-inventory method are as follows:

1. Estimated interim inventories can be obtained easily without taking a physical inventory.

2. When the customary annual physical inventory is taken, it can be priced at retail and easily converted to cost without time-consuming examination of individual invoices.

3. It provides an easy means of testing the reasonableness of an inventory taken by some other method.

4. It permits the costing of an inventory even when its cost price is not available.

To apply the retail method effectively, the accountant must understand the meaning of the following terms:

1. *Original retail:* the price at which goods are first offered for sale

2. *Markup* (*mark-on*): the amount added to cost to establish the selling price

3. *Additional markup:* an increase above original retail

4. *Markup cancellation:* a reduction in selling price after one or more additional markups but leaving the selling price equal to or greater than the original selling price

5. *Net markups:* additional markups minus markup cancellations

6. *Markdown:* a reduction in selling price below the original retail price

7. *Markdown cancellation:* an increase in selling price after one or more markdowns but leaving the adjusted price equal to or less than the original retail price

8. *Net Markdowns:* markdowns minus markdown cancellations

The retail-inventory method will produce an inventory value

that is considered to approximate cost or market, whichever is lower, if net markups only are used in computing the cost–selling-price ratio. This is the more generally favored method, because it yields a lower value and hence a more conservative inventory and because it provides better matching of costs and revenues period by period.

The alternate method—considering both net markups and net markdowns—yields an inventory value generally considered to approximate cost.

The following problem is solved by each of the methods just discussed:

PROBLEM DATA

	Cost	Retail
Beginning inventory	$ 30,000	$ 60,000.00
Purchases	100,000	200,000.00
Freight-in	10,000	
Additional markups		25,000.00
Markup cancellations		(5,000.00)
Markdowns		(50,000.00)
Markdown cancellations		3,333.33
Sales		150,000.00

INVENTORY CALCULATION BY RETAIL METHOD[a]

	Cost	Retail
Beginning inventory	$ 30,000	$ 60,000.00
Purchases	100,000	200,000.00
Freight-in	10,000	
Additional markups		25,000.00
Markup cancellations		(5,000.00)
Goods available for sale	$140,000	$280,000.00
Cost–retail ratio ($140,000 ÷ $280,000)	50%	
Less		
Sales		$150,000.00
Markdowns		50,000.00
Markdown cancellations		(3,333.33)
Total (total sales and net markdowns)		$196,666.67
Estimated inventory at retail		$ 83,333.33
Estimated inventory at lower of cost or market	$41,666.67	

[a] Yielding a cost at the lower of cost or market.

INVENTORY CALCULATION BY RETAIL METHOD[a]

	Cost	Retail
Beginning inventory	$ 30,000	$ 60,000.00
Purchases	100,000	200,000.00
Freight-in	10,000	
Additional markups		25,000.00
Markup cancellations		(5,000.00)
Markdowns		(50,000.00)
Markdown cancellations		3,333.33
Goods available for sale	$140,000	$233,333.33
Cost–retail ratio ($140,000 ÷ $233,333.33)	60%[b]	
Less: sales		150,000.00
Estimated inventory at retail		$ 83,333.33
Estimated inventory at cost	$ 50,000[b]	

[a] Yielding approximate cost value.
[b] Rounded.

LONG-TERM CONTRACT. Contracts for the construction of ships, large buildings, dams, bridges, and so forth often require several years to complete. For firms specializing in these types of production, the usual cost-oriented methods of valuing work-in-process inventory are often inadequate as well as inappropriate.

A contractor working on one or more long-term contracts (i.e., contracts having a life of more than one year) may use consistently either of the following long-term contract methods of valuing work in process:

1. Completed-contract method
2. Percentage-of-completion method

It is important that this selection be made carefully because it will greatly affect the timing of the recognition of income.

Completed-Contract Method. This method is the conventional cost-oriented method of valuing work in process, whereby all costs (but only costs) incurred in connection with the long-term contract are accumulated in a work in process account, typically referred to as "construction in process." No income is recognized on the contract until its completion. By this method, a firm operating under a single long-term contract may report no income or possibly even a loss for several years and then report a very large profit in the year in which the contract is completed. This, of course, is in accordance with the principles that inventories should be valued at cost and that profit should not be recognized upon the purchase or production of goods but deferred until the goods are sold. However, such a procedure may result in unrealistic reporting of periodic profits. Its principal advantage is that costs and profits are based on finally determined results, rather than on preestablished estimates. Its principal disadvantage is that it does not accurately report current operating results.

Percentage-of-Completion Method. Under this method, not only are all costs incident to the completion of the long-term contract charged to the construction in process account as they are incurred but estimated amounts of profit are also periodically charged to this account. This profit accumulation may be accomplished on either of two generally accepted bases:

1. Ratio of cost incurred to estimated total cost
2. Stage of completion based on engineers' or architects' estimates

Each of these methods has advantages. A close correlation does not necessarily exist between cost incurrence and productive effort expended. For example, perhaps most or all material is acquired before production on the contract starts. On the other hand, the stage of completion as established by engineers or architects does not always indicate the portion of total productive effort already expended.

For purposes of explanation, consider the following example: On January 2, 1973, the Rite Way Construction Company signed a contract with a customer to erect a building with a completion date of December, 1975. The price agreed upon was $6,000,000. It was also agreed that the customer should be billed for 80 percent of actual incurred costs as of the end of each of the first two years but that the customer should pay only 90 percent of such billing until the completion of the contract. The original cost estimate was $3,000,000. The following data were developed during the construction period:

	1973	1974	1975
Cost incurred to year-end	$1,000,000	$2,500,000	$4,500,000
Estimated cost to complete	2,000,000	1,500,000	0
Total	$3,000,000	$4,000,000	$4,500,000

The profit for each of the three years may be calculated as follows:

1973

Sales price		$6,000,000
Less		
Cost incurred to date	$1,000,000	
Estimated cost to complete	2,000,000	3,000,000
Estimated profit		$3,000,000
Profit recognized in 1973		
[($1,000,000/$3,000,000) × $3,000,000]		$1,000,000

1974

Sales price		$6,000,000
Less		
Cost incurred to date	$2,500,000	
Estimated cost to complete	1,500,000	4,000,000
Estimated profit		$2,000,000
Profit for 1974		
Profit recognized to date		
[($2,500,000/$4,000,000) × $2,000,000]		$1,250,000
Profit recognized in prior year		1,000,000
Profit recognized in 1974		$ 250,000

1975

Sales price		$6,000,000
Less: Cost incurred to completion		4,500,000
Total actual profit		$1,500,000
Profit recognized in prior years		1,250,000
Profit recognized in 1975		$ 250,000

The following journal entries should be made to record the transactions:

	1973		1974		1975	
	Dr.	Cr.	Dr.	Cr.	Dr.	Cr.
Construction in process	$2,000,000		$1,750,000		$2,250,000	
Material						
Labor }		$1,000,000		$1,500,000		$2,000,000
Factory overhead						
Profit		1,000,000		250,000		250,000
Construction accounts receivable	800,000		1,200,000		4,000,000	
Partial billings on construction in process		800,000		1,200,000		4,000,000
Cash	720,000		1,080,000		4,200,000	
Construction accounts receivable		720,000		1,080,000		4,200,000
Partial billings on construction in process					6,000,000	
Construction in process						6,000,000

When the percentage-of-completion method of handling long-term contracts is used, such contract balances are customarily shown on the balance sheet below the receivables but above the inventories. The balance of this account should be composed of actual cost incurred, plus the profit recognized on the contracts, less all billings against them. Thus, the current assets section of the balance sheet for December 31, 1973, would list (among other items) the following:

Construction contracts receivable		$ 80,000
Construction in process	$2,000,000	
Less: Partial billings on construction in process	800,000	1,200,000

It should be remembered that the percentage-of-completion method is a deviation from normal valuation procedures; therefore, it should be used only when definitely warranted because of the time involved. It should not be used when reliable estimates of costs cannot be made.

The principal advantage of this method of valuing work in process is periodic recognition of income as production progresses. Its principal disadvantage is the great reliance placed on estimates.

The federal-income-tax regulations permit the recognition of profits on a percentage-of-completion basis for contracts extending for more than one year.

CHAPTER 4

Current Assets: Inventory Flows

Business operations involve a number of *flows* such as *cash flows, income flows,* and *asset flows.* One of the most important flows is inventory flows. For a meaningful analysis and control of inventory flows, the inflows and outflows must be measured on a similar basis. For example, if at the time of acquisition, units are charged to inventory at invoice price, less discount, plus freight-in, then when units are removed from inventory, they must be removed at that same value.

FLOW ASSUMPTIONS AND THE VALUATION OF INVENTORIES

The inflows and outflows of inventory may be matched on either a specific identification basis or on any of several generally accepted *assumed* flow bases. It should be observed that the assumed flow does not have to coincide with the actual physical flow.

First-in, First-out (FIFO). A common assumed inventory flow is *first-in, first-out*. This method is based on the logical assumption that costs should be charged out in the chronological order of their incurrence. It is especially logical in the case of perishable products, in that usually the oldest stocks are physically removed from inventory first, always leaving the freshest stock in inventory. This is a practical means of minimizing deteriorated or obsolete stock, even when some other assumed flow is utilized for accounting purposes.

The FIFO method has a distinct advantage over the last-in,

first-out method for balance-sheet presentation because by this method, the inventory listed on the balance sheet is recorded at the most recent acquisition prices. This results in the current asset, inventory, being valued at rather-current values. However, it does have a concomitant disadvantage: a poorer matching of income and expense on the income statement than that provided by the last-in, first-out method (under which the most recent purchase prices are used in making charges to production or to cost of goods sold). Another advantage of the FIFO method of inventory keeping is that it is easily understood and easily computed. This method is unique among assumed-flow methods in that it is the only one that yields essentially the same results by either the periodic or the perpetual-inventory methods, as the following example demonstrates:

PURCHASES

Date	Units	Unit Price	Total
Jan. 1	100	$1.00	$ 100
Jan. 5	200	1.25	250
Jan. 10	200	1.40	280
Jan. 15	100	1.50	150
Jan. 20	100	1.75	175
Jan. 25	200	1.70	340
Jan. 30	200	1.80	360
	1,100		$1,655

SALES

Date	Units
January 12	200
January 22	300
January 31	300
	800

If the periodic-inventory method is used, the calculation of the cost of goods used (or sold) and the ending-inventory value will be calculated as follows:

	Units		Cost
Total available	1,100		$1,655
Less: Ending inventory			
January 30	200	$360	
January 25	100	170	
Total	300		530
Total used or sold	800		$1,125

If the perpetual-inventory method is used, a running record of the transactions will be kept. In simplified form, it will be as follows:

	Received			Issued			Balance		
Date	Quan-tity	Unit Price	Total	Quan-tity	Unit Price	Total	Quan-tity	Unit Price	Total
Jan. 1	100	$1.00	$100				100	$1.00	$100
5	200	1.25	250				100	1.00	100
							200	1.25	250
10	200	1.40	280				100	1.00	100
							200	1.25	250
							200	1.40	280
12				100	$1.00	$100	100	1.25	125
				100	1.25	125	200	1.40	280
15	100	1.50	150				100	1.25	125
							200	1.40	280
							100	1.50	150
20	100	1.75	175				100	1.25	125
							200	1.40	280
							100	1.50	150
							100	1.75	175
22				100	1.25	125	100	1.50	150
				200	1.40	280	100	1.75	175
25	200	1.70	340				100	1.50	150
							100	1.75	175
							200	1.70	340
30	200	1.80	360				100	1.50	150
							100	1.75	175
							200	1.70	340
							200	1.80	360
31				100	1.50	150	100	1.70	170
				100	1.75	175	200	1.80	360
				100	1.70	170			

The total cost of goods used or sold is $1,125, the sum of the value of the units shown as having been issued. The ending inventory is assumed to be composed of all the last purchase and one-half of the next-to-the-last purchase.

Jan. 30	200 units @ $1.80	$360
Jan. 20	100 units @ $1.70	$170
		$530

Last-in, First-out (LIFO). The *last-in, first-out inventory method* is based on a chronologically reversed flow. Those who have difficulty reconciling such a reversed flow with the need in many cases of physically removing the oldest units from inventory first (in order to minimize deterioration and obsolescence) should be reminded that for accounting purposes, it is the *cost flow* rather than the commodity flow that is recognized. One of the most important reasons for the adoption of the LIFO inventory method is the tax savings or deferment in periods of rising prices, as compared with some other methods, especially FIFO. Also, this method has a tendency to smooth the profit curve in periods of changing prices. The acceptance of the LIFO method versus the FIFO method is made possible from a theoretical point of view by the shift in emphasis from the balance sheet to the income statement. In periods of rising prices, if the ending inventory is equal to or greater than the beginning inventory, there is a close matching of costs and revenues, inasmuch as there is close correspondence between the price paid for goods removed from inventory and the figure used in charging them to cost of sales or to production.

However, the LIFO method leaves something to be desired from the balance-sheet point of view. In periods of rising prices, this method will cause the current asset, inventory, to be valued below current costs. It is always possible to raise the question of just what constitutes cost; but if it is accepted that the application of the LIFO method to inventories distorts current asset values, then it follows that the working capital and current ratio may also be distorted. Because goods sold or used today must be replaced at current prices, the LIFO method provides management with a good basis for making price and cost decisions.

Aside from the illogic of the assumed flow as seen by some, the greatest disadvantage may be the complexity of the calculations required by this method. The IRS requires that when the LIFO method is used for tax purposes, it must also be used in annual reports to the public.

The LIFO method may be applied on either a periodic or a perpetual basis. Using the data given on page 56, the cost of goods sold and the ending inventory would be calculated as follows on a periodic LIFO basis:

		Units	Cost
Total available		1,100	$1,655
Less: Ending inventory			
Jan. 1	100		$100
Jan. 5	200		250
Total		300	350
Total used or sold		800	$1,305

If the perpetual-inventory method is applied, a simplified inventory record will be kept as illustrated on p. 60.

The ending inventory is valued at $395, and the cost of goods removed from the inventory amounts to $1,260.

It should be pointed out that the IRS does not permit the replacement of inventory at earlier costs, even when that inventory has been involuntarily liquidated. Neither does it permit the write-down to market in those cases in which market is less than LIFO cost. However, such a write-down is permitted for public financial reports.

The timing of the adoption of the LIFO method of inventorying goods is important because the method is often instituted primarily to reap tax benefits. The LIFO method should be adopted when prices are rising. If prices fall shortly after the adoption of this method, the firm may suffer a tax disadvantage. Also, it is advisable to institute the LIFO method when the inventory is rather small because if the inventory is reduced below the amount at the installation of this method, the firm will also be at a tax disadvantage. After the inception of the LIFO method, the firm should strive to maintain normal inventory levels, at least at year-ends, because if the levels are increased too much, the firm may find it necessary to record the removal of the excess

Date	Received Quantity	Received Unit Price	Received Total	Issued Quantity	Issued Unit Price	Issued Total	Balance Quantity	Balance Unit Price	Balance Total
Jan. 1	100	$1.00	$100				100	$1.00	$100
5	200	1.25	250				100	1.00	100
							200	1.25	250
10	200	1.40	280				100	1.00	100
							200	1.25	250
							200	1.40	280
12				200	$1.40	$280	100	1.00	100
							200	1.25	250
15	100	1.50	150				100	1.00	100
							200	1.25	250
							100	1.50	150
20	100	1.75	175				100	1.00	100
							200	1.25	250
							100	1.50	150
							100	1.75	175
22				100	1.75	175	100	1.00	100
				100	1.50	150	100	1.25	125
				100	1.25	125			
25	200	1.70	340				100	1.00	100
							100	1.25	125
							200	1.70	340
30	200	1.80	360				100	1.00	100
							100	1.25	125
							200	1.70	340
							200	1.80	360
31				200	1.80	360	100	1.00	100
				100	1.70	170	100	1.25	125
							100	1.70	170

at values that are no longer current. Interim fluctuations will not affect the LIFO calculation of the inventories for tax purposes.

DOLLAR-VALUE LIFO. One of the major disadvantages of the use of the common LIFO method just described is the amount of work involved in keeping the necessary records. The records for common LIFO applications must be kept in both physical units and dollar values for each type of item in inventory. In order to save time and expense, a simplified method, referred to as the *dollar-value LIFO method,* has been developed. It should be noted that this method is accepted by the IRS for tax purposes.

Under the dollar-value LIFO method, an inventory pool is established at base-year costs as of the beginning of the first year of the adoption of the method. So long as subsequent inventories are equal to or greater than the beginning inventory, this base inventory pool remains intact. Increases in subsequent inventories are considered to be additional layers of inventory. Decreases in inventories are deducted from the previous increase layers in reverse chronological order.

Inventories are taken at current prices. Both the beginning and ending inventories (at current prices) are then reduced to base-year prices by the application of appropriate index numbers. The difference between the beginning and ending inventories valued at base prices indicates the amount of inventory increase or decrease at base prices. This tends to indicate the change in quantity. Any inventory increase valued at base prices must be adjusted to current prices by the application of the appropriate index number, and it should be added to the base inventory carried at a base price. A decrease in inventory is considered an inventory reduction and should be removed by subtraction from the built-up layers of inventory in reverse chronological order.

For example, the ending inventories for each of five years at both base and current prices are as follows:

| | Ending Inventories | | Index Numbers[b] |
Year	At Base Prices	At Current Prices	(Percent)
0[a]	$ 50,000	$ 50,000	100.0
1	60,000	72,000	120.0
2	80,000	88,000	110.0
3	100,000	125,000	125.0
4	60,000	67,500	112.5

[a] Ending inventory of 0 year is beginning inventory of year 1.
[b] Current prices ÷ base prices = index number.

YEAR 1

Beginning inventory—base prices	$ 50,000
Ending inventory—base prices	60,000
Increase—base prices	$ 10,000
Beginning inventory—base prices	$ 50,000
Increase adjusted to current prices ($10,000 × 1.20)	12,000
Ending inventory—LIFO	$ 62,000

YEAR 2

Beginning inventory—base prices	$ 60,000
Ending inventory—base prices	80,000
Increase—base prices	$ 20,000
Beginning inventory—LIFO	$ 62,000
Increase adjusted to current prices ($20,000 × 1.10)	22,000
Ending inventory—LIFO	$ 84,000

YEAR 3

Beginning inventory—base prices	$ 80,000
Ending inventory—base prices	100,000
Increase—base prices	$ 20,000
Beginning inventory—LIFO	$ 84,000
Increase adjusted to current prices ($20,000 × 1.25)	25,000
Ending inventory LIFO	$109,000

YEAR 4

Beginning inventory—base prices	$100,000
Ending inventory—base prices	60,000
Decrease—base prices	$ 40,000
Beginning inventory—LIFO	$109,000

Deductions

Year	base prices	× index	= current price	
3	$20,000	1.25	$25,000	
2	20,000	1.10	22,000	47,000

Ending inventory—LIFO	$ 62,000

RETAIL LIFO. The retail-inventory method may be adapted to yield an approximation of LIFO values. The *retail LIFO method* is a variation of the dollar-value LIFO method. The inventory at retail values is divided into a base-year portion at retail and additional layers (increases) at base-year retail values. The base-year portion at retail is reduced to cost by multiplying the retail value by the base year's cost-retail ratio. Each layer of increase is converted to average cost for the year of acquisition by multiplying first that layer by the price index for that year and then multiplying that result by the cost-retail ratio applicable to that year. The total inventory valued at retail LIFO is the sum of the costs of the base quantity and the costs of the layers of inventory increases.

For example, the Ace Hardware Company carries its inventory at retail. The company's ending inventory on December 31, 1972 (its base year), was valued at $60,000 retail and at $36,000 cost. The firm's inventory on December 31, 1973, was $88,000 at retail. The firm's 1973 cost-retail ratio was 60 percent. There has been an industry-wide price increase of 10 percent during 1973. The retail LIFO value of the ending inventory is calculated as follows:

Ending inventory at retail base prices ($88,000 ÷ 1.10)	$80,000
Beginning inventory at retail	60,000
Inventory increase at retail	$20,000
Inventory increase at current prices ($20,000 × 1.10)	$22,000
Inventory increase at cost ($22,000 × .60)	$13,200
Cost of beginning inventory	36,000
Ending inventory at retail LIFO	$49,200

Average Cost. Inventories are often valued by some form of average-cost method. The three average-cost methods most frequently used are discussed in the following paragraphs.

SIMPLE AVERAGE. A simple arithmetic average is obtained by adding the unit cost involved in each transaction and then dividing that sum by the number of transactions. Then the inventory value may be calculated by multiplying the number of units in the inventory by the average price. This method is illustrated in the following example:

Quantity	Purchases, Unit Cost	Total Cost
100	$1.00	$ 100
200	2.00	400
300	3.00	900
400	4.00	1,600
1,000		$3,000

Of the 1,000 units, 800 have been sold.

$$\frac{\$1.00 + \$2.00 + \$3.00 + \$4.00}{4} = \$2.50 \text{ unit cost}$$

The value of the inventory is calculated as follows: (1000 − 800) × \$2.50 = \$500.

WEIGHTED AVERAGE. Under the *weighted-average method*, the total value of the transactions is divided by the total number of units involved to establish the weighted-average value. The value of the inventory is calculated by multiplying the number of units on hand by the weighted-average price.

Using the same data as given in the illustration of the simple-average method, the inventory would be calculated as follows:

Total cost (\$3,000) divided by total units (1,000) equals \$3.00 weighted-average unit cost. Inventory is valued at 200 × \$3.00, or \$600.

MOVING AVERAGE. The *moving-average method* usually requires that a new average cost be calculated after each purchase. In some cases, a new cost is computed after each transaction, either purchase or return of merchandise. In other cases, a new average cost is calculated only at predetermined intervals, for example, at the end of each month. Under such a system, goods are removed from inventory during the entire period at the cost in effect at the beginning of the period. The inventory is charged with the actual cost of goods received during the period. The average unit cost to be used during the next period is determined by dividing the dollar balance of the inventory by the number of physical units in the inventory.

The true moving-average method requires the use of a perpetual-inventory system; whereas the weighted-average method is usually employed with the periodic type of inventory. Perhaps it should be observed here that the moving-average method is also a weighted-average method and differs from the so-called weighted-average method only by the frequency with which the average moves, that is, is recalculated. For example, under the weighted-average method, a new average cost may be computed only at the end of each accounting period; but under the moving-average method, a new average may be calculated after each purchase.

Using the same data for purchases given in the example of the simple-average method and the additional information that 200 units were issued between the second and third purchases and another 600 units were issued after the last purchase, a perpetual-inventory card could be prepared in the following manner:

	Receipts			Issues			Balance		
Date	Units	Unit Cost	Total	Units	Unit Cost	Total	Units	Unit Cost	Total
Jan. 1	100	$1.00	$ 100				100	$1.00	$ 100.00
4	200	2.00	400				300	1.66⅔	500.00
8				200	$1.66⅔	$ 333.33⅓	100	1.66⅔	166.66⅔
15	300	3.00	900				400	2.66⅔	1,066.66⅔
20	400	4.00	1,600				800	3.33⅓	2,666.66⅔
25				600	3.33⅓	2,000.00	200	3.33⅓	666.66⅔

Specific Cost. Specific costs of identified units sold or used may be charged against revenue under some circumstances. In order that this method may be used, it is necessary that each lot of physical units purchased be identified with a specific invoice. Thus, this method cannot be used in cases where homogeneous items acquired at different prices are mixed together. It is not possible to assume a flow of goods in a specific-cost application, as can be done in the use of the FIFO or LIFO methods. Because of the difficulty of identifying each physical unit with a specific price, this method is not widely used.

Selling Price. Selling prices are not generally accepted as a basis for valuing inventories for two important reasons: (1) Accountants are hesitant to depart from a conservative and objectively determined cost value. (2) The inventorying of goods at selling price anticipates profits and results in poor matching of costs and revenues. However, there are instances in which because of the difficulty of establishing reliable cost prices or because of rather-fixed selling prices that will not be materially affected by one firm's decision to sell or not to sell, net realizable sales prices may be used for valuing the inventory.[1]

It would seem that even when there is not a fixed controlled price for gold and silver, they could still be valued at net selling prices as can "minerals and agricultural" products.

Base Stock. The *base-stock,* or *normal-stock, method* rests on the assumption that a minimum permanent stock of goods is essential to the efficient operation of the business. Proponents of the base-stock method hold that such a minimum stock is really equivalent to a permanent asset and should not be affected by fluctuations in current prices. Therefore, costs of current produc-

1. See quotation on p. 46.

tion or sales requirements should be charged with current costs.

The base-stock portion of the inventory should be valued at the original base cost. The portion of the inventory that is regarded as temporary should be valued at current cost as determined by FIFO, LIFO, average cost, or some other acceptable basis. Any reduction in the base-stock quantity is considered a temporary borrowing from the base stock in order to meet current sales or production requirements and is charged against current revenues at current replacement costs.

The application of the base-stock method is illustrated by the solution to the following problem: A firm started operations with an inventory of 1,000 units at a unit cost of $1. This was determined to constitute the base stock. At the end of the first year, the inventory consisted of 1,100 units. The current cost at that time was $1.25. At the end of the second year, the inventory consisted of only 900 units, and the current replacement cost was $1.10. The ending inventory for each year may be determined in the following manner:

INVENTORY AT THE END OF FIRST YEAR

Base stock (1,000 units @ $1)	$1,000
Excess over base stock (100 units @ $1.25)	125
Total inventory	$1,125

INVENTORY AT END OF SECOND YEAR

Base stock (1,000 units @ $1)	$1,000
Deficiency of base stock (100 × $1.10)	110
Total inventory	$ 890

The second-year inventory may be reported at $890 or at $1,000, less a deficiency allowance of $110. The allowance account should be closed out at the time of the next purchase.

The base-stock method is quite similar to the LIFO method in its attempt to match current costs with current revenues. It was, in fact, a forerunner of LIFO. Since LIFO was approved for tax purposes, it has generally replaced the base-stock method, which is not accepted for tax purposes. However, it is used frequently enough to warrant an understanding by students of accounting.

Standard Cost. The *standard-cost method* is especially designed for use by manufacturing firms. Its greatest value lies in its use as a cost-control device and the possibility of improving efficiency through analytic means. It is better suited to cost-control purposes than to inventory pricing. Although in a broad sense, anything that is predetermined is estimated, a standard cost is a scientific predetermination of what cost *should* be. On the other hand, an estimated cost (as used in accounting) is a scientific predetermination of what cost is *expected* to be. Thus, it is apparent that standard costs reflect not actual costs but, rather, some ideal or hoped-for cost. Since standard costs do not reflect actual costs, they are not acceptable to the IRS and the AICPA for reporting purposes. A firm may use standard costs for internal control and management decision-making purposes and then adjust them to an actual-cost basis for public-reporting purposes.

For control purposes, the differences, variances, between the standard costs and the actual costs of a job or process should be broken down and isolated according to their functional causes in order that appropriate steps may be taken to bring actual costs in line with the standard costs or to correct the standards used in establishing such standard costs if they are found to be faulty. The reader should consult a book on cost accounting for details on the setting of standards and the analysis of variances.

Next-in, First-out (NIFO). From the point of view of matching costs and revenues, the *NIFO method,* which attempts to match current revenues with current costs (the cost of replacing physical units), is ideal. However, this represents a departure from the cost basis of valuing inventories and for this reason is not acceptable for inventory pricing. This method is mentioned here only because proponents recurrently advocate its adoption.

INVENTORY PLANNING AND CONTROL TECHNIQUES

Inventory planning is the determination in advance of the types and quantities of goods to carry in inventory with the view of minimizing the cost of carrying the inventory while giving consideration to the needs of inventory for maximizing revenue, efficient production, and/or sales operations.

Inventory control is the restraint or direction exercised over the current asset, inventory, either by accounting methods or by physical methods or by both, with the intention of safeguarding the assets of the firm.

Inventory Planning. The cost of carrying inventories can easily be reduced simply by decreasing their physical quantities. However, unless reductions are wisely planned, they may result in serious curtailments of production and/or sales because of "stock-outs" of certain items. Of course, "stock-outs" can be avoided by maintaining large quantities of possibly needed items, but this would entail a heavy financial burden. Ideal inventory planning should maximize the profit resulting from the inventorying function and the producing and/or selling function by minimizing the cost of carrying the inventory in a way consistent with the most efficient operation of the production and/or sales function. A number of useful guides that may be used in inventory planning are discussed in the following paragraphs.

OPTIMUM ORDER SIZE. *Optimum order size,* also known as *economic order quantity,* is the number of units to be ordered at a single time in order to minimize the inventory acquisition and carrying costs and thus maximize the benefits.

There are many different types of costs incurred in acquiring and carrying inventories. However, they can be isolated into two groups: those costs that result periodically from repetitious transactions or events and those costs that result from the continuous act of carrying goods in inventory. Common repetitious costs are the costs of issuing purchase requisitions, writing purchase orders, order follow-ups, and writing receiving reports. Common continuous costs of carrying the inventory are property taxes, insurance, cost of invested capital, deterioration, and obsolescence.

As the number of orders increases, the total repetitious costs increase, but the total continuous costs decrease. As the number of orders decreases, the total repetitious costs decrease, but the total continuous costs increase. The optimum order size would be the one that would result in the smallest combined total of the two types of costs.

The following formula has been developed for the purpose of determining the optimum order size.

$$OOS = \sqrt{\frac{2 \times AR \times PC}{CC}}$$

where OOS = optimum order size (in units)

AR = annual requirements (in units)

PC = cost (repetitious) of placing and receiving an order

CC = cost (continuous) of carrying a unit in inventory

The application of this formula may be illustrated as follows: A firm requires 9,000 units a year that cost $4 each. The cost of placing and receiving an order amounts to $10 per order, and the cost of carrying a unit is $.50 based on a carrying-cost percentage of 12½ percent of $4.

$$OOS = \sqrt{\frac{2 \times 9,000 \times \$10}{.50}} = \sqrt{\frac{180,000}{.50}} = \sqrt{360,000} = 600$$

REORDER POINT. The *reorder point* is the number of units to which the inventory of a particular item must decrease in order to indicate a need for placing a purchase order. In the case of very inexpensive items, the reorder point is arbitrarily set high enough to prevent any possibility of a stock-out. However, in the case of expensive items, the cost of carrying inventory should be equated against the cost of stock-outs in order to minimize the total cost of providing goods for use or sale.

The reorder point can be determined by formula if the following data are available: optimum order size, unit carrying costs, usage, lead time (expected elapsed time between the placing of an order and its receipt), and stock-out costs.

$$RP = OOS \times \frac{S}{C + S} - U$$

where RP = reorder point

OOS = optimum order size

S = annual cost of stock-out of one unit

C = unit carrying cost

U = usage during lead time

If the optimum order size is 400 units, the carrying cost per unit is $1; the usage during lead time, 200 (50 per week for four weeks); and the estimated stock-out cost, $15 per unit. The reorder point, which is 175 units, is calculated as follows:

$$RP = 400 \times \frac{\$15}{\$1 + \$15} - 200 = 175 \text{ units}$$

It is significant that the higher the stock-out cost, the higher the reorder point would be in order to reduce the risk of stock-out losses.

It is very difficult to establish stock-out costs. An alternative method of calculating the reorder point is:

$RP = U + F$ (where F = safety factor, a quantity allowance for excess usage during lead time or for delayed delivery)

Using the facts given in the preceding example, plus a safety factor of 50 units, the reorder point is calculated as follows:

$$RP = 200 + 50 = 250 \text{ units}$$

MINIMUM INVENTORY. The *minimum inventory* is the quantity of goods expected to be in inventory just prior to the receipt of the next shipment, based on normal usage and normal delivery. If the lead time could be calculated exactly, and if the usage between the time of placing an order and its receipt could be determined exactly, the minimum inventory could theoretically be reduced safely to zero. But because of uncertainties with respect to both the usage function and the delivery function, a safety factor is necessary in establishing the estimated minimum inventory size. Thus, in setting a minimum inventory size, maximum usage during the lead time and reasonable delivery delays are included in establishing lead time, rather than normal or average figures, as in the calculation of the reorder point.

For example, if the maximum usage is estimated to be 60 units per week (rather than 50 units), with a maximum lead time of five weeks (rather than four weeks, as in the previous example), then the reorder point changes from 175 units to 300 units, as the following calculation demonstrates:

$$RP = 60 \times 5 = 300 \text{ units}$$

If an order is placed for 400 units when the inventory is reduced to 300 units and normal conditions prevail until the goods are received, the inventory will be reduced to 100 units just prior to the receipt of the goods.

Units on hand when order is placed		300
Normal weekly usage	50 units	
Normal lead time	× 4 weeks	
Normal usage		200
Inventory prior to receipt of new shipment		100

MAXIMUM INVENTORY. The *maximum inventory* is the quantity of goods expected to be on hand just after the receipt of a shipment. If the minimum inventory is 100 units just prior to receipt of 400 units, then after the receipt, the maximum inventory becomes 500 units.

COST OF STOCK-OUT. *Stock-out* is the failure to have a particular item available when needed either for use or for sale. So many possible variables are involved in the case of a stock-out that it is almost impossible to determine the cost. The cost of a stock-out includes the profit lost on the potential sale if the sale is lost. If the customer accepts a substitute item, the loss includes the difference in profit between the original item and the substitute item. If the customer waits for the original article, all costs incident to expediting quick delvery of the article represent a stock-out cost. These costs may be determinable, but it is impossible to calculate the lost profits if a customer becomes so dissatisfied that he takes his business elsewhere permanently. If stock-outs happen too often, a firm's reputation will suffer. The determination of the value of the resulting loss of goodwill almost defies calculation.

In the case of a manufacturing firm, all costs resulting from production delays or inefficiencies brought about by stock-outs are stock-out costs.

Inventory Control. Inventory control is the exercise of direction or restraint over the various types of inventories (e.g., merchandise, raw material, work in process, finished goods, and supplies). Control of inventories may be obtained by accounting and physical methods. It is suggested by some authorities that the physical control of inventory is not an accounting function, but there must be good accounting control in order for physical control to be effective.

Accounting control is effected by use of records and analyses. These records may include stock or stores ledger cards, ledger accounts, and so forth. Various analyses and comparisons may be made as a means of improving accounting control. The physical control involves the physical acts of receiving, storing, handling, and issuing goods. It will also involve stock or inventory taking. Inventory control includes all methods of detecting and preventing waste and loss of inventories.

Obsolescence is a carrying cost of inventory. Items of seasonal or technological value are especially subject to obsolescence. Therefore, the inventories of such items should be kept small, with a resulting rapid turnover.

Deterioration is a carrying cost especially applicable to perishable items such as vegetables and grain.

Shrinkage may occur as a result of such causes as evaporation or normal spillage or such causes as abnormal spillage or theft. In any event, the cost relates to the carrying of the inventory.

Cost of money, real or imputed, is a cost of carrying the inventory. If the inventory is financed with borrowed funds, the actual interest cost should be charged to the cost of carrying the inventory. In the event that the inventory is financed with the firm's funds, a reasonable amount of interest should be imputed as a carrying charge for decision-making purposes. It must be remembered, however, that costs cannot be imputed for accounting purposes per se.

INVENTORY TURNOVER. Inventory turnover is the number of times that the investment in goods or merchandise is replaced during a given period, usually a year. The inventory turnover indicates the period of time that an investment is committed to a given stock of goods or merchandise. The importance of such a ratio is dependent upon the size of the investment.

The inventory turnover is computed by dividing the cost of goods used during the period by the average cost of the inventories.

To be most significant for analysis and control purposes, the turnover of each major inventory group should be computed separately. For example, if a firm has large inventories of sheet steel and of plywood, the turnover of each should be calculated separately. In a merchandising firm, the inventory turnover is calculated as follows:

Inventory turnover = cost of goods sold ÷ average inventory

An alternate, but certainly less desirable, method of calculating the inventory turnover for a retail establishment that values its inventory at selling price is:

Inventory turnover = sales for the period ÷ average inventory taken at selling price

In a manufacturing firm, three kinds of inventory turnovers may be calculated as follows:

Finished-goods turnover = cost of goods sold during period ÷ average finished-goods inventory

Work-in-process turnover = cost of work completed during the period ÷ average work-in-process inventory

Raw-material turnover = cost of material placed in process during period ÷ average raw-material inventory

Some accountants express the turnover in terms of days by dividing 365 by the number of turnovers as calculated by these formulas.

Since the objective of the turnover ratio is to determine the rapidity with which goods pass through inventory, it is important to determine as typical an average inventory as possible because given a specific cost of goods used, the smaller the average inventory, the more rapid the turnovers. Normally (this is especially true of seasonal businesses reporting on a natural business-year basis), the year-end inventory is taken when the inventory is at or near its lowest level. A turnover based on an average of only the year's beginning and ending inventories would yield an inflated turnover number. Where monthly inventory figures are available, it would be much better to calculate the average inventory by adding together the amounts of the beginning inventory for the first month and the ending inventory for each of the twelve months and dividing the sum by 13.

Too slow an inventory turnover may well indicate inefficient overstocking. This, in turn, can increase the investment cost and the risk of obsolescence, deterioration, and theft, as well as such costs as storage, insurance, taxes and similar costs.

On the other hand, too rapid an inventory turnover may be

brought about by stocking too few items, resulting in lost sales or inefficient production.

A firm should strive for an optimum-size inventory with an optimum turnover rate.

NUMBER OF DAYS SALES IN INVENTORY. A similar and useful ratio is the number of days sales in the inventory. It is computed as follows:

$$\text{Days sales in ending inventory} = 365 \times \frac{\text{ending inventory}}{\text{cost of goods sold}}$$

CONTROL OF EXPENSIVE ITEMS VERSUS CHEAP ITEMS: THE ABC METHOD. Control of inventory items differs in three major ways: (1) the frequency of the review of the status or quantity of the particular items, (2) the level of personnel used for making the review, and (3) the detail and cost expended in making the review.

In many cases, about 10 percent of the units in a given total inventory account for approximately 50 percent of the total inventory value. Another 40 percent of the units may account for roughly 30 percent of the total inventory value. In terms of physical units, 50 percent of the inventory may account for as little as 20 percent of the total value of the inventory.

Good management dictates that control procedures should differ for each such significant group in the inventory. This has given rise to the so-called *ABC inventory-control method*. The few expensive items are considered to compose the A group. The B group is composed of the intermediate-valued items. The C group is composed of the great number of relatively inexpensive items.

The cost of controlling and safeguarding the several types of inventory must be equated against the potential savings that such a program may be expected to effect. Thus, more careful supervision by higher-salaried personnel can be justified for the relatively expensive items than for the many cheap items.

In the case of expensive units, weekly or even daily reviews of quantities and requirements by a responsible person may be required. In a manufacturing organization, for example, a responsible person in the production-planning department may closely coordinate promised delivery dates and quantities with production schedules to be sure that an adequate, but not too great, quantity of such items will be available as needed.

In the case of the very cheap items, the use of a high-salaried, responsible person for checking inventories cannot be economically justified. It is more economical to set an arbitrary high reorder point and authorize the inventory clerk to place an order for a predetermined quantity whenever the quantity on hand drops to the reorder point. It is more economical to have an excess quantity on hand and run the risk of some loss and deterioration than to spend large sums of money to obtain fine control over such cheap items.

Items of intermediate value would justify a moderate expenditure in behalf of their control and safeguarding.

CHAPTER 5

Current Assets:
Temporary Investments and Prepayments

Temporary investments and prepayments have a common claim to classification as current assets under the opinion expressed by the AICPA, which states that "cash and other assets or resources . . . which are reasonably expected to be realized in cash or sold or consumed during the normal operating cycle of the business"[1] should be designated as current assets.

NATURE OF TEMPORARY INVESTMENTS

Temporary investments may be distinguished from long-term or fixed investments by the requirement of ready marketability and the intent to sell during the current operating cycle.

Certain securities, even though they are currently marketable, should not be treated as temporary investments and thus as current assets if any of the following conditions are applicable:

1. The securities are treasury stock, that is, reacquired shares of the company's own stock.
2. The securities are not *intended* to be realized (converted into cash) during the current operating period.
3. The securities were acquired in order to obtain control of the particular company.
4. The securities were acquired in order to improve or maintain business relations with the company that issued them.

1. *Accounting Research and Terminology Bulletins,* Final Edition (1961), p. 20.

Marketability. The term *marketability* as used in regard to temporary investments (sometimes referred to as *marketable securities*) refers not only to the ease and speed with which these securities may be converted into cash but also to the stability of the price during the holding period, as well as to the effect that the sale of the securities may have on the price. Usually, marketable securities are acquired by a firm in order to earn some return on otherwise seasonally idle and thus unproductive cash. Therefore, a potentially high rate of return is sacrificed in favor of greater liquidity and security. In order to be considered marketable, the security under consideration should be traded on a daily basis in such volume that the amount held by the particular investor would not materially affect the price if sold at one time.

Short-term government securities are especially favored for temporary investments, even with their low yield, because of the relatively stable prices and large sales volume of such securities. Corporate bonds and preferred stock are suitable for temporary investments if they meet the requirements of relative stability of price and ready salability. Normally, common stocks do not have sufficient price stability to be appropriate for temporary or short-term investment.

Stocks and bonds that are not widely held or actively traded cannot properly be classified as temporary investments.

Intent to Sell. It is generally agreed that marketability is a prerequisite of classifying a security as a temporary or short-term investment and thus as a current asset. Some accountants believe that marketability alone is a sufficient basis for treating an investment as a current asset. However, most accountants hold that intent to sell the security within the current operating period is also a prerequisite of classifying it as a temporary investment. The AICPA expresses it as follows: "The term current assets is used to designate cash or other assets . . . reasonably expected to be realized in cash . . . during the normal operating cycle of the business. Thus, the term comprehends . . . marketable securities representing the investment of cash available for current operations."[2]

2. Ibid., p. 20.

VALUATION OF TEMPORARY INVESTMENTS

Temporary investments are essentially composed of marketable securities. Marketable securities may be divided into two general types: stocks and bonds. At time of acquisition, the securities should be recorded at cost, plus cost of acquisition, even though there are alternate ways of valuing them after acquisition.

Cost. Under the *cost method,* the securities should be recorded and carried at the price paid for them, plus all costs of acquisition, such as brokers' fees or commissions and transfer taxes.

When bonds are bought at either a premium or a discount, a valuation account may be used for recording the premium or discount separately. However, especially in the case of temporary investments, it is preferable to ignore the valuation account and to record the investment at cost net of premium or discount. This is appropriate because over a short period of time, the failure to amortize premium or to accumulate discount would not materially distort income. Day-to-day market prices would have a greater effect on earnings of short-term investments than the amortization of premium or the accumulation of discount would. In the case of bonds bought between interest dates, the bonds are usually quoted at a market price plus accrued interest. Under such circumstances, the accrued interest is an asset separate from the bond and should be recorded in a separate account.

Stock bought as a temporary investment may be recorded initially and carried at cost, that is, market price plus acquisition costs. Any premium or discount is normally considered part of the acquisition cost and is not shown as a separate account. Thus, the recognition of any gain or loss per se is deferred until the securities are sold, at which time the proceeds of the sale may be compared with the costs of acquisition. Interest earned on the investment is considered ordinary income rather than a capital gain.

There is a marked difference between the earnings on bonds and the earnings on stock. Interest on bonds accrues; dividends on stock do not accrue. Therefore, in the case of the use of stock as a temporary investment, there is no problem of recording accrued income.

Lower of Cost or Market. Even when the lower-of-cost-or-market method of valuing temporary investments is used, the initial recording of the securities should be at market price plus cost of acquisition, just as in the cost method. However, when statements are being prepared subsequent to the acquisition of the securities, the value of these securities should be reduced to current market value if indeed the present market value has declined below the original cost.

The AICPA supports this method, stating that "in the case of marketable securities where market value is less than cost by a substantial amount and it is evident that the decline in market value is not due to a mere temporary condition, the amount to be included as a current asset should not exceed the market value."[3]

In those instances where the lower-of-cost-or-market method is used in valuing temporary investments, the method is usually applied to the group of short-term investments as a whole, rather than to each security. Such reductions in the value of the investments may be recorded directly in the asset account. However, they are frequently recorded in a separate valuation account, thus leaving the original cost figure intact in the asset account.

It should be pointed out that the lower-of-cost-or-market method is not acceptable for income-tax purposes.

Market. The AICPA recognizes the importance of showing the current market value of temporary investments. The Institute supports the use of market value when values are declining, by approving the lower-of-cost-or-market method; but it does not give full support to a market-value method when prices are rising because it hesitates to value temporary investments above cost, just as it disapproves of valuing inventories above cost. The Institute does recommend, however, that current market value be shown parenthetically.

Evaluation of the Three Methods. The cost method has the advantages of providing the most objectively determined valuation, of being generally accepted by the accounting profession, of being accepted for income-tax purposes, and of being the easiest and simplest method to apply. It is said that temporary investments are the nearest thing to cash that a firm has, other than cash itself. A major disadvantage of the cost method is the failure to show on the balance sheet the realizable value of the securities except perhaps by a parenthetical insertion or footnote.

3. Ibid., p. 23.

Another disadvantage is that any gain or loss is deferred until the sale of the investment.

The lower-of-cost-or-market method has the advantage of the unqualified approval of the AICPA and the acceptance by the accounting profession. Furthermore, when prices are declining, this method provides an indication in the balance-sheet accounts of the current net realizable value of the investments, and correlatively, the income statement will show any loss on the securities sustained during the period. The major disadvantage of this method is lack of consistency. Current net realizable value and periodic loss are shown when prices are declining, but when prices are rising, neither net realizable values nor periodic gains are shown in the accounts. Other disadvantages of this method are its complexity and lack of acceptance for income-tax purposes.

The major advantage of the market-value method is its consistency. Current net realizable value is reflected in the accounts both when prices are rising and when they are declining, and both periodic gains and periodic losses are recognized. This method has one overriding disadvantage: the lack of acceptance by the AICPA, the accounting profession, and the IRS. Although many people favor this method as a means of showing the cash equivalent of such a liquid asset, the general lack of support almost rules it out as a usable method at this time.

ACCOUNTING FOR PURCHASE AND SALE OF TEMPORARY INVESTMENTS

There is a slight difference between the accounting treatment of bonds held as a temporary investment and stocks held temporarily because interest on bonds accrues with the passage of time; whereas dividends on stock do not accrue but, rather, become a legal liability of the stock issuer only if and when such dividends are declared. Therefore, accounting for bonds and for stocks will be discussed separately.

Accounting for Temporary Investments in Bonds. Regardless of which of the three methods of accounting for temporary investments in bonds is used, the acquisition will be recorded in the same manner: at cost.

For example, assume the purchase of a $1,000 8 percent bond for $900 plus accrued interest on September 30. The interest is payable on June 30 and December 31 of each year. The market value of the bond declined to $800 as of December 31.

Regardless of method used, the entry to record the purchase on September 30 would be as follows:

Investment in bonds	$900	
Accrued interest receivable	20	
Cash		$920

On December 31, when the interest payment is received, the following entry would be appropriate under any of the three methods:

Cash	$40	
Accrued interest receivable		$20
Interest income		20

Under the cost method, no entry is required on December 31 to give recognition in the investment account to the decline in value of the bond. However, if either the lower-of-cost-or-market method or the market-value method is used, the loss in market value should be recorded by an entry such as the following:

Loss on investment in bonds	$100	
Allowance for loss on investment in bonds		$100

Assume that the market value rose to $1,000 by December 31, instead of declining to $800. The entries to record the purchase and receipt of the interest would be the same as those given in the preceding example. However, under this changed situation, no entry would be required under the cost method or the lower-of-cost-or-market method to adjust the investment account. The following entry would be required under the market-value method:

Allowance for gain on investment in bonds	$100	
Gain on investment in bonds		$100

It should be observed that since original cost data must be preserved for income-tax purposes, it is convenient to carry the unadjusted cost in the investment account and to record any adjustments necessitated by changes in market values in an evaluation account, as in the preceding entries. However, some accountants prefer to make such adjustments directly to the investment account. Thus, the adjustment indicated in the previous example could be recorded as follows:

Investment in bonds	$100	
Gain on investment in bonds		$100

Accounting for Temporary Investments in Stocks. Assume the purchase of 10 shares of $100 par value 6 percent stock for $900 on September 30. Dividends normally are declared on December 31. Assume that the market value of the stock declined to $80 per share as of December 31.

Under any of the three methods of carrying temporary investments, the following entry should be made to record the acquisition:

Investment in stocks	$900	
Cash		$900

Under any of the three methods, the receipt of the declaration of the dividend would be recorded as follows:

Dividends receivable	$60	
Dividend income		$60

Under the cost method of carrying investments, no entry is required as of December 31 to adjust the investment account to current market value.

However, if either the lower-of-cost-or-market method or the market-value method is being used, the following entry should be made:

Loss on investment in stocks	$100	
Investment in stocks		$100

It should be observed that this credit could have been to allowance for loss on investment in stock.

PREPAID EXPENSES

Prepaid expenses represent expenditures for goods or services (usually of a recurring nature) that have not yet been consumed but that are expected to be used up during the coming year or operating cycle. For this reason, they should be treated as current assets. At one time, accountants did not distinguish between prepaid expenses and deferred charges. Currently, accountants hold that a distinction should be made between prepaid expenses (sometimes referred to as *prepaid items*) and deferred charges (to expense). Currently, the application of the term *deferred charges* is generally restricted to expenditures that are not recognized as expenses in the period in which they are incurred but that will be a benefit to two or more future periods; therefore, they are charged to expense during the periods benefited. Because such items will not be expensed in their entirety during the next year or operating period, they are classified as noncurrent assets.

Nature of Prepaid Expenses. Prepaid expenses would not qualify as current assets under the old definition of a current asset, which required that a current asset be cash or other assets which would be converted into cash or sold during the current operating cycle of the firm. However, prepaid expenses do qualify as current assets under the current definition of a current asset as cash or other assets that will be converted into cash, sold, or consumed during the current operating cycle.

The current-asset classification of prepaid expenses is justified on the basis that if such items had not been acquired prior to the beginning of the current period, cash would have to be expended during the period for their acquisition so that the firm could continue to operate efficiently.

Typical prepaid expenses are operating supplies, prepaid interest payable, prepaid insurance, prepaid taxes, prepaid wages, and prepaid advertising. Under a firm's normal operating conditions, such items will not be converted into cash or sold but will be consumed by the firm in its normal operations.

Evaluation of Prepaid Expenses. Because of the general acceptance of the going-concern concept (the concept that the firm is currently operating and is expected to continue operating), prepaid expenses are valued at cost. This is true even though many items, such as letterheads, would have practically no realizable cash value.

CHAPTER 6

Noncurrent Assets: Plant and Equipment (Tangible Fixed Assets)

An asset that has an expected life under its intended use of more than one accounting cycle or one year, whichever is longer, is properly considered a *noncurrent asset*. Such noncurrent assets may be divided into two major categories: tangible and intangible.

Tangible noncurrent assets are things that have physical substance and that will have value in their intended use for more than one accounting cycle or one year, whichever is longer.

Intangible noncurrent assets are valuable rights, privileges, advantages, or services that will extend over more than one accounting cycle or one year, whichever is longer, but that lack physical substance. However, an intangible item may be evidenced by some physical substance, for example, a bond is considered to be intangible, but its existence and ownership are established by a physical substance, a piece of paper known as a *bond* or a *bond certificate*.

Noncurrent assets are frequently subdivided into three groups: fixed assets, investments, and deferred charges. The term *fixed assets* is applied to noncurrent assets used in the regular operations of the business. The term *investments* is applied to noncurrent assets not used in the usual operations of the business but held in anticipation of future gain. Thus, land on which a firm's operating plant is situated may properly be classified as a fixed asset, but land that the firm has bought with the idea of using it for a plant site sometime in the future or perhaps of selling it at a profit should be classified as an investment. Not all firms distinguish between fixed assets and investments.

Deferred charges are discussed in Chapter 9. They are mentioned here only because they are a part of the total noncurrent assets, as contrasted with current assets. This is important because total assets are composed of current assets plus noncurrent assets.

NATURE OF PLANT AND EQUIPMENT

The group of tangible noncurrent assets used in the regular operations of a business may be referred to as *property, plant, and equipment,* or *plant and equipment,* or simply *fixed assets.* Regardless of the term applied to these assets, they have three significant common characteristics:

1. They have a life expectancy of more than one accounting cycle or year.
2. However, with the exception of land, they will have a limited life.
3. They will be used in the usual operations of the business.

Land. The accounting concept of the term *land* is much more restricted than the legal concept is. As an accounting term, land refers to the earth's surface that can be owned and used to grow crops and to support man-made structures, and for general (surface) use by mankind. This restricted definition excludes minerals and similar useful substances within the earth, as well as the rights to air above the earth's surface.

By contrast, the legal definition of land includes not only the earth's surface but also rights to the earth's subsurface and its contents to its very center, as well as the air as high as the heavens. One must point out that this old definition is currently undergoing some modification in the area of air rights because of modern air transportation and space travel.

The fact that accountants use a restrictive definition of land should not imply that they do not recognize the value of things within the earth or above it. Accountants have subdivided this whole into a number of parts. The natural resources within the earth and even trees growing in their natural state are referred to as *crops* or *wasting assets.* Air rights above the land are owned by the landowner subject to public-domain claims. In metropolitan areas, these rights are separable from the land itself and may be sold or leased separately from the land. Land improvements or betterments are produced by man and are attached to the land.

Noncurrent or fixed assets are sometimes referred to as *permanent assets,* but this definition is not accurate in the strictest sense. It may be reasonably true in comparison with current assets; however, with the exception of land, all such assets will be consumed eventually or worn out. Land (with the possible exception of valuable air rights) is the only truly permanent asset to be accounted for. Land is not depreciable. One notable exception to treating land as a fixed asset is land held as stock-in-trade by land developers. Under such circumstances, it should be considered as inventory and included with the current assets.

Buildings. Buildings are long-lived assets intended not to be resold but to house and shelter another large group of fixed assets referred to as *machinery and equipment* and also to provide working space for the firm's operations.

Machinery and Equipment. *Machinery and equipment* consist of a varied array of industrial, agricultural, and office equipment, including large tools and movable and immovable items such as stationary cranes, mobile cranes, transportation vehicles, and containers. Often, there is no clear-cut distinction between buildings on the one hand and machinery and equipment on the other. For example, elevators, wiring, plumbing, and various other types of built-in equipment are in some cases included as part of the building and in other cases listed separately as equipment. Theoretically, it would be better to list such major built-ins separately because their useful life may be somewhat shorter than that of the building itself.

Improvements or Betterments. *Improvements or betterments* are changes or modifications of an existing facility or asset in a way that substantially extends its useful life, increases its potential rate of output, increases its operating efficiency, or decreases its operating cost. These factors distinguish betterments from repairs or maintenance, which tend to keep a facility in or near its original efficiency without materially adding to its life, productivity, or efficiency.

Additions. An *addition* is an increase in the size of an existing asset or group of assets. It may take the form of a new room or wing added to an existing building or an entirely new building added to (but not physically attached to) an existing group of buildings.

The essential difference between improvements or betterments and additions is that improvements result in an increase in quality; whereas additions result in an increase in quantity or size.

Tools, Jigs, Patterns, and Fixtures. Although this is a heterogeneous group of assets, the items generally have two elements in common: a relatively small unit value and an uncertain life. As a group, they often represent a significant investment. The term *tools,* as used here, implies "small tools," as contrasted with "large tools," which is used in connection with machinery and equipment.

Because of their small unit value and uncertain life, such items are often charged to expense when acquired. An alternative but less favored method is to capitalize the cost of the items and then to expense their replacements.

VALUATION

Generally, fixed assets should be valued at cost. This is a rather straightforward statement, but the determination of which items are properly includable in the cost calculation under particular circumstances may become quite complex. Although fixed or noncurrent assets may differ widely according to type, they have many common and similar costing problems.

Acquisitions by Cash Purchase. *Cost* is understood to mean the cash consideration or its equivalent exchanged in an arms-length transaction (a transaction in which both the buyer and the seller are each able to act freely in seeking his own best economic interest, position, or price) for a particular asset, good, or service. Specifically, an asset that is purchased for cash should be recorded at the amount of cash paid out for that asset, but this gives rise to questions concerning whether cash payments or discounts were directly connected with the acquired asset or with a related function. For example, is the cash paid for freight to get the asset delivered a part of the cost of the asset, or is it an operating expense? Is the cost of material used and destroyed in the initial breaking-in and adjusting of the machine a part of the cost of the machine, or is it an operating expense? Is the cash discount received for prompt payment a reduction in the asset cost, or is it financial income?

It is generally held that all costs (at cash value) incurred to get a fixed asset in position and operating properly may be capitalized as part of the fixed asset's cost.

In the case of land, there are unique costing difficulties because of the peculiar physical characteristics and legal problems involved in acquiring the land and preparing it for its intended use. Included among such costs are the purchase price, cost of surveys, legal fees, costs of perfecting or insuring title, any liabilities or liens against the land (the liens at time of purchase must be paid by the purchaser—but they may be paid subsequent to purchase) which must be paid by the buyer at date of purchase, accrued taxes, and the cost of clearing, filling, grading, and draining the land in preparing it for use. In some cases, permanent improvements are included in the land cost. Frequently, such improvements are charged to a separate land improvement account.

The cost of removing an old building is charged to the land, but the cost of excavating for the basement of a new building is charged to the building.

Improvements such as drives, walks, curbs, fences, and landscaping added by the owner preferably should be charged not to the land but to separate improvements accounts in order that they may be depreciated over their estimated useful lives.

Care should be taken to discover any hidden interest or finance charges. If any are discovered, they should be excluded from the asset accounts and charged to expense.

In the case of existing usable buildings bought with land, the problems are the same as those discussed in connection with land except for the additional problem of allocating the costs between the nondepreciable asset land on the one hand and the depreciable asset buildings on the other hand. This is necessary so that proper periodic depreciation charges can be made for the buildings.

Land and buildings have common costing problems because the laws of real estate apply to both.

Because machinery, equipment, tools, jigs, patterns, and fixtures are legally considered personal property rather than real estate, the problems and thus the cost of establishing legal title to them are not so great as in the case of land and buildings. The cost of such personal property will include the invoice price, less available cash discount, plus transportation costs, installation costs, and breaking-in costs, if any, including cost of material damaged during this period. Costs of necessary foundations and building modifications also should be charged to the asset that necessitated the expenditure.

Small tools and so forth may be either capitalized at their net delivered cost or expensed upon acquisition.

Acquisition by Credit Purchase. In the case of credit purchases, a purchaser is confronted with the same potential cost inclusions and exclusions as in the case of cash purchases, plus one additional problem: the cost of credit. The cost of credit, interest, should be excluded from the cost price of the asset. The reason for the exclusion is quite evident when both a cash price and a credit price are given. The difference between the cash price and the deferred-payment price should be considered by the buyer to be the cost of borrowing money, and therefore, it should be treated as a financial expense. The fact that the buyer elects to pay more than the cash price does not make the asset any more valuable. Certainly, if the buyer elected to borrow the funds from a financial institution and take advantage of the seller's cash price, the interest paid to the financial institution could not be considered a part of the asset cost.

Often, only a cash price is quoted, and credit terms are specified separately, for example, 6 percent on the unpaid balance or 4 percent on the initial amount for the full term of the loan or deferred-payment plan. When credit terms are specifically set forth in this or a similar fashion, it is quite clear that they should not be charged to the asset.

The costing problem becomes more involved when the seller quotes only one price and is willing to accept payment over a prolonged period. The question may be asked: Is there interest included in the quoted price? And if so, how much? Theoretically, the buyer should reduce the cost of the asset by a normal interest charge. However, this procedure is not commonly followed.

Acquisition by Issuance of Securities. When a firm issues its own securities, either bonds or stock, in exchange for assets, questions may be raised concerning the most appropriate basis for valuing the assets received. The basis that would provide the most reliable valuation should be used.

If the securities are currently being traded frequently on one of the large organized exchanges, the current market price listed by the exchange probably would provide the most realistic value for the assets received, based on the assumptions that the securities could have been issued for cash at the quoted price and that the cash could then have been used to purchase the assets. If there are only occasional small transactions in the securities involved, the prices may not be typical. Also, an issue of the securities that is large enough to pay for the assets could depress the market value of the securities. Occasionally, in a single transaction, some stock will be issued at par for cash, and additional stock will be issued to the same party for noncash assets. There has been an improper tendency to value the noncash assets at the par value of the balance of the securities exchanged. Such a transaction is hardly a typical arm's-length deal and, therefore, probably will not provide a reliable market price for the securities.

In some instances, the market value of the assets themselves may be a more reliable indication of their value than the market value of the securities exchanged for them.

When bonds are issued for assets, there is a strong tendency to value the assets received at the face value of the bonds. Such a valuation is correct only when the actual interest rate and the nominal rate are the same. The assets received should be valued at the present value of the bonds exchanged for them.

Sometimes it is difficult for the buyer to establish a reliable market value for either the assets or the securities; in such cases, an independent professional appraisal should be obtained as a means of establishing a value for the assets.

In the past, it has been a common practice to value assets at the par or stated value of the securities exchanged for them. In the absence of fraud, the courts have allowed the boards of directors absolute authority in valuing property under such exchanges.

Securities frequently are exchanged for assets in order to effect a merger or consolidation. When the procedure results in a transfer of the assets to a new owner, the transaction is said to be a *purchase*, and the assets are recorded at their cost to the new owner. When the program results in the continuation of the original ownership, the transaction is said to be a *pooling of interests*, and the assets are carried forward at the values as shown on the books of the acquired firm.

Acquisition by Exchange of Other Assets. When one asset is exchanged for another, the new asset should be recorded at the fair market value of the old or the new asset, whichever value can be determined most reliably. Any difference between the book value of the old asset and the recorded value of the new asset should be recorded as a gain or loss on the exchange.

When cash is involved in the exchange, an option of three common valuation methods exists. (1) The *secondhand-market-price method* fixes the value of the new asset at the market value of the old asset, plus or minus the amount of cash given or received. This method is theoretically sound and is generally favored. (2) The *list-price method* fixes the value of the new asset according to the listed retail price. (3) The *income-tax method* fixes the value of the new asset at the book value of the old asset, plus or minus the amount of "boot" (money or other property given or received in order to equalize the exchange; this is especially significant in tax-free exchanges) given or received plus any recognized tax gain or less any recognized tax loss on the exchange. This method lacks theoretical and logical support because it may result in carrying forward cost elements of an asset no longer owned or in capitalizing losses from former assets. It does have the practical result of making separate property records for tax purposes unnecessary. This method is acceptable from an accounting point of view only if it does not result in a substantial misstatement of asset values.

Acquisition by Own Construction. Sometimes assets are constructed by a firm for its own use in order to save on construction costs, to use men and facilities more efficiently, to maintain a work force, or to exercise greater control over the quality of construction. When a firm undertakes such construction, three unique problems arise: the allocation of overhead costs, the charging of interest during construction, and the treatment of profit on self-construction.

There are three possible alternate solutions to these overhead problems.

ALLOCATE ONLY INCREMENTAL OVERHEAD TO THE SELF-CONSTRUCTED ASSET. This is the most logical and most generally favored method because it does not disturb the firm's usual treatment of fixed overhead, that is, charging it to regular production (inventory). It is assumed here that true fixed costs would not be affected by the additional activity but that any increase in variable costs would be occasioned by the additional activity. It is therefore believed that this method would result in charging production with amounts of overhead reasonably comparable with amounts charged to production in periods when self-construction was not engaged in and also in charging the self-construction with a justifiable amount of overhead.

ALLOCATE A PORTION OF OVERHEAD, BOTH FIXED AND VARIABLE, TO THE SELF-CONSTRUCTED ASSET. This method enjoys fair acceptance and is supported by the argument that all production, regardless of type or purpose, should bear a portion of all overhead. If all fixed overhead is charged to inventory, the fixed asset's cost is understated. It is argued by a few that the failure to distribute fixed overhead to all production would result in lack of comparability of inventory costs between years when there was self-construction and years when there was no self-construction.

CHARGE NO OVERHEAD TO THE SELF-CONSTRUCTED ASSET. This is the least acceptable method because it would undervalue the fixed asset and overstate inventory costs.

Interest is generally regarded as a financing cost, rather than a production cost. Public utilities are permitted to capitalize actual or imputed interest during the construction period for rate-making purposes. Because of this interest treatment accorded public utilities, nonpublic utility companies are permitted, although with reservations, to capitalize actual interest costs incurred during construction. There is more reason to capitalize interest during the initial construction period before any revenue is produced than to capitalize it for subsequent additions. Failure to capitalize the actual interest incurred during the initial construction period would cause the firm to begin operations under the handicap of a deficit. However, if the interest is capitalized, it is better to charge it to some intangible asset account as *start-up costs* than to charge it to the tangible asset.

Profit on self-construction should not be recognized. If a firm receives a low bid of $100,000 for the construction of a plant addition but constructs the facility for itself at a cost of $90,000, the addition should be recorded at $90,000. The $10,000 decrease in construction cost effected because of self-construction is a *saving*, not a profit. The profit will be realized later through the use and/or sale of the asset. On the other hand, if the owner rejected bids of $100,000 because it was believed that the addition could be built for $90,000 but, because of unexpected costs and inefficiencies, it cost the owner $110,000 to build, the entire $110,000 cost may be charged to the self-constructed asset on the basis that actual costs should be recognized and capitalized. However, if it is evident that the cost is excessive for the quality of the asset obtained, the excess cost (here apparently $10,000) may be charged off immediately as an extraordinary expense. This will prevent future production from being burdened with excessve depreciation charges.

Acquisition by Gift or Discovery. It is generally held that cost is the most objectively determined and reliable basis for measuring the value of an asset; however, when an asset is received as a gift or is unexpectedly discovered, there is no reliable cost figure to use. If a gift of substantial value were recorded at no value, this would result in understating assets and capital. Income in future periods would be overstated by such factors as the amount of depreciation, depletion, or amortization which should have been taken but were not. Also, the earnings-to-assets and earnings-to-capital ratios would be misstated. For these reasons, the gifts should be appraised and recorded at fair market value. For example, assume that a gift of land with a market value of $50,000 and with a building on it worth $100,000 was received by a corporation. The gift should be recorded as follows:

Land	$ 50,000	
Building	100,000	
Donated capital—plant donation		$150,000

Sometimes the gift is contingent upon the meeting of certain conditions, for example, the hiring of at least fifty men for the next five years. Under such conditions, the entry might be made as follows:

Contingent asset—land	$ 50,000	
Contingent asset—building	100,000	
Contingent donated capital		$150,000

After five years, if the conditions of the gift have been met, the following entries would be made:

Land	$ 50,000	
Building	100,000	
Contingent asset—land		$ 50,000
Contingent asset—building		100,000
Contingent donated capital	150,000	
Donated capital—plant donation		150,000

Although there may be a cloud on the legal title to the property during the five-year period, the firm holding the contingent gift should record depreciation on the building as if it held a clear legal title to it. To do otherwise would understate costs for the first five years of the life of the gift, with resulting overstated costs during the balance of the gift's life.

Unexpected discoveries of natural resources should be handled similarly to gifts because here again cost fails to provide an adequate basis for valuing the property. For example, assume that oil reserves reliably appraised at $100,000 are suddenly discovered under land already owned by a particular firm. An entry such as the following would be in order:

Oil reserves discovered	$100,000	
Appraisal capital—discovered oil		$100,000

Lump-Sum Acquisition or Basket Purchase. Two or more assets may be acquired for a single amount without an indicated breakdown for each individual asset. For accounting and control purposes, such a cost should be allocated among the assets. This is especially true where the several assets have different life expectancies. If two assets are involved and the value of one can be reliably determined, the value of the other may be assumed to be the balance of the purchase price. When an objective value cannot be developed for either of the two assets, an appraisal may be in order. If the appraised values equal the total purchase price, the appraised values may be used. If the total appraised value is either more or less than the total purchase price, the purchase price may be allocated according to the relationship of the appraised value of each unit to the total appraised value.

For example, assume that three assets were purchased for $45,000. An appraisal established values for items A, B, and C at $10,000, $20,000, and $30,000, respectively. The following allocation could be made:

Asset	Appraised Value	Fractional Allocation	Cost Allocation
A	$10,000	1/6 (or 10,000/60,000)	$ 7,500
B	20,000	2/6	15,000
C	30,000	3/6	22,500
Total	$60,000		$45,000

Now assume that the assets bought for $45,000 were appraised at $5,000, $10,000, and $15,000. The allocation could be made as follows:

Asset	Appraised Value	Fractional Allocation	Cost Allocation
A	$ 5,000	1/6 (or 5,000/30,000)	$ 7,500
B	10,000	2/6	15,000
C	15,000	3/6	22,500
Total	$30,000		$45,000

An alternate solution in this case, in which the appraised value of the tangible assets is less than the total purchase price when a going concern is taken over, is to record the tangible assets at their appraised value and to record the balance ($15,000) of the purchase price as an intangible asset, goodwill.

Capital versus Revenue Expenditures. A *capital expenditure* is one that is intended to benefit future periods, whereas a *revenue expenditure* is expected to benefit only the current period. Capital expenditures usually increase the book value of fixed assets by increasing the quantity of fixed assets through the acquisition of new units or additions to existing units, by increasing the efficiency of existing assets through improvements, or merely by increasing the life expectancy of the existing assets.

REARRANGEMENTS. *Rearrangements,* often referred to as *reinstallation* (in the case of machinery and equipment) or *remodeling* (in the case of buildings), create some interesting cost-allocation problems. Rearrangements of machinery refers to relocating production units in order to improve the production route or flow of work in process. In the case of buildings, or remodeling, rearrangement refers to changing the structure to improve the work flow by altering partitions, doorways, and in some cases even floors and roofs.

Presumably, the reason for rearranging machinery and equipment or remodeling a building is to make the asset more efficient and thus increase profits during the useful life of the rearrangement. Therefore, many accountants urge that such costs be capitalized into the affected asset's account or, better, charged to an adjunct account for rearrangement costs. In either case, the depreciated cost of the original installation or construction of the involved equipment or portion of building should be removed from the asset accounts. It is sometimes impossible to determine the cost of the original installation or construction. In such cases, it is acceptable practice to charge a rearrangement or remodeling account with such costs without removing the book value of the original installation or prior remodeling costs from the asset account, even though this admittedly results in an overstatement of asset values.

Machinery may be rearranged many times at short intervals during its useful life. Therefore, for reasons of practicality, some accounting authorities recommend that the first installation or construction costs be charged in the original asset costs and depreciated over the useful life of the asset and that all subsequent costs of rearrangements be expensed as incurred.

Often under the terms of commercial or industrial real estate leases, the tenant is required to make desired rearrangements and alterations at his own expense. Under these conditions, the costs should be charged to a leasehold improvement account and amortized during the term of the lease or the life of the alteration, whichever is shorter.

IMPROVEMENTS. Improvements, sometimes referred to as betterments, result from expenditures that extend the useful life of an existing fixed asset, increase its output capacity, increase its operating efficiency, lower its operating costs, or in other ways make it more valuable to the firm than just the cost of added repairs. An improvement *increases* the *quality* of an asset. An addition *increases* the *quantity* of an asset. A repair *maintains* an asset in something of its *original condition.* Patching the worn asphalt surface of a parking lot would constitute a repair; the installation of an entirely new asphalt surface in place of the old one would constitute a replacement; the installation of a new cement surface in place of the asphalt one would be an improvement. In practice, it is sometimes difficult in borderline cases to distinguish between improvements and replacements. However, this should not create a serious accounting problem because *major* improvements and replacements will be accounted for in the same way. In either case, the asset account and the allowance for depreciation account should be relieved of the amounts applicable to the asset (or part of asset) being replaced either in like kind or in better quality, and an asset account should be charged with the cost of the replacement or improvement. In either case, the following entry should be made:

Asset (new)	XX	
Allowance for depreciation	XX	
Asset (old)		XX
Cash		XX

In the case of *minor* improvements or replacements, similar treatment is acceptable. Theoretically, small expenditures for either improvements or replacements should be handled in the same manner as major expenditures; however, for reasons of practicality, such small expenditures are treated as repairs and are charged directly to expense, without involving the fixed asset accounts.

MAINTENANCE AND REPAIRS. In practice, it is often difficult to distinguish between maintenance and repairs, even though there is a clear distinction according to the respective definitions. Limited expenditures made to *keep* fixed assets in normal operating condition are referred to as *maintenance*. Limited expenditures made to *restore* fixed assets to normal operating condition are referred to as *repairs*. Maintenance is preventive in nature; repairs are restorative or curative in nature. There must be some limitation on the amount of expenditure to be classified as either a maintenance expense or a repair expense. If the expenditure would be very large, an improvement or a replacement may be indicated.

Maintenance should always be charged against current revenue. Some accounting authorities believe that there are two types of repairs: *ordinary* and *extraordinary*. These authorities consider such things as the frequent replacement of parts, which involves small expenditures, to be ordinary repairs. These should be charged to expense. These same authorities consider such things as infrequent replacement of parts to be extraordinary repairs. They suggest that in such cases, the cost of the original parts should be removed from the asset account along with the removal of the proper amount from the account for accumulated depreciation, and the cost of the repairs should be added to the asset account. It should be observed that this procedure is similar to the treatment accorded major replacements (discussed in the preceding section "Improvements"). Thus, it follows that extraordinary repairs may be considered replacements.

Because repair costs may vary from year to year and even from month to month, and because there is no direct correlation between production and repair costs, a few accountants attempt to relate the cost of repairs equally period by period or to the product on a production basis, regardless of when the actual cost was incurred, by recourse to an allowance for repairs account. This method is similar to the method used in accruing depreciation. The repair costs for the life of the asset would be estimated. The life of the asset would be estimated in terms of time periods or units of output. A repair rate would then be established by dividing the estimated total cost by the number of periods or the number of units of asset life. If the allowance is based on time, the amount would be the same for each period. If it is based on production, the amount involved would be the product of the units produced multiplied by the unit rate. In either of these ways, the amount of the following entry would be determined without regard to actual cost incurred:

Repair expense	XX	
Allowance for repairs		XX

The following entry would be made for the actual repair cost when incurred:

Allowance for repairs   XX
  Cash   XX

SPECIAL PROBLEMS PERTAINING TO TOOLS, JIGS, PATTERNS, AND FIXTURES. This diverse group of assets has several common characteristics that give rise to special accounting problems. They are all fixed assets, but their actual useful lives may differ greatly from their physical lives. They all have relatively small unit values. They are all somewhat portable.

Some accountants use a two-way breakdown of tools: large tools and small tools. Generally, such large tools as lathes, drill presses, and motors are classified as machinery and equipment. The small tools such as hammers, saws, and other hand tools, as well as small machine tools such as drill bits and various cutting attachments, are often referred to simply as *tools*. Generally, when *tool* is used alone, the restrictive term *small* is implied.

How should an asset such as a hand hammer, which may last for ten years but which may be lost or stolen tomorrow, be accounted for? It is impractical to set up property and depreciation records for each such item. It is more practical and a generally accepted practice for control purposes to treat such tools as inventory. At the end of each accounting period, a physical inventory of the tools is taken, at which time the tools are valued at approximate cost. If substantial deterioration is evident, the approximate cost may be written down proportionately. Some accountants will list a minimum or initial amount as an asset and charge all subsequent acquisitions to expense as acquired. A modification of this method is to treat the tools as assets when acquired but to charge them to expense when issued.

Jigs and patterns may have a long physical life but a short useful life. They may be used in the production of so many stock items that they will wear out physically, or they may be suited for use only on a special job of such small size that they will be only slightly worn by the time the special job is completed. Although it is possible that there will be repeat orders for special jobs on which these special jigs and patterns may be used, conservatism dictates that their cost be charged to the first order.

Of course, the jigs and patterns used for the production of stock items should be expensed to the time periods or the total expected quantity that is to benefit from them. If they should last through more than one accounting cycle, they may be depreciated.

The term *furniture and fixtures* covers a vast variety of items, ranging from wastebaskets to chairs, desks, safes, counters, and partitions. The normal physical life of these assets is greater than one year; thus, they could be capitalized and depreciated over their lifetime. However, because of the great variances of actual life of similar items and the relatively small unit value of some types of items, it is advisable to set a minimum unit value that may be capitalized. Then any item costing less than the established capitalizable minimum would be immediately charged to expense, even though it may last for several years.

Retirement. *Retirement* refers to the removal from use of a whole or partial unit of a fixed asset, such as a building or a piece of equipment. Retirement may be occasioned because of a change in production methods and procedures, a curtailment of a particular activity, or the liquidation of the firm. The retired unit may be sold, scrapped, abandoned, or even traded. If it is traded for a similar unit, the retirement may be considered as the first half of a replacement transaction (see p. 101).

When a fixed asset is retired, the accumulated depreciation must be brought up to date. Then the asset account and its adjunct account should be closed out and the gain or loss recorded.

For example, an asset that cost $1,000 is depreciated 50 percent to date and is sold for $200 cash. The following entry would properly record the retirement:

Cash	$200	
Allowance for depreciation	500	
Loss on retirement	300	
Asset		$1,000

Involuntary Conversions. *Involuntary conversion* is the substitution of another asset, including cash, for property given up by the owner unwillingly or without consent. Typical examples of involuntary conversion are property seized in condemnation proceedings, stolen property, and property destroyed by storm, flood, fire, and so forth. An involuntary conversion may be a conversion into cash or into similar or dissimilar assets.

If property is converted into property that is similar or related in use to the property replaced, there is no taxable gain if the amount realized is equal to or less than the cost of the replacement property. If the amount realized on the conversion exceeds the cost of the replacement property, gain is recognized to the extent of the excess. For these tax rules to apply, the replacement must be made within a stipulated time period, the replacement must be in kind, and the taxpayer must elect to apply the rules.

Although under some circumstances for tax purposes, an involuntary conversion may be considered as resulting in no (or only a limited) gain or loss, it is generally accepted accounting practice to record the involuntary conversion as a replacement and thus to recognize the full amount of the gain or loss.

Assume that a building with a cost value of $90,000 and accumulated depreciation of $40,000 is destroyed by fire, that the amount of insurance collected is $60,000, and that a similar building is acquired at a cost of $70,000. Consider the comparative recordings of the transactions.

The involuntary conversion recorded in summary form according to tax rules that permit the deferral of taxable gain or loss would be:

Cash (received)	$60,000	
Building (new) (old book value[a] + "boot")	60,000	
Allowance for depreciation	40,000	
Building (old)		$90,000
Cash (paid out)		70,000

[a] The book value surrendered to the insurance company is zero. Or, the basis of the new building is cost ($70,000) less unrecognized gain ($60,000−$50,000) or $60,000.

The entry on a replacement or on a nontax basis would be:

Cash (received)	$60,000	
Building (new)	70,000	
Allowance for depreciation	40,000	
Gain		$10,000
Building (old)		90,000
Cash (paid out)		70,000

In providing insurance protection, the possibility of a coinsurance clause in the policy and its effect on the coverage must be considered. A *coinsurance* clause limits the liability of the insurer to a loss no greater than the amount determined by multiplying the amount of loss by the ratio of the amount of insurance carried to the amount required by the coinsurance clause for full coverage. The percent of required coverage may vary, but 80 percent of the asset's market value is common.

Assume the following example: A building with a book value of $100,000 had an estimated replacement value of $200,000 at the time that a fire loss of $60,000 was sustained. The firm's fire insurance policy for $120,000 carried an 80 percent coinsurance clause.

The amount of the insurance claim would be calculated as follows:

$$\frac{\$120,000 \ (\text{insurance carried})}{.80 \times \$200,000 \ (\text{coinsurance requirement})} \times \$60,000 = \$45,000$$

Accounting for Returnable Containers and Pallets. Accounting for returnable containers and other product-handling equipment furnished as a convenience to customers and occasionally to suppliers creates varying problems based on the probability of their return and their billed price as compared with cost or book value.

In cases where the unit value of the container is small and there is a history of a high percent of returns, no accounting record of containers issued is kept. This procedure is justified on the grounds that it is more economical to lose some containers than to incur the cost of establishing controls. In other cases, only memorandum records of containers issued to customers are kept. In an increasing number of cases, however, the customer is billed for the containers or handling equipment issued to him and is credited for the same amount upon their return. The customer may be billed at cost, depreciated cost, or above cost.

Assume, for example, that a customer purchases merchandise worth $100, delivered in returnable containers that cost $4 and that are billed at $5. The following entry should be made to record the sale:

Accounts receivable—J. Doe	$105	
Sales		$100
Allowance for returnable containers		5

The return of the containers may be recorded as follows:

Allowance for returnable containers	$5	
Accounts receivable—J. Doe		$5

If the customer decides to keep and pay for the containers, the following entries are in order:

Cash	$5	
Accounts receivable—J. Doe		$5
Allowance for containers	5	
Containers		4
Containers income		1

In the case of cash sales, a liability account should be set up for the cash deposits on containers. Assume the same facts given in the preceding example except that the sale is for cash. The following entries would be in order:

Cash	$105	
Sales		$100
Liability for container deposits		5

Upon the return of the containers, the following entry should be made:

Liability for container deposits	$5	
Cash		$5

In some cases, the customer would be billed for the actual cost of the container; then $4 would be used where $5 is used in the preceding entries, and no income would be recorded on the sale of the containers.

It is customary not to accumulate depreciation against containers because of their uncertain life. A glass carboy may be as good as new after hundreds of uses, or it may be completely destroyed with one use.

Often containers are treated as supplies, and losses are determined through the taking of periodic inventories.

In the case of producers of fruits and vegetables, it is common for the processor to provide the grower with baskets or crates for the mutual convenience of both in handling the produce. In such cases, the processor provides a quantity of baskets to the grower at the beginning of the season; and as the season's demand increases, the processor may issue additional quantities, all of which are charged to the grower's account. As deliveries of produce are made in baskets, they are replaced with an equal number of baskets, plus replacement of any broken baskets returned. This is done without any accounting entries. At the end of the season, the grower returns all baskets to the processor and is given credit for them, plus a quantity arrived at by multiplying the number issued by an established percentage to cover unidentified but normal loss and breakage. This is over and above the broken baskets returned during the season. The remaining net charge for baskets (if any) is settled by a reduction in the amount paid the grower for the produce.

CHAPTER 7

Noncurrent Assets:
Depreciation and Depletion

The terms *depreciation, depletion,* and *amortization,* although differing in specific meanings and applications, have much in common: Each term refers to the allocation of the cost of a noncurrent asset to the periods benefited.

Depreciation is the systematic periodic allocation of the total cost of a man-made long-term tangible asset to the periods benefited by its use. *Depletion* is the systematic allocation of the total cost of a wasting asset or natural resource (other than land) to units extracted or produced. *Amortization* is the systematic periodic allocation of the total cost of an intangible asset to the periods benefited by such asset. As a generic term, *amortization* may be used to refer to the systematic write-down of any long-term but limited-life asset or even liability.

Depreciation and depletion are discussed in this chapter. Amortization is discussed in Chapters 9 and 10.

NATURE OF DEPRECIATION

The AICPA has defined depreciation accounting as follows:

Depreciation accounting is a system of accounting which aims to distribute the cost or other basic value of tangible capital assets, less salvage (if any), over the estimated useful life of the unit (which may be a group of assets) in a systematic and rational manner. It is a process of allocation, not of valuation. *Depreciation for the year* is the portion of the total charge under such a system that is allocated to the year. Although the allocation may properly take into account occurrences during the year, it is not intended to be a measurement of the effect of all such occurrences.[1]

Depreciation has different meanings and applications for different people. To an economist, depreciation is a decrease in value resulting from wear and tear, action of the elements, inadequacy, obsolescence, or accident. To an engineer, depreciation is the decrease in efficiency or the physical deterioration of a tangible fixed asset. To the financier, depreciation is a decrease in value caused by market action, obsolescence, and so forth. But to the accountant, depreciation is a *method of cost allocation* rather than a *method of valuation*. Actually, depreciation is a function of the use of existing assets, rather than of their replacement cost. This view reflects the accountant's belief that the purpose of depreciation accounting is to spread the cost of a fixed asset methodically over the periods or units benefited by the asset.

Accountants generally consider depreciation to be a part of the total bundle of services originally thought to be contained in a fixed asset. *Depreciation* is the cost of the expired portion of this total. A current asset such as raw material is consumed in production, identifiable unit by identifiable unit. But a fixed asset is not consumed or reduced in size unit by unit as each unit of product is made; rather, it loses production potential through use or passage of time without decrease in physical size. The confusion between the valuation concept of depreciation held by some nonaccountants and the cost-allocation concept held by accountants may be lessened if depreciation is considered as being taken on the investment in an asset, rather than on the asset itself.

Depreciation Base. The depreciation base should include the cost of acquiring, installing, and start-up costs, less net salvage value.

Serviceable Life. The serviceable life of an asset is the usefulness to a particular owner expressed in units of either time or use. The physical life of an asset is the total of the units of usefulness to all successive owners of that specific asset. The service life of an asset cannot be greater than its physical life and often

1. *Accounting Research and Terminology Bulletins,* Final Edition 1 (1961), p. 25.

will be less than the physical life. For example, a firm may follow the policy of trading its automobiles after 50,000 miles, even though they have a potential of 100,000 miles. For this firm, the automobiles have a service life of 50,000 miles, even though they have a physical life of 100,000 miles. To a second owner, they may have a service life of not more than 50,000 miles. In accounting for depreciation, the service life to the current owner should be used. The serviceable life of an asset may be affected by both physical and economic factors.

PHYSICAL DEPRECIATION. There are several causes of physical depreciation.

Deterioration and Decay. Deterioration and decay occur simply because of the passage of time and the action of the elements. Periodic maintenance and repairs may retard the deteriorating effects of the elements but cannot halt them entirely. The maximum life of an asset is determined by the actions of the elements through time. The periodic painting of a wood and steel structure may retard decay and rust, but ultimately decay and rust will make the structure useless.

Wear and Tear. Wear and tear is occasioned by the use of the asset. As has been mentioned, the maximum life of an asset may be limited by the action of the elements. However, this life may be further reduced by use. An asset of steel may not rust out for twenty years, but because of use, it may become worn to the point of uselessness by the end of ten years.

Damage or Destruction. Damage or destruction, including accidents, may further shorten the life of an asset already limited by the action of the elements and wear and tear. Reasonably predictable damage should be considered in establishing the estimated life of an asset. Heat generated by a controlled fire in a furnace will have an effect on the life of the furnace, and its effect must be considered in estimating the life of the furnace. It is, of course, possible that an accidental and uncontrolled fire would develop within the plant and damage the furnace to such an extent that it is immediately rendered useless, but such a possibility should not be considered in estimating the life of the furnace.

ECONOMIC DEPRECIATION. *Economic,* or *functional,* depreciation may occur in conjunction with, or independently of, physical depreciation. A number of factors affect the economics of functional usefulness of an asset, even though its physical qualities may not be affected.

Obsolescence. Obsolescence results from the loss of economic usefulness brought about by causes external to the asset, as opposed to loss of physical usefulness, which is brought about by internal causes. In a broad sense, obsolescence includes both inadequacy and supersession. It results from cultural changes, new inventions, new production methods, or style changes.

Obsolescence may be classified as ordinary or extraordinary. *Ordinary* obsolescence results from normal or expected reasonable changes in style demands and changes in production brought about by invention and the use of new materials or machines. *Extraordinary* obsolescence results from a sudden major unforeseeable decrease in the economic usefulness of an asset, occasioned by a sudden change in production methods or by a sudden change in the demand for the output of a specialized asset.

In the 1920s, in the Midwest, several companies were formed to produce sugar by processing sugar beets. Consequently, many farmers bought specialized equipment for use in planting, cultivating, and harvesting sugar beets. It was, of course, expected that from time to time, technological improvements would be made in such equipment resulting in a relative decrease in the economic or functional usefulness of the old equipment. This gradual, expected decrease in usefulness should be considered ordinary obsolescence. However, suddenly and without warning, the processing companies closed down. This caused specialized agricultural equipment that was still in good physical condition suddenly to become practically worthless from a functional point of view. This sudden and unexpected major decrease in economic usefulness should be considered extraordinary obsolescence.

For accounting and income-tax purposes ordinary obsolescence is included in the depreciation provision. Extraordinary obsolescence is not provided for in advance of its determination.

Inadequacy. Inadequacy is a specific type of obsolescence. Inadequacy frequently results from expansion of operations. A machine that had a large-enough potential output to meet the needs of a given production program may not be able to meet the production requirement if the program is doubled. Thus, from the current owner's point of view, the asset has become inadequate and has lost economic usefulness, even though its physical qualities have not been impaired. A piece of equipment may be inadequate for one firm but quite adequate for another; therefore, such equipment may have a high salvage value.

Supersession. Supersession is another specific type of obsolescence. In depreciation accounting, supersession means the replacement of one asset by another of greater economic or functional usefulness; for example, the replacement of a manually operated machine with an automatic machine.

METHODS OF CALCULATING DEPRECIATION CHARGE

Three factors must be considered in determining the total depreciation to be charged to expense during the life of the asset and the amount allocated to each period. They are:

1. *Original cost,* which includes not only the billed cost but also the cost of transportation, installation, breaking in, and other capitalizable costs incident to putting the asset in use.

2. *Estimated life,* which will, of course, be affected by the repair and maintenance program followed. The estimated life may be expressed in units of time, such as months or years, in units of service, such as working hours, or in units of output.

3. *Estimated net salvage or residual value,* is the amount that can probably be obtained for the asset at the end of its service life. The net salvage value is the total salvage value less the probable costs of dismantling and removal.

It should be observed that estimated salvage value theoretically should be considered in determining the total amount of depreciation (cost expiration) to be charged to operations during the service life of an asset. However, for practical reasons, this factor is often ignored on the bases that such future salvage value cannot be reliably estimated, that it probably will be a relatively insignificant amount, or that the cost of removal may be as great as (in some cases even greater than) the gross salvage value.

The purpose of all depreciation methods is to spread the net cost of an asset systematically over its output during its life.

The following formulas may be used in calculating depreciation charges:

$$D = \frac{C - S}{N}$$

$$R = \frac{C - S}{N}$$

where C = cost

D = depreciation for the period

N = estimated life (expressed in units of time or product)

R = rate of depreciation (not expressed as a percentage)

S = salvage value (net)

Straight-Line Depreciation. *Straight-line depreciation* is the simplest and most frequently used of all depreciation methods. Under this method, an equal amount of depreciation is charged to each time period.

For example, assume an asset that cost $52,000 and that is expected to have a net salvage value of $2,000 at the end of its service life of either 5 years, 5,000 hours, or 20,000 units.

The actual hours of asset use and production for each year were as follows:

Year	Hours Used	Units of Output
1	800	3,000
2	1,000	4,000
3	1,200	5,000
4	900	3,700
5	800	3,500
Total	4,700	19,200

Depreciation by the straight-line method (for each year) would be calculated as follows:

$$D = \frac{\$52,000 - \$2,000}{5} = \$10,000$$

Service-Output Depreciation. *Service-output depreciation* may be based on use expressed either in terms of hours that the asset was used or in terms of units of production. Both the units-of-output and the hours-of-service methods take account of the fact that although some deterioration may occur because of the passage of time, many assets will lose value more quickly if used full time than if used only part time. Also, those periods during which the asset is used full time receive greater benefits than those periods during which the asset is used only part time. In support of the service-output method, it is argued that depreciation should be charged according to the benefits received.

UNITS OF OUTPUT. The *units-of-output method* of calculating depreciation applied to the asset described in the discussion of the straight-line method would yield the following results:

$$R \text{ (per unit)} = \frac{\$52,000 - \$2,000}{20,000}$$

$$R = \$2.50$$

Year	Units Produced	Rate	Depreciation	Book Value
1	3,000	$2.50	$ 7,500	$44,500
2	4,000	2.50	10,000	34,500
3	5,000	2.50	12,500	22,000
4	3,700	2.50	9,250	12,750
5	3,500	2.50	8,750	4,000
Total	19,200		$48,000	

HOURS OF SERVICE. The *hours-of-service method* would produce the following results when applied to the same asset.

$$R \text{ (per hour)} = \frac{\$52,000 - \$2,000}{5,000}$$

$$R = \$10$$

Year	Service Hours	Rate	Depreciation	Book Value
1	800	$10	$ 8,000	$44,000
2	1,000	10	10,000	34,000
3	1,200	10	12,000	22,000
4	900	10	9,000	13,000
5	800	10	8,000	5,000
Total	4,700		$47,000	

Decreasing Charge (Accelerated). *Decreasing-charge,* or *accelerated, methods* of calculating depreciation charges relate the expense to the passage of time, rather than to services or benefits provided. In this respect, the decreasing-charge methods are similar to the straight-line method, but they differ in that each succeeding period's charge is less than the preceding period's.

The logic of the various decreasing-charge methods is defended on several bases. It is suggested that the total cost of an asset's use for a period of time is composed of repair and maintenance costs and the cost of depreciation. Because the repair and maintenance costs are expected to increase as the asset ages, the periodic depreciation charges should decrease as the asset ages, so that the total of the two expenses will be the same for each time period. It should be observed, however, that although repair costs may increase with the aging of the asset, there need not be a correlation between the repair costs and systematic depreciation charges.

It is also suggested that an asset's efficiency decreases with age and that, therefore, greater benefits are provided by the asset in its early life than in its later life; therefore, less depreciation should be charged in the later periods than in the early periods of the life of the asset.

One of the most compelling reasons for using an accelerated-depreciation method is the tax advantage that such an approved method provides. The quicker the cost of an asset is charged to operations, the quicker a tax benefit is obtained.

It is occasionally suggested that since an asset loses value more rapidly when new than when older, some decreasing-charge method of depreciation should be used. The lack of merit in this argument becomes apparent when it is recalled that depreciation charging is a means of cost allocation rather than a means of valuation.

SUM OF YEARS' DIGITS. *The sum-of-years'-digits method,* also referred to as the *sum-of-life-periods method,* is best explained as follows: The depreciable cost $(C - S)$ is multiplied by a fraction. The denominator of this fraction is the sum of the digits representing the periods of the asset's service life, and the numerator is the number of the life period in reverse order.

Referring again to the example in the section "Straight-Line

Depreciation," depreciation by the sum-of-years'-digits method is calculated as follows:

DEPRECIATION SCHEDULE, SUM OF YEARS' DIGITS

Year	Fraction	Cost — Salvage	Depreciation	Book Value
1	5/15	$50,000	$16,666.67	$35,333.33
2	4/15	50,000	13,333.33	22,000.00
3	3/15	50,000	10,000.00	12,000.00
4	2/15	50,000	6,666.67	5,333.33
5	1/15	50,000	3,333.33	2,000.00
15			$50,000.00	

DECLINING BALANCE. The *declining-balance methods* produce results quite similar to those obtained by the sum-of-the-years'-digits method. However, in these methods, the rate remains constant, but the value to which the rate is applied decreases; whereas in the sum-of-the-years'-digits method, the rate (fraction) decreases, but the multiplicand remains constant.

Double-Declining-Balance Method. The double-declining-balance method of calculating depreciation is acceptable for certain assets for income-tax purposes. For such approved assets, the law provides that a rate double the applicable straight-line rate may be used. The tax law does not require that salvage value be considered in applying the rates. An asset cannot be depreciated below its net salvage value.

The following depreciation schedule, prepared by the double-declining-balance method, is based on the original problem in the section "Straight-Line Depreciation":

DEPRECIATION SCHEDULE, DOUBLE-DECLINING BALANCE

Year	Beginning Balance	Rate[a] (percent)	Depreciation	Ending Balance
1	$52,000.00	40	$20,800.00	$31,200.00
2	31,200.00	40	12,480.00	18,720.00
3	18,720.00	40	7,488.00	11,232.00
4	11,232.00	40	4,492.80	6,739.20
5	6,739.20	40	2,695.68	4,043.52
Total			$47,956.48	

[a] The straight-line rate for five years is 20 percent.

Limited-Declining-Balance Method. The limited-declining-balance method is identical with the double-declining-balance method except that the rate is less than 200 percent of the straight-line depreciation rate. As indicated, for tax purposes the law permits depreciation on certain types of assets to be taken on the declining balance at 200 percent of the allowed straight-line rate. On certain other types of assets, for tax purposes the law permits the taking of depreciation on the declining balance at 150 percent of the allowed straight-line rate. Thus, it is not unusual to associate 150 percent of the straight-line rate with the limited-declining-balance method. This is the rate used in preparing the following depreciation schedule, again based on the original data.

DEPRECIATION SCHEDULE, LIMITED DECLINING BALANCE
(150%)

Year	Beginning Balance	Rate (percent)	Depreciation	Ending Balance
1	$52,000.00	30	$15,600.00	$36,400.00
2	36,400.00	30	10,920.00	25,480.00
3	25,480.00	30	7,644.00	17,836.00
4	17,836.00	30	5,350.80	12,485.20
5	12,485.20	30	3,745.56	8,739.64
Total			$43,260.36	

If the asset is still usable at the end of the fifth year, the same method of taking depreciation may be continued year after year until the asset's book value is reduced to its salvage value. Also, with the permission of the IRS, a taxpayer may change to the straight-line depreciation method when the annual charges under the declining-balance method become smaller than they would be under the straight-line method. If the change to the straight-line method is made, then the annual charge is computed by dividing the unrecovered cost, less estimated net salvage, by the estimated remaining years (periods) of service life.

Group and Composite Depreciation. *Group- and composite-depreciation methods* utilize an average service life for a number of assets on which depreciation for the entire group is then taken as a single unit. Specifically, the group-depreciation method should be restricted to use in those cases where a collection of similar units is treated as a single unit, and the composite-depreciation method should be used in cases where a collection of dissimilar assets is treated as a single unit. However, the methods are so similar in principle and application that the terms are sometimes used interchangeably.

GROUP DEPRECIATION. The group-depreciation method (as has been mentioned) may be applied to a group of similar assets. The expected physical life of each unit, therefore, is the same, even though it is an established fact that two identical machines may have different actual lives. Under the group-depreciation method, depreciation is taken on all the assets in the group as if they were a single unit.

As units in the group are disposed of, the depreciation is calculated on the remaining units only. Probably some units will have shorter actual lives than expected, but this may be compensated for because some will have longer actual lives than expected. Those units still in use after the expiration of their average life should continue to be depreciated until they are fully depreciated (i.e., until the balance in the valuation account, plus estimated salvage value, is equal to the cost of the remaining units). The depreciation is based on the expected average life of the group.

The accumulated depreciation is recorded in a single valuation account. Because the amount of accumulated depreciation is identified only with the group of assets and not with the individual units, no gain or loss can be recognized upon the disposal of individual units. Upon the disposal of a unit, the asset account will be credited with the unit's cost, and the valuation account will be charged with cost, less salvage value.

The method may be illustrated by the following example. Five identical machines were bought at the same time at a total cost of $50,000. They are expected to have an average life of five years, after which they will be worthless. At the end of the third year, one machine is disposed of for $1,000. At the end of the fourth year, another machine is disposed of for $2,000. At the end of the fifth year, another machine is sold for $1,000. At the end of the sixth year, another machine is scrapped. The last machine is still in use after the end of the seventh year.

Year Disposed	Units	Cost	Depre-ciation	Accumulated Depreciation Debit	Accumulated Depreciation Credit	Accumulated Depreciation Balance	Book Value
1	5	$50,000	$10,000		$10,000	$10,000	$40,000
2	5	50,000	10,000		10,000	20,000	30,000
3 before	5	50,000	10,000		10,000	30,000	20,000
3 after	4	40,000		$ 9,000		21,000	19,000
4 before	4	40,000	8,000		8,000	29,000	11,000
4 after	3	30,000		8,000		21,000	9,000
5 before	3	30,000	6,000		6,000	27,000	3,000
5 after	2	20,000		9,000		18,000	2,000
6 before	2	20,000	2,000[a]		2,000	20,000	0
6 after	1	10,000		10,000		10,000	0
7	1	10,000	0			10,000	0

[a] It should be noted that in the sixth year, the recognized depreciation is only $2,000, rather than $4,000, because a $2,000 credit to the valuation account reduces the book value of the two remaining assets to zero. In the seventh year, no depreciation is recorded for the group (of one) because the book value was previously reduced to zero.

COMPOSITE DEPRECIATION. *The composite-depreciation* method, sometimes referred to as the *average-life* or *mean-life* method, is quite similar to the group-depreciation method as far as results are concerned; but because such a collection of assets may be composed of assets with varying service lives, the method of computing the composite amount will be slightly different from that for calculating group depreciation.

The development of a composite rate is illustrated by the following schedule:

Asset	Cost	Salvage	Depreciation base (cost − salvage)	Esti-mated Life (years)	Annual Depreciation
A	$ 30,000	$10,000	$ 20,000	4	$ 5,000
B	60,000	20,000	40,000	8	5,000
C	80,000	20,000	60,000	12	5,000
D	130,000	40,000	90,000	15	6,000
Total	$300,000	$90,000	$210,000		$21,000

Composite life: $210,000 ÷ $21,000 = 10 years
Composite rate: $21,000 ÷ $300,000 = 7%

As in the case of the group-depreciation method, the accumulated depreciation for the collection of assets is kept in a common account. Therefore, when an asset is disposed of, its cost is removed from the asset account; cash, or another appropriate account, is charged with the value received; and the difference is charged to the accumulated depreciation account. Thus, no gain or loss is recognized until the collective net book value· is reduced to zero or the last unit in the collection is disposed of.

If the composite collection of assets is considered to be a closed-end collection, the composite rate is applied to the balance in the collective asset account. Thus, referring to the schedule, the depreciation for the first four years (based on A, B, C and D) would be $300,000 × 7 percent, or $21,000. If asset A were disposed of at the end of the fourth year, depreciation for the fifth year (based on B, C and D) would be ($300,000 − $30,000) × .07, or $18,900.

In no case should the assets be depreciated below their net salvage value.

In some cases, the composite collection of assets is considered to be an open-end collection; that is, as assets are removed from the collection, they will be replaced by assets of similar lives, so that the initial rate may continue until there is evidence that the cost-life composition of the collection has changed.

Inventory (Appraisal). The *inventory method* of calculating depreciation, sometimes referred to as the *appraisal method,* endeavors to measure depreciation in terms of loss of value of the assets by direct reductions of the asset balances to an appraised value (based on original cost) at the end of each period. In making the appraisals, extreme care must be exercised to exclude value increments resulting from inflation, increases in market or replacement costs, and going-concern values. The inclusion of such value increments in the "inventory valuation" in periods of rising prices would result in mixing appreciation values with expense measurement, thus overstating the cost value of the asset balance and reducing the charge to depreciation expense. Such results would be improper in that profit would be anticipated in the form of unrealized appreciation of assets. It would also fail to recognize depreciation properly when depreciation is correctly defined as some systematic method of assigning asset costs to periods benefited.

Perhaps the greatest disadvantage of this method is the difficulty and in some cases the actual impossibility of excluding such appreciation from the appraisal. The most practical way of apply-ing the inventory method is as follows: First, determine the quantity of depreciable assets involved and their original cost, broken down into life-expectancy groups that are in turn broken down into age groups. Then, apply a percentage to the cost value to establish the present carrying values. The percentages used should be based on life expectancies and ages of the various asset groups involved. This method is usually applied only to relatively inexpensive fixed assets with indeterminate lives, such as small hand and machine tools, returnable containers, and in the food-service industry, kitchen and dining room utensils.

The inventory method is used in such cases not because of its accuracy but because of its practicality. In fact, in some cases, it is practical to carry certain types of assets at or close to their original cost during their entire lives. For example, a hand hammer may be as serviceable just before it is lost or stolen as it was when new. Also, such a tool may last in normal use for many years, or it may be lost or stolen during the first day of use.

Replacement. Under the *replacement method* of taking depre-ciation, the asset accounts are charged with the acquisition cost of each original unit. No depreciation charge is recorded until the original asset (or later, its replacement) is replaced. At the time of replacement, depreciation is charged with the cost of the replacing asset, less the net salvage value (if any) of the replaced asset. Thus, the asset accounts will always show the unallocated cost of the original assets. Also, depreciation is charged not on a systematic periodic basis but on a random basis, as assets are replaced.

Retirement. Under the *retirement method* of taking depreci-ation, the asset accounts are charged with the acquisition cost of each original unit, as they are under the replacement method. Also, no depreciation is recorded until a retirement occurs. At the time of retirement, the asset account is relieved of (credited with) the total cost of the asset being retired, and the depreci-ation account is charged with that total cost, less any net salvage. Then the asset account is charged with the total cost of the new asset. Thus, the asset accounts will always reflect the unallocated costs of the existing fixed assets, and the depreciation charge will be the total cost, less salvage of the retired fixed asset. As under the replacement method, depreciation will be charged not on a systematic periodic basis but on a random basis as assets are retired.

Either the replacement or the retirement method may be used in cases involving large numbers of similar units having relatively small unit values. These methods have been popular with public utilities. They have been applied especially to poles, ties, rails, and similar items.

DEPRECIATION AND MANAGEMENT DECISIONS

Management is confronted with the necessity of making a decision only when alternate courses of action are available, but the alternatives may be as simple as either to continue a given course of action or to cease such action. Management is continually searching for better, more economical, and more profitable ways of utilizing its capital. This frequently involves the acquisition and/or the replacement of depreciable assets. In such cases, it is important to understand the nature of several different kinds of costs in order to determine which ones to consider and which ones to ignore.

In decision making, only future costs (to the exclusion of sunk costs) should be considered. *Future costs* are those costs the incurrence of which are contingent upon a present or future decision. *Sunk costs* are expenditures made in the past that cannot be changed by a present decision.

Costs are said to be *relevant* or *irrelevant* according to whether or not they are pertinent to the problem being considered. A cost that will not be changed by the alternate courses under consideration is irrelevant. Only relevant costs should be considered in decision making. Differential costs are relevant costs in decision making because by definition they are costs that are contingent on specific courses of action.

Opportunity costs are profits foregone by diverting an investment or asset from one use to an alternate use. Therefore, they are relevant in decision making.

Whether depreciation is relevant or irrelevant in decision making depends on several factors. If depreciation in the given situation is considered to be a function of use, it is a differential cost and, therefore, relevant. However, if depreciation is a function of time, it becomes a sunk cost because it results from a prior decision that cannot be changed at the present time. It, therefore, may be irrelevant to the problem under consideration.

Out-of-pocket costs are costs that will require cash or near-cash outlays in the period under consideration.

A decision to keep or replace a depreciable fixed asset should be based on relevant future differential costs such as out-of-pocket costs, opportunity costs, and the most troublesome one of all, depreciation. Several examples are presented in the paragraphs that follow.

Depreciation as a Fixed Expense. A special-purpose machine was purchased six years ago at a cost of $100,000. It is being depreciated on a straight-line basis over a ten-year period at the rate of $10,000 per year, on the assumption that at the end of ten years, it will have no salvage value. It has an annual capacity of 100,000 units. Material and direct labor cost $1.00 and $2.00 per unit, respectively. Maintenance costs resulting from usage amount to $.50 per unit of output. Maintenance resulting from the passage of time amounts to $4,000 per year. Insurance is $1,000 per year, and annual taxes are $2,000. The machine is currently being used at 50 percent of capacity to produce items that sell for $5.00 each. A salesman has located a potential customer who will buy 40,000 units if he can acquire them at a unit cost of $3.75. Management has to decide whether or not to accept this offer. The decision should be based on the following facts and comparisons:

	Costs of first 50,000 units	Costs of additional 40,000 units
Material	$ 50,000	$ 40,000
Direct labor	100,000	80,000
Maintenance, resulting from use	25,000	20,000
Maintenance, resulting from passage of time	4,000	0
Insurance	1,000	0
Taxes	2,000	0
Depreciation	10,000	0
Total costs	$192,000	$140,000
Sales revenue (50,000 × $5.00)	250,000	
(40,000 × $3.75)		150,000
Profit	$ 58,000	$ 10,000

Although the unit cost of producing the usual quantity is $3.84 ($192,000 ÷ 50,000), it is profitable to sell additional units produced with existing facilities at only $3.75. This is possible because only the differential (additional) costs of producing the extra units are relevant to this decision.

Depreciation as a Differential Expense. Now assume the same facts given in the preceding example with the exception that depreciation is considered to be solely a function of use rather than of time and that the machine will have produced 1,000,000 units by the time it becomes worthless. The following costs and comparisons are appropriate:

	Costs of first 50,000 units	Costs of additional 40,000 units
Material	$ 50,000	$ 40,000
Direct labor	100,000	80,000
Maintenance, resulting from use	25,000	20,000
Maintenance, resulting from passage of time	4,000	0
Insurance	1,000	
Taxes	2,000	
Depreciation (50,000 × .10)	5,000	
(40,000 × .10)		4,000
Total costs	$187,000	$144,000
Sales revenue	250,000	150,000
Profit	$ 63,000	$ 6,000

By changing the assumed cause of the incurrence of depreciation from a time basis to a production basis, the depreciation expense changes from a fixed expense that was irrelevant in costing the extra production to a differential cost that is relevant in costing the additional production.

Depreciation in Cases of Replacements. Assume now that the decision confronting management is whether to continue using the old machine or to purchase a new machine. The original data for the example given in "Depreciation as a Fixed Expense" concerning the old machine are still valid. However, a current trade-in or market value for the old machine is established at $10,000. The new machine under consideration would cost $120,-000 and would last for ten years, after which time it would be worthless. It, too, would have a capacity of 100,000 units per year; but because of improvements in design, it would reduce per-unit material and direct-labor costs to $.80 and $1.50, respectively. Maintenance resulting from usage would be $.75 per unit, but maintenance required because of passage of time would be only $1,000 per year. Because of the greater value of the new machine, insurance would be $4,000 per year, and taxes would be $5,000. The firm can borrow money currently at 6 percent.

As an aid in arriving at a decision, the following costs and comparisons should be considered:

	Cost of using present machine	Cost of using new machine
Material	$ 50,000	$ 40,000
Direct labor	100,000	75,000
Maintenance, resulting from use	25,000	37,500
Maintenance, resulting from passage of time	4,000	1,000
Insurance	1,000	4,000
Taxes	2,000	5,000
Depreciation ($10,000 spread over 4 years)	2,500	12,000
Opportunity cost	300	3,600
	$184,800	$178,100
Annual saving by purchase of new machine		6,700
	$184,800	$184,800

In making comparisons of this kind, depreciation on the old machine should be based on the current market value of the asset rather than on the original cost. However, if the old machine is kept, then for cost purposes, depreciation must be calculated, as in the preceding example, on cost. The opportunity cost, the value of capital for an alternate use, is 6 percent. The average amount of capital invested in the old machine for decision-making purposes is ($10,000 + 0)/2, or $5,000, and for the new machine, the average investment is ($120,000 + 0)/2, or $60,000. It is important to observe that for decision-making purposes, the present market value ($10,000) is used, rather than the book value ($40,000). The difference ($30,000) is considered a sunk cost and is irrelevant to the problem. It should also be remembered that opportunity costs are imputed costs used for decision-making purposes only; they are ignored in accounting for costs.

DEPRECIATION AND INCOME MEASUREMENT

Depreciation is an expense and, as such, has a direct bearing on the measurement of income. In fact, the purpose of depreciation accounting is to allocate systematically the cost of long-term assets to the periods benefited by them and to reduce income accordingly. As was pointed out earlier in this chapter, the amount of depreciation charged against income in a particular period will depend upon the depreciation method. In selecting a depreciation method, consideration must be given to its effect on the measurement of net income and the effect that the resultant net income will have on income taxes, dividend policy, and capital-investment decisions.

NATURE OF DEPLETION

Depletion is the direct physical exhaustion or consumption of a natural resource (also referred to as a *wasting asset*). Depletion differs from depreciation in that depletion recognizes a *quantitative exhaustion*, that is, an actual physical reduction in the available supply of a natural resource; whereas depreciation recognizes a *service exhaustion* of a replaceable fixed asset brought about by use, obsolescence, or inadequacy.

Depletion Base. Usually, a natural resource is acquired in conjunction with a nonwasting asset, for example, oil or minerals under surface land. In such cases, the total cost should be allocated between the recoverable natural resources and the residual value of the land. In order to facilitate accounting for the separate values, two separate accounts should be established. In the event that costs are incurred in restoring the residual land to use after the removal of the wasting asset, they should be charged to the wasting asset account, rather than to the residual land account. Thus, these costs become a part of the depletion base.

COST AS A DEPLETION BASE. Almost universally, cost is used as the depletion base except for income-tax purposes. Cost in such cases includes the total cost of the property, less the net residual value of the land, plus *development costs,* such as costs of exploring, drilling, excavating, and construction preliminary to general operations for the removal of the wasting asset. Preferably, development costs should be charged to a third separate account, even though they are to be included in the depletion base. After production starts, further development costs may be capitalized or charged to expense. In fact, some large companies expense even the preliminary development costs. On the other hand, some firms anticipate future development costs and thus include them in the original depletion base.

COST-PLUS AS A DEPLETION BASE. In some cases, the cost paid for the wasting asset is unrealistically low, and a valuation greater than cost may be permissible.

Discovery Value. In many cases in the past, land was purchased for its value as surface land only, without any knowledge of its subsurface natural resources. The subsequent discovery of the existence of a subsurface natural resource increased the value of the property without any increase in cost. Thus, to give a realistic value to the property, it was written up by the estimated value of the discovered natural resource.

This base is mentioned here because of its past popularity. It is now almost obsolete, having been replaced by percentage depletion, which is discussed in "Gross Income as a Depletion Base."

Accretion. Accretion is matter added to the original unit through adhesion or growth. Accretion is especially applicable in cases of tracts of growing timber. Here, through time, accretion may add substantially to the value of the depletable asset.

Some accountants approve of recording the increase in value occasioned by accretion on the theory that the failure to recognize such increases constitutes the omission of a part of a firm's assets.

If accretion is recognized, it should be accomplished by a charge to an asset account and a credit to an unrealized increment account. After the recording of accretion, depletion should be based on the new total valuation. According to conservative accounting theory, no portion of the unrealized-increment balance should be transferred to retained earnings until depletion charges amount to the original cost of the natural resource. By the same token, if accretion is treated as unrealized (deferred) income, the costs of maintaining and improving the natural resources should also be deferred.

Many accountants take the position that accretion merely adds to the firm's resources and should not be recognized until those added units are utilized or sold.

Timber has long been the classic accretion example, but its use as such may well be waning because of the change in attitude of most large timber processors. Timber is losing the most important attribute of a wasting asset, irreplaceability, because in recent years the large timber companies have been practicing scientific reforestation. Many large timber tracts are now being operated on a crop basis, so that after a stand of timber is cut, the land is cleared and replanted. In such a case, all costs of developing the new timber stand should be capitalized and depleted or depreciated as the new timber is cut.

GROSS INCOME AS A DEPLETION BASE. Gross income as a depletion base is not usable for accounting purposes; it may be used only for purposes of determining income-tax liability. The *percentage*, or *statutory*, depletion method has been applicable since 1926 to oil and gas wells and was later made applicable to many other minerals and metals. The rates vary from 22 percent of gross income for oil and gas production to as little as 5 percent of gross income on some natural resources. The allowance may not exceed 50 percent of the taxpayer's taxable income computed without the allowance for depletion.

Like depreciation, cost depletion cannot exceed the cost or adjusted base of the asset. However, percentage depletion may exceed the cost of the wasting asset.

Depletion Methods. There are two distinct depletion methods.

PRODUCTION METHOD. The *production method* is almost universally used for accounting purposes and in many cases for tax purposes as well. The unit of measure should be a standard measure of the usable or salable natural resource (such as an ounce of gold or silver, a pound of copper, a ton of coal), rather than a ton of raw ore because of the great variation in value between high- and low-grade ore even if it is taken from the same mine. The unit-depletion charge may be computed by the following formula:

$$\text{Unit depletion} = \frac{\text{cost} + \text{capitalized development costs}}{\text{total estimated recoverable units}}$$

PERCENTAGE METHOD. The *percentage method* is used for tax purposes only. It is computed by applying a rate that varies (depending on the nature of the natural resource) from 5 to 22 percent of gross income but is limited to 50 percent of net income before an allowance for depletion.

ACCOUNTING FOR DEPLETION

Accounting for depletion and accounting for depreciation have much in common in that in both cases, attempts are made periodically to match systematically the cost of the asset against the revenues resulting from the asset's use or consumption. Accounting for depletion is more involved than accounting for depreciation because it is more difficult to determine the number of commercially recoverable units in the mine, well, or tract. It is also difficult to determine the total development and carrying costs for the project.

The problems of accounting for depletion may best be explained by an example. Assume that the Great Western Mining Company acquired a tract of land for $1,000,000. It was estimated that there were 500,000 tons of commercially recoverable mineral under the surface of this land. After the mining operations are completed, it will cost $50,000 to place the land in legally required condition, at which time it can be sold for $60,000. The development costs during the first year amounted to $100,000. During the first year, 100,000 tons of mineral were mined and sold. During the second year, the capitalizable development costs amounted to $200,000. The remaining recoverable mineral at the beginning of the second year was reestimated at 600,000 tons. During the second year, 200,000 tons were sold. The first year's depletion may be calculated as follows:

$$\frac{\text{Total cost} + \text{development cost} - \text{net residual land value}}{\text{Total estimated recoverable tons}} = \text{unit-deple-}$$
$$\text{tion charge} \times \text{units sold} = \text{depletion charge}$$

$$\frac{\$1,000,000 + 100,000 - \$10,000}{500,000} = \$2.18 \times 100,000 = \$218,000$$

The second year's depletion may be calculated as follows:

$$\frac{\$1,000,000 + \$100,000 - \$10,000 - \$218,000 + \$200,000}{600,000} = \$1.78\tfrac{2}{3}$$
$$\$1.78\tfrac{2}{3} \times 200,000 = \$357,333.33$$

The entries that should be made for the first year are:

Mineral deposits	$990,000	
Residual land—net	10,000	
Cash		$1,000,000
Mineral deposits	100,000	
Cash		100,000
Cost of goods sold	218,000	
Mineral deposits		218,000

The development costs could have been chargd to an account such as development costs rather than to mineral deposits, but that would have required the calculating of two separate depletion rates.

CHAPTER 8

Noncurrent Assets:
Revaluation of Plant and Equipment

There is general agreement among accountants that cost, or amortized cost, is the most acceptable basis for valuing assets except in special cases. It may be advisable to depart from a cost or amortized-cost basis in situations where a transfer of ownership is contemplated, to establish an equitable tax basis, or for credit or financing purposes. Under some circumstances, a small number of accountants will recommend a revaluation of plant and equipment as a means of improving the periodic matching of expenses and revenues.

For many years, accountants have recognized the acceptability of property revaluation under certain circumstances. Today their concern is: Should revaluation continue to be restricted to exceptional cases, or should it become generally accepted practice?

ARGUMENTS FOR AND AGAINST REVALUATION

In order to avoid bias, the arguments pro and con must be considered.

For Revaluation

1. Management should be judged on the effectiveness of the use of the assets under its control. When there is a difference between book value based on cost and market value, a more realistic evaluation of management's effectiveness may be made if assets are valued at market price. For example, a firm that acquired its fixed assets at a time when prices were low may seem to be efficiently managed when compared with a firm that bought its fixed assets more recently and when prices were higher because of larger depreciation charges incurred by the latter firm.

2. Although it is admitted that the function of depreciation taking is to allocate systematically the cost of the long-term assets to the periods benefited rather than to serve as a valuation method, the revenue produced through the use of such assets must be sufficient to provide for the replacement of such assets when they are exhausted.

3. Although competition plays a large part in the pricing of a firm's products, costs cannot be ignored. If a firm costs its production on historical costs rather than on current values in periods of rising prices, a distorted matching (on current values) of expenses and revenues will result. Such a result may mislead management, investors, and creditors.

4. Management must provide not only for the recovery of the cost of an asset but also for its anticipated replacement at prices in effect when the replacement becomes necessary.

5. A realistic matching of periodic expenses and revenues is possible only when common current values are used; that is, 1960 expense dollars cannot be compared effectively with 1970 revenue dollars.

6. Comparability of financial statements would be improved because dollars of common size would be used in their preparation.

Against Revaluation

1. There will be a loss of objectivity. The most objectively established value of any item is that price established in an arm's-length transaction between a knowledgeable and willing buyer and a knowledgeable and willing seller. Reliability of values decreases as subjectivity in their establishment increases.

2. If revaluation were to be allowed, then the unanswered questions of which assets should be revalued and how often revaluations should be made become very important.

3. Comparability of financial statements would not be improved because there is no universally accepted definition of a common-size dollar.

4. Asset replacement and income measurement are two separate problems.

5. If management has the foresight to purchase long-term assets in periods of low prices in anticipation of price increases, such judgment should be reflected in the measurement of income.

6. Management may, if it wishes, use current costs for internal

reports and decision making and even for auxiliary public reports, but the primary reports to the public should still be based on historical costs.

The APB in its Opinion No. 6 holds that "property, plant and equipment should not be written up by an entity to reflect appraisal, market or current values which are above cost to the entity."[1]

CAUSES AND TREATMENT OF REVALUATION

The problem of revaluation is occasioned by a discrepancy between the book value of an asset and its current market value. Any one or more of several factors may cause the discrepancy, and the method of recording the revaluation and its subsequent treatment will depend on the causes giving rise to the revaluation.

Change of Life Expectancy. The estimated life of a long-term asset will, after several years, have a bearing on the book value of an asset and indirectly may cause a discrepancy between the book value and the market or use value. For example, assume that a machine purchased for $10,000 was estimated to have a useful life of ten years, at which time it would be worthless. It was depreciated $1,000 a year for five years, at which time it was estimated that the asset had a remaining useful life of fifteen years. Based on the original estimated useful life of ten years, the machine would be 50 percent depreciated at the end of the fifth year and thus would have a book value of $5,000. However, in light of the revised estimated life of the asset, only 25 percent of the use value has been consumed; therefore, the remaining use value (75 percent of cost) would be $7,500.

Changing the estimated life of an asset may change the book value of the asset and the amount of the periodic depreciation charge, but the valuation is still cost-oriented. Its main result is the allocation of the asset cost over a different number of accounting periods than was originally intended.

Errors in accounting for plant and equipment on a cost basis may occur not only because of errors in estimating the life of an

. 1. "Status of Accounting Research Bulletins," *Opinions of the Accounting Principles Board*, No. 6 (1965), p. 42.

asset but also because of failure to charge the asset with certain applicable costs, such as freight-in, additions, and betterments.

In contrast with errors such as these, consider changes in value discussed in the following paragraphs.

Change in Value Appreciation. *Appreciation* is the increase in value of an asset over its appropriately amortized cost; it is a nonoperating increase in value. It may occur because of a restriction on the supply of a particular asset in relation to increases in demand; for example, appreciation in the value of land because of its relatively fixed supply in relation to an increasing demand brought on because of increasing population. Or as is frequently the case (apparent) appreciation may occur because of a decrease in the value of the unit of measure, namely, the dollar.

Accountants are generally agreed that appreciation is not realized income as it occurs but that the appreciation is realized when the asset is disposed of at a value greater than its depreciated cost.

There is a difference of opinion concerning the proper treatment of the appreciation prior to the disposal of the asset. Some accountants hold that plant and equipment should be revalued from time to time in order to bring the account balances in line with current replacement costs.

The position of the AAA is expressed by its Committee on Concepts and Standards as follows: "The Committee recommends that current cost be adopted immediately as the basis of valuation for land, buildings, and equipment wherever the amounts involved are significant."[2]

The APB takes a different position: "The Board is of the opinion that property, plant, and equipment should not be written up by an entity to reflect appraisal, market, or current values which are above cost of the entity."[3]

Recording Appraisal Increases. Following the dictates of the APB, appreciation would not be recognized and, therefore, would not be recorded. However, the AAA recommends that if the appreciation is significant, it should be recorded. Because of

2. "Accounting for Land, Buildings, and Equipment—Supplementary Statement No. 1," *Accounting Review* (July 1964), p. 698.
3. "Status of Accounting Research Bulletins," *Opinions of the Accounting Principles Board*, No. 6 (1965), p. 42.

a general lack of approval, long-term assets are not written up to appraised values except in unusual circumstances. When such appraisal increases are recorded, both an asset account and a capital account must be increased.

For example, assume that a tract of land was purchased twenty-one years ago for $50,000 and that it has just been appraised at $100,000. Also, during the first year of ownership of the land, the firm constructed a building on it at a cost of $400,000. The building at the time of completion had, and still has, a total life expectancy of forty years. Depreciation for the past twenty years has been taken at the rate of $10,000 per year. The building is now appraised at replacement cost new of $800,000. The appraisal would be recorded as follows:

Land—appraisal increase	$ 50,000	
Building—appraisal increase	400,000	
Accumulated depreciation—building		
—appraisal increase		$200,000
Appraisal capital—land		50,000
Appraisal capital—building		200,000

Recording Depreciation Subsequent to an Appraisal Increase. Subsequent to an appraisal increase, depreciation may be taken either on the appraised value or on the actual cost of the asset.

DEPRECIATION BASED ON APPRAISED VALUE. Many accountants believe that appraisal increases should not be recorded; but if they are recorded, then, to be consistent, operations should be charged with depreciation based on such increased values. It is suggested that if the income statement cannot bear the increased depreciation expense, the increased value of the asset on the balance sheet cannot be justified. The AICPA states its position as follows: "Whenever appreciation has been recorded on the books, income should be charged with depreciation computed on the written up amounts."[4]

Using the same data given for the example in "Recording Appraisal Increases," depreciation would be recorded as follows:

Depreciation—building	$40,000	
Accumulated depreciation—building		$20,000
Accumulated depreciation—building		
—appraisal increase		20,000

4. "Status of Accounting Research Bulletins," p. 42.

DEPRECIATION BASED ON ACTUAL COST. Other accountants agree that appraisal increases should not be recorded. However, they do not feel that the commission of such an error is a valid reason for committing a second error, that of departing from a cost basis for the recognition of depreciation. This group of accountants would continue to compute depreciation on actual cost.

Using the data from the same example, the entry would be as follows:

Depreciation—building	$20,000	
Appraisal capital—building	20,000	
Accumulated depreciation—building		$20,000
Accumulated depreciation—building		
—appraisal increase		20,000

A series of ten entries such as this would eliminate the balance in the appraisal capital—building account and would increase the balance in the accumulated depreciation—building—appraisal increase account by $200,000, bringing the balance in that account to $400,000. This is equal to the amount charged to the building—appraisal increase account when the appraisal was recorded.

It should be observed that the recorded depreciation was $40,000 when it was calculated on the appraised value but only $20,000 when it was calculated on actual cost.

Because land is nondepreciable, there is no question that the increase in the land value of $50,000 resulting from the appraisal cannot be realized until it is sold. This is not the case, however, with depreciable assets. For example, in the case under consideration, $20,000 more is charged to depreciation each year by the appraised-value method than by the cost method. This difference occurs because under the appraisal method, the appraisal capital—building account is left intact; whereas, under the cost method, that account is decreased by $20,000. Thus, during the remaining life of the building, the original credit of $200,000 to appraisal capital—building is offset (realized) by ten debits of $20,000 each to that same account.

The question may well be raised concerning when the $200,000 of net appraisal increase should be recognized under the appraisal method. Some accountants believe that the value of the appraisal increase should be recognized periodically by credits to income (in this case, $20,000 annually). Thus, there would be a $20,000 net charge for depreciation against income by either method. This is true even though accountants in general would treat the extra $20,000 credit under the appraisal method as an extraordinary item rather than as an operating item.

The annual entry would be as follows:

Appraisal capital—building	$20,000	
Profit from appraisal		$20,000

Thus, the actual cost of depreciation by the appraisal method is the same as that by the cost method, and it can truly be said that the appraisal increase is recognized (as income) periodically.

Some accountants believe that an appraisal increase should be recognized periodically but should not appear on the income statement. They would recommend the following entry:

Appraisal capital—building	$20,000	
Retained earnings		$20,000

A few accountants recommend that the periodic credit to retained earnings ($20,000) not be made but that a single entry for the total amount ($200,000) be made at the expiration of the life of the asset.

Recording Asset Devaluations. Appreciation has been defined as an increase in value. Depreciation has been defined, in non-accounting terms, as a decrease in value. However, for accounting purposes, depreciation has been defined as a method of systematically allocating the cost of a fixed asset to the periods benefited. Thus, in accounting, there is no word that can be used as the opposite of appreciation. The recording of depreciation results in a devaluation or write-down of an asset. The devaluation or write-downs under consideration here are in addition to normal depreciation charges. They may be occasioned by general price-level decreases, extraordinary obsolescence, or loss of utility to the particular owner.

For example, assume that a machine having an estimated life of thirty years was purchased for $60,000. It was depreciated for ten years at the rate of $2,000 per year. At the beginning of the eleventh year, it was appraised at $30,000 replacement cost new. The remaining useful life was estimated to be twenty years. The write-down would be recorded as follows:

Capital adjustment—building	$20,000	
Allowance for devaluation—building	10,000	
Building—devaluation		$30,000

The annual entries for depreciation would be as follows:

Depreciation	$1,000	
Allowance for devaluation	1,000	
Allowance for depreciation—building		$2,000
Income and expense	1,000	
Capital adjustment—building		1,000

Quasi-Reorganization. The method of recording a devaluation illustrated in the preceding example is ideal in cases where only one or a small number of assets are to be written down. However, when a substantial portion of the assets of a firm are to be devalued, either because of a significant and apparently permanent price-level decrease or because of operating and financial difficulties of the particular firm, a quasi-reorganization would be in order.

Using the data given for the preceding example, the asset would be reduced to current sound cost by the following entry:

Retained earnings (if any)	$20,000	
Allowance for depreciation—building	10,000	
Building		$30,000

The annual depreciation entry would be as follows:

Depreciation—building	$1,000	
Allowance for depreciation—building		$1,000

It is significant to note that under the fresh start provided by the quasi-reorganization, there is a direct write-down of the assets. The allowance for depreciation balance is reduced in proportion to the reduced value of the asset, and the resulting loss is charged to retained earnings. Any deficit in retained earnings should be charged off against capital surplus. After a quasi-reorganization, there should be a zero balance in the retained earnings account.

CHAPTER 9

Noncurrent Assets:
Intangibles Other than Investments

An *intangible asset* is one that lacks substantive or material value. Its value is derived from the rights, privileges, protections, or competitive advantages that it provides. An intangible asset lacks physical substance, but its existence may be established by a physical substance. The existence of a patent, which is an intangible asset, may be evidenced by a physical substance, a document from the U.S. Patent Office. It is significant to note that the value rests not in the material document itself but, rather, in the rights and privileges which are granted and protected by it.

Although it is evident from these statements that in a broad sense, stocks and bonds are intangibles, discussion of such items will be reserved for Chapter 10.

NATURE OF INTANGIBLES

The major characteristic of intangible assets is lack of physical substance, but there are other delimiting factors. Stocks and bonds are, according to both the general definition and the legal definition, intangibles, but accountants usually exclude them from the intangible classification. Also, bank deposits and accounts receivable lack tangibility, but they are not classified as intangibles by accountants.

For accounting purposes, there are a limited number of intangible assets, all of which fall into one of two groups as follows:

Limited-Life Intangibles (Type A)	Unlimited-Life Intangibles (Type B)
Copyrights	Brand names
Franchises, fixed term	Franchises, perpetual
Goodwill, of limited life	Goodwill, permanent
Leases and leaseholds	Trademarks
Licenses	Trade names
Patents	Secret formulas
	Secret processes
	Subscription lists
	Organization costs

There are some similarities between tangible and intangible assets. Both are dependent on earning power for their value. Both should be valued at cost or amortized cost. In both cases, cost is determined by the amount of expenditures made for their acquisition, and economic value is dependent upon the amount of revenue that they are expected to produce.

Limited-Life Intangibles (Type A). The AICPA has developed two classes of intangibles: type A and type B. Type A includes "those having a term of existence limited by law, regulation, or agreement, or by their nature (such as patents, copyrights, leases, licenses, franchises for a fixed term, and goodwill as to which there is evidence of limited duration)."[1]

The cost of such limited-life intangibles should be amortized (written off) systematically over their useful lives.

Unlimited-Life Intangibles (Type B). The AICPA defines type B as including "those having no such limited term of existence and as to which there is, at the time of acquisition, no indication of limited life (such as goodwill generally, going value, trade names, secret processes, subscription lists, perpetual franchises, and organization costs)."[2]

An unlimited-life (type B) asset may be carried at unamortized cost until it acquires the characteristics of a limited-life (type A) asset, at which time a program of amortization should be established for it. This is expressed by the AICPA as follows:

1. *Accounting Research and Terminology Bulletins,* Final Edition, (1961), p. 37.
2. Loc. cit., p. 37.

When a corporation decides that a type (b) intangible may not continue to have value during the entire life of the enterprise it may amortize the cost of such intangible by systematic charges against income despite the fact that there are no present indications of limited existence or loss of value which would indicate that it has become type (a), and despite the fact that expenditures are being made to maintain its value.[3]

The AICPA's opposition to an immediate write-off of either type A or type B intangibles is expressed by the following statement:

Lump-sum write-offs of intangibles should not be made to earned surplus immediately after acquisition nor should intangibles be charged against capital surplus. If not amortized systematically, intangibles should be carried at cost until an event has taken place which indicates a loss or a limitation on the useful life of the intangibles.[4]

As has been indicated, the AICPA recognizes only two types of intangible assets: (1) those having limited lives and (2) those having unlimited lives. However, it does recognize the fact that an intangible having an apparently unlimited life may change character in such a way that it develops a limited life. Also, it is generally agreed that an intangible with a definite legal life may have a shorter useful life. Thus, in many instances, the actual useful life of an intangible is indeterminable at the outset; therefore, an estimate of its useful life must be made.

CARRYING VALUE OF INTANGIBLES

As is the case with assets in general, intangibles should be carried at cost or amortized cost. Because of the very nature of intangibles, it is often more difficult to establish costs for them objectively than it is for tangible assets. For this reason (although the same costing principles may be applied to intangible and to tangible assets), there is a tendency to expense the costs of intrafirm-developed intangibles, even though it is agreed that, theoretically, the costs of developing an intangible (with the excep-

3. Loc. cit., p. 39.
4. Loc. cit., p. 40.

tion of goodwill) should be capitalized, just as the cost of a purchased intangible should be capitalized. In those cases in which purchased intangibles are recorded as assets and developed intangibles are expensed, dual standards of reporting are created.

Cost. All intangible assets, whether developed (except goodwill) or purchased, should be recorded initially at cost. When a single intangible is purchased for cash, there is no problem in determining the cost of the item; it is the amount paid for the item. Problems of costing arise when intangible assets are acquired through the exchange of stock or other assets or together with other assets in a lump-sum, or basket, purchase.

When stock is issued in exchange for an intangible asset, the cost of the intangible should be recorded at the fair current market value of the stock or the asset, whichever is established more reliably. Most likely this would be the stock if it is actively traded.

In many cases, the cost of the asset is set at the par value of the stock, which is an error except in the rare instances in which the market value of the stock happens to coincide with its par value. In the case of a basket purchase involving both intangible and tangible assets, there is the same problem of selecting an allocation basis as in the case of a basket purchase of tangible assets only, but it is complicated by the dissimilar characteristics of the two types of assets. Sometimes, the tangible assets acquired are simply recorded at the previous owner's values, and the balance is assigned to the intangible assets. Such a practice is faulty and should be guarded against.

As has been mentioned in Chapter 6, all costs incident to the acquisition of a long-term asset should be capitalized rather than expensed. However, because of the difficulty of identifying various costs with the resulting intangible assets, there is a theoretically improper, although practical, tendency to charge them to expense as they are incurred.

An intangible asset may be carried at cost, without amortization, so long as it appears to have an unlimited life.

Amortized Cost. Amortization of an intangible is similar in principle to depreciation of a tangible asset in that the periodic write-down of the asset depends on the net cost of the asset and the length (in periods or units) of its useful life. However, there is a difference in recording the periodic credits. The offsetting credit for depreciation expense is to an asset valuation account; whereas, the offsetting credit for amortization expense usually is directly to the asset account.

There is a conservative tendency to assign rather short lives to intangible assets, thus writing them off rather quickly.

SOME COMMON INTANGIBLES

Although it is impossible to cover all intangibles, a number of the more common ones are discussed in the following paragraphs.

Patents. A patent is a right granted by a government (in the United States, the U.S. Patent Office) to an inventor, giving him the exclusive right to produce and use or sell his invention for seventeen years. Legally, a patent cannot be renewed; but in practice, its life may be extended indefinitely by obtaining a series of patents on slightly modified versions of the preceding product just prior to the expiration of the preceding patent.

A patent may become obsolete or fail to withstand an infringement suit and thus become worthless long before the expiration of seventeen years. The economic value of a patent depends on the reduction of costs and/or increases in revenue made possible by the monopolistic condition it provides.

Revenue may be obtained by assigning the patent rights in part or in the entirety under licensing agreements whereby royalties are paid to the owner of the patent.

The useful life of a patent is often less than the legal seventeen years. In such cases, it should be amortized over the shorter period.

Patents should be recorded at cost. This is the common practice when they are purchased. In some cases where patents are developed within the firm, such costs are charged to expense. The better practice, theoretically, is to capitalize all costs of developing and proving a useful patent. These would include research and development costs, costs of drawings and models, legal fees, and costs of infringement suits. However, for tax purposes, the litigation expenses must be expensed in the year incurred, and the research and development costs may be either expensed as incurred or capitalized and amortized over the life of the patent.

Copyrights. In the United States, a *copyright* is an exclusive right granted by the federal government to an author, artist, or other creator to publish, sell, and control the reproduction and use of the creator's artistic products for a period of twenty-eight years. A copyright may be renewed for a second twenty-eight-year period. Thus, an artist or author may have his creations protected from unauthorized use or reproduction for fifty-six years. However, there is pending legislation to extend the life of a copyright to fifty years beyond the death of the author.

The copyright protection may be granted on books, pamphlets, designs, drawings, maps, pictures, photographs, moving pictures, musical compositions, and so forth. A copyright prohibits the unauthorized reproduction, publication, or use, of any part of the copyrighted material.

Copyrights may be assigned or licensed; occasionally, free use of specified parts of the material copyrighted may be authorized by the copyright owner.

The cost of a copyright includes all costs of producing the artistic work and obtaining the copyright. Copyrights are transferable. If one is bought, its recorded cost should be the total of all expenditures made for its acquisition.

It is important to note that the useful or economic life of a copyright frequently is much shorter than the fifty-six-year possible legal life and that the cost should be amortized over the estimated economic life of the copyright.

Trademarks. A *trademark* is a name, label, symbol, or mark used to distinguish or identify goods or services offered for sale. Trademarks and their ownership are protected under common law. Greater protection may be obtained under the statutory law by the registration of the trademark with the U.S. Patent Office. A trademark may be registered for a twenty-year period and may be renewed an indefinite number of similar periods. A registrant, in order to obtain full legal protection of the trademark, must give notice of such registration by displaying one of the following notations along with the trademark: "Registered U.S. Patent Office," "Reg. U.S. Pat. Off.," or an encircled "R."

The cost of a developed trademark should include all developmental and designing costs, filing and registry fees, and all litigation costs.

The cost of a purchased trademark is the cash paid or fair market value of other assets exchanged for it.

Because trademarks have unlimited lives and, therefore, are theoretically not subject to amortization, they should be carried at cost. However, in practice, they are written off entirely or written down to $1 over a short period. For federal-income-tax purposes, trademark costs incurred after December 31, 1955, may be written off over a period of not less than sixty months.

The economic value of a trademark is dependent upon its ability to develop additional revenue for its owner.

Trade Names. *Trade names* are very similar to trademarks, with the major difference that, normally, trade names and brand names, as such, cannot be registered with the U.S. Patent Office.

Research and Development Costs. Research and development (R and D) can be broken down into three distinct functions: basic research, applied research, and development. *Basic research* is involved with the discovery and investigation of fundamental scientific principles and phenomena. *Applied research* is effort directed to the discovery or design of goods in a certain area. *Development* is the cost of making the results of research commercially useful. However, the three functions are often so intertwined that for practical reasons the costs are lumped together.

Most large firms continually spend large sums for research and development. It is argued that a firm's competition is continually seeking new and improved products as well as more efficient ways of producing them and that for this reason, continual research and development on the firm's part are necessary; therefore, the costs are necessary operating expenses. Consequently, many firms charge off research and development costs in the period in which they are incurred. This procedure avoids the problem of how to handle capitalized costs of research programs that ultimately prove worthless.

In many industries, the costs of research and development are increasing. A significant number of firms are devising cost methods by which the costs of the various research programs can be kept separately so that the costs of each program can be capitalized separately. The capitalized costs of a successful program should be amortized over the beneficial, or economic, life of the results of the program. It should be observed that many successful research programs result in patentable products. The accumulated costs may be transferred to the appropriate patent accounts. The capitalized costs of an unsuccessful program should be charged off immediately.

Some accountants suggest that in large firms with special research and development departments or divisions, the costs of maintaining the departments are rather indirect continuing costs and should be expensed as incurred.

For income-tax purposes, such costs can be expensed either in the period paid or incurred or over a period of sixty months or more.

Exploration and Development Costs. *Exploration and discovery* in extractive industries is quite similar to the research function in manufacturing industries. Exploration is performed to determine whether a certain area has sufficient natural resources to be extracted profitably on a commercial basis. Development is the work performed in preparing for the extraction of the natural resource on a commercial basis. In some cases, such costs are added to the cost of the tangible product. In other cases, they are treated as intangible assets. In still other cases, they are expensed as incurred.

Franchises. A *franchise* is a contract by which one group or body confers stipulated monopolistic privileges on another person or group, usually in return for the acceptance of certain obligations by the second person or group.

Perhaps the most important franchises are those issued by government units to public utilities. For example, the exclusive right to sell electric power in a certain area is granted to a public utility company by a governmental unit in exchange for the utility's promise to provide all customers in the area with service under prescribed conditions.

Also, one firm may issue a franchise to another firm. For example, an automobile manufacturer may, under stipulated conditions, grant a dealer the exclusive right to sell the manufacturer's products within a prescribed territory.

The cost of a franchise includes all legal fees and expenses incurred in obtaining it. When an existing franchise is purchased from another firm, the amount paid the other firm and any necessary legal, transfer, and recording fees constitute the franchise cost.

A limited-life franchise should be amortized during that limited life. The life of a franchise may be limited either by the terms of the franchise or by the loss of economic value of the granted rights and privileges. The cost of a perpetual franchise may be capitalized and carried forward indefinitely. When a franchise is terminable at the option of the grantor, it should be amortized by the grantee over a relatively short time.

Perpetual-life franchises should appear on the balance sheet at unamortized cost. Limited-life franchises should be reported at amortized cost.

In some cases, the holder of a franchise is required by the terms of the contract to build and maintain certain tangible assets, such as bridges and streets. The cost of such construction should be capitalized and written off over the life of the asset or the remaining life of the franchise, whichever is shorter. The normal cost of maintaining such assets should be charged to expense as incurred.

Organization Costs. *Organization costs* include any costs incurred in promoting, organizing, or establishing a firm (usually a corporation), including promotional costs, legal fees, accounting fees, incorporation fees, taxes, costs of preparing stock certificates, underwriters' fees, commissions, and so forth.

Typical items that should *not* be included as organization costs are stock and bond discounts and operating deficits.

Organization costs should benefit many operating periods. To recognize such costs as expenses of preoperating periods would burden the firm with a deficit, even before beginning operations. Therefore, it is advisable to treat such costs as intangible assets.

There are three alternate ways of treating organization costs after they have been established as intangible assets: (1) Since organization costs will provide benefits to the firm during its entire life, the costs should be viewed as a permanent asset and carried at unamortized cost until the end of the firm's existence. (2) Since organization costs have no sale or disposal value, they should be amortized over a short time, perhaps three to five years. (3) Since the value of organization costs does not decrease on a systematic basis, these costs should be carried at unamortized cost until there is evidence of loss of value, at which time they should be written off in a lump sum.

Theoretically, the best treatment of organization costs is to carry them at unamortized cost during the life of the firm. However, in the interest of valuing assets conservatively, many accountants prefer to amortize organization costs rather quickly. This method is given impetus by the tax code, which (since 1954) allows a firm during its first year, under certain circumstances, to elect to write off organization costs over a period of at least sixty months.

Goodwill. *Goodwill* is that portion of the value of the firm in excess of the net book value of its other assets. It is the present value of the expected future income in excess of a normal return on assets, other than goodwill, for the type of operations and degree of risk involved. It is the difference between the price paid for a business as a whole and the sum of the individual values of the net assets involved other than goodwill. It is a master valuation account.

NATURE OF GOODWILL. Of all intangible assets, goodwill is the one to which it is most difficult to assign a realistic value. Anything that will contribute to above-normal earnings will also increase goodwill.

Goodwill may be affected by factors such as the attitudes of investors, credit institutions, trade creditors, employees, and customers; advantageous locations (not included in the cost of the location); and momentum. In the vast majority of cases, goodwill is positive; that is, the account is charged with the amount involved. In fact, the usual definitions of goodwill consider only positive goodwill. Occasionally, however, it is appropriate to consider and record negative goodwill.

Positive Goodwill. Positive goodwill exists when the potential earnings of the total of a firm's assets used as a whole are greater than the potential total earnings of all of the assets when utilized individually. By the same token, when the expected earnings of the total assets used as a unit are less than the expected earnings of those same assets when utilized individually, *negative goodwill* is said to exist.

Negative Goodwill. If negative goodwill is recorded, it results in a credit balance in an asset account (which is illogical) or a reduction in a previous debit balance. Because the existence of negative goodwill indicates that the firm would be better off selling its assets piecemeal than continuing to operate, it is usually not recorded. In the event an unprofitable firm is sold as a going concern, the recording of negative goodwill by the purchaser is avoided by reducing the carrying value of the tangible assets acquired to the purchase price.

RECOGNITION OF GOODWILL. Goodwill should be recognized in the books of account only when it is *purchased*. This very conservative principle prevents firms that have *developed* goodwill through the years (as evidenced by a return on their tangible assets above the normal rate for that particular firm or industry) from recording the goodwill that was developed.

Because it is based on earnings, goodwill cannot be purchased separately from other assets; it can be purchased only when all, or a substantial part, of a firm is purchased.

Because of the intangibility of goodwill and the fact that it cannot be sold separately, there is a tendency to amortize it over a relatively short time. This tendency is increased by the lack of objectivity in establishing its value.

On the other hand, some accountants take the position that without specific evidence that purchased goodwill has been exhausted, it should be carried on the books indefinitely at unamortized cost. The assumption is that the conditions, such as efficient management, which caused the development of the purchased goodwill, will continue indefinitely and that therefore it should not be amortized. However, a logical counterargument to this is that even though above-normal earnings continue because of efficient management or good customer relations, the purchased goodwill is gradually exhausted and replaced by goodwill developed by the new owners and therefore the purchased goodwill should be amortized.

It is now generally agreed that goodwill should not be charged off to retained earnings as a lump sum immediately after acquisition. The preferable conservative treatment is to amortize it rather quickly. Some firms follow the practice of writing goodwill down to $1 because the officers are uncertain of the continuing value of the goodwill but want to show that goodwill has been purchased.

Some firms carry goodwill at unamortized cost. This treatment is given weight by the fact that for tax purposes, the IRS will not recognize amortization of goodwill as an expense.

ESTIMATING THE AMOUNT OF GOODWILL. The actual price of goodwill usually results from arm's-length negotiations between the buyer and the seller. Although there are many ways of calculating the goodwill, certain basic elements are common to most methods:

1. An estimate of future earnings (based, among other things, on past earnings)
2. Establishment of the value of net assets excluding goodwill
3. Determination of rate of return based on steps 1 and 2
4. Determination of normal rate of return for the trade or industry
5. Use of the data developed in the preceding steps to determine the possible value of goodwill

It should be remembered that the value of purchased goodwill is actually the excess of the total purchase price over the value assigned to purchased net assets other than goodwill. Hence, the following calculations of goodwill only indicate possible values for goodwill for negotiating purposes rather than an exact value.

For example, assume the following facts: The seller's net assets, excluding goodwill, are worth $400,000. The income for the past four years averaged 20 percent, or $320,000 for the four years. The normal rate is estimated at 10 percent.

YEAR'S PURCHASE OF AVERAGE EXCESS EARNINGS

Average earnings	$80,000
Normal earnings (10% of $400,000)	40,000
Annual excess earnings	$40,000

If it is believed that goodwill should be worth two years' excess earning, it would be valued at $80,000; if it is thought to be worth three years' excess earnings, it would be valued at $120,000; and so forth.

CAPITALIZATION OF EXCESS EARNINGS

Excess earning [(.20 −.10) × $400,000]	$ 40,000
Excess earning capitalized at normal rate ($40,000 ÷ .10) = goodwill	$400,000
Other net assets	400,000
Total assets, including goodwill, that yield 10% return	$800,000

PRESENT VALUE OF EXCESS EARNINGS. This method is based on the assumption that the goodwill has a limited life. Assume, as in the previous example, that the average excess earnings amount to $40,000 per year and that interest is 10 percent. Assume also that the goodwill will be worthless at the end of five years.

The value of the goodwill may be established at the present value of five installments of $40,000 each, discounted at 10 percent. Present-value tables indicate that the present value of an annuity of $1 for five periods at 10 percent is $3.7908.

The present value of an annuity of $40,000 (the annual amortization of goodwill) would be $40,000 × $3.7908, or $151,632.

Leases and Leaseholds. A *lease* is a contract between a landlord (the lessor) and a tenant (the lessee) setting forth the conditions for the lessee's use of the asset and his obligations, as well as the lessor's obligations. There is a striking similarity between some long-term leases and property financed by mortgages. It is this similarity that has caused some accounting authorities to recommend reporting leases and the property under the lease on the balance sheet.

A *leasehold* is an interest in property, real or personal, provided under the terms of a lease. A leasehold provides the tenant, or lessee, with only a right to the use of the asset, not a legal title to the asset; therefore, if the lessee has any asset, it is an intangible one evidenced by the lease, rather than a tangible one evidenced by legal title to the asset itself.

Many leases simply provide that the lessee make stipulated periodic payments for rent and so forth in return for the use of the property, without accumulating any apparent equity in the property. Under such conditions, the lessee should show neither an asset nor a liability on the balance sheet in regard to the leased property. Such executory contracts as these leases should be shown in separate schedules or notes to the financial statements.

On the other hand, some lease agreements are essentially equivalent to installment purchases of property. In such cases, the substance of the arrangement, rather than its legal form, should determine the accounting treatment. The property and the related obligation should be included in the balance sheet as an asset and a liability, respectively, at the discounted amount of the future lease rental payments, exclusive of payments to cover taxes and operating expenses other than depreciation. Further, in such cases, it is appropriate to depreciate the capitalized amount for property over its estimated useful life rather than over the initial period of the lease.[5]

If the early rental payments are substantially greater than the expirations of the economic value of the property and the lessee has the right either to purchase the property at the expiration of the lease at a price considerably less than its probable value at that time or to renew the lease at a much-reduced price, this indicates that the transaction should be treated as an installment purchase rather than as a lease per se.

Leasehold Improvements. *Leasehold improvements* are improvements, additions, or betterments added to leased property by the lessee. Because such improvements revert with the original property to the lessor at the expiration of the lease, they should be capitalized and then amortized by the lessee over the physical life of the improvement or the remaining life of the lease, whichever is shorter.

Deferred Charges (to Expense). A *deferred charge* is an expenditure that is not recognized as an expense in the period in which it is incurred but is carried forward to be written off over one or more future periods and that may not properly fall into some other long-term asset classification.

In a very general sense, all noncurrent assets are deferred charges because they are assets waiting to be charged to expense in some future period. Thus, in a very general way, machinery, plant and equipment, and all the intangible assets specifically mentioned in this chapter are deferred charges. But in the interest of clarity, accountants are striving to keep the deferred-charge group as small as is practical. In fact, many items formerly

5. The American Institute of Certified Public Accountants, *APB Opinion* 5 "Reporting of Leases in Financial Statements of Lessee," p. 30.

classified as deferred charges are now classified as prepaid items; those expenditures that may be deferred over a short period, such as twelve months, are now commonly treated as prepaid items and are classified as current assets.

Discount on bonds payable is probably the one item that appears most frequently on the balance sheet under the Deferred Charge caption. Goodwill is often classified as a deferred charge rather than as an intangible asset.

CHAPTER 10

Noncurrent Assets: Investments

Investment, in a generic sense, refers to the act and the result of exchanging money or other capital for some other property or asset that is expected to return a profit or service. In such a general sense, the acquisition and holding of almost any asset might be considered an investment. For example, the acquisition and/or holding of property (real or personal, tangible or intangible) for a short or long period of time could be viewed as an investment.

In this chapter, the term is used in a restricted accounting sense to apply to assets that are incidental to the primary operations of the firm. The major portions of this chapter will be devoted to intangible-asset investments, rather than tangible-asset investments. The emphasis here is on long-term investments, those that may properly be listed on the balance sheet below the current assets under the general caption Investments.

It is important to distinguish between long-term and short-term investments. Long-term investments involve a rather-permanent or long-term commitment of funds; whereas temporary or short-term investments involve a short-term commitment of current working capital.

NATURE OF INTANGIBLE INVESTMENTS

As previously noted in Chapter 9, intangible assets are items lacking physical substance, their value depending on the rights and benefits that they confer on their owner. Thus, the benefits resulting from intangible investments are auxiliary to values or benefits developed by the primary operations of the firm.

Includes Long-Term Holdings. Noncurrent intangible investments include long-term commitments for stock (both common
and preferred), bonds, mortgages, and other long-term debt instruments.

Excludes Short-Term Holdings. One may invest in a three-
month note or a three-year note. The three-month note should appear on the balance sheet as a current asset under such a caption as Marketable Securities, whereas the three-year note (unless the holder expects to sell the note within the year) should be
listed among the noncurrent assets under the general caption
Investments. Many firms with temporary excess working capital
will invest such temporarily idle funds in marketable securities
during short periods of low cash requirements. Such procedures
are especially appropriate for firms in seasonal industries. Such
temporary investments should be classified as current assets.

The term *investment,* as used in this chapter, excludes the
short-term commitment of funds except for the purpose of drawing distinctions.

DEALER's INVENTORIES. The securities held by a broker or a
dealer in such intangibles constitute his stock in trade or inventory and therefore should be treated as current assets for the
same reasons that a merchandising firm treats its inventory of
goods held for sale as a current asset. For tax purposes, security
dealers are permitted to value their securities inventory at market
value, cost, or the lower of cost or market.

MARKETABLE SECURITIES INTENDED FOR QUICK TURNOVER. Marketable securities that were acquired as a means of profitably
employing otherwise temporarily idle working capital but that
will be converted into cash in the near future as increased working capital becomes necessary should be classified as current
assets. These temporary investments should be valued at the
lower of cost or market for accounting purposes. However, for
information purposes, it is advisable to include in the reports a
parenthetical statement or footnote setting forth the alternate of
the cost-or-market figure used in the accounts in order that a
reader may be informed of both the cost of the securities and
their present market value.

EQUITY INSTRUMENTS

In a broad sense, an *equity instrument* is any document that establishes a valuable claim against assets. This broad definition encompasses both ownership and creditor claims. However, in the generally accepted restricted sense (the one used in this chapter) an equity instrument is considered to be any document that proves ownership; documents that establish claims of creditors are excluded in this definition. Under this definition, corporate equity instruments are restricted to common- and preferred-stock certificates.

Frequently, one corporation buys stock of another corporation in order to improve the effectiveness and profitability of its own operations. For example, a firm may buy stock of a corporation that supplies the purchasing firm with materials in order to control a critical source of supplies. Or a firm may buy stock of a sales organization in order to be assured of an outlet for the production of the purchasing firm. In such cases where the stock is acquired in order to obtain control of that corporation, the investment is a permanent one and should be classified as a noncurrent asset, even though there is a ready market for the stock, because the intent to market the stock in the near future is lacking.

The corporation that controls another corporation by virtue of the ownership of a majority of that corporation's voting stock is referred to as a *holding,* or *parent, company,* and the controlled company is referred to as a *subsidiary company.*

Valuation of Stock. Since temporary investments in the stock of another firm should be treated as current assets, they should be valued at the lower of cost or market. The lower-of-cost-or-market principle is commonly applied to the portfolio as a whole rather than to each specific item within the portfolio. The initial cost of the investment normally is charged to a single account, ignoring, as such, any premium or discount from the par value. The decrease in value resulting from the write-down of the portfolio should be credited to a contra-account and the (nontax) loss should be charged against income. It is important to maintain a permanent record of the original cost because for tax purposes, a gain or loss will be recognized only at the time of disposal of the stock. The difference between the purchase price and the selling price normally provides the basis for determining taxable gain or loss.

Market value of property may be used instead of cost for determining the tax liability in three instances:

1. When acquired by gift
2. When acquired by inheritance
3. When acquired by any method prior to March 1, 1913

Long-term investments are usually carried at cost except in those cases where the decline in value appears to be permanent and substantial. Minor declines in the market value are ignored because it is quite possible that the market will recover before the stock is to be sold. However, for purposes of information, it is advisable to state the current market value on the financial statements by means of a parenthetic expression or footnote. The cost of stock includes all expenses incurred directly in acquiring and keeping the stock, such as brokerage fees, commissions, and taxes, as well as any assessments levied against the stock during the ownership period.

The cost will be reduced by the return of capital as a result of dividends out of capital or (on a per-share basis) as a result of stock dividends or stock splits.

The cost of acquiring the investment should be recorded in a single account, with no recognition being given to a possible par value and premium or to a discount from that par value.

Dividends on Stock. *Dividends on stock* may constitute either a return of invested capital or income on invested capital, depending on the source of cash or other assets used in paying the dividend. A stock dividend has no effect on the investor's financial position.

CASH DIVIDENDS. *Cash dividends* are dividends paid in cash and are the most common type of dividend. When no limiting phrase is used in connection with the term *dividend*, it is safe to assume that it will be paid in cash. Usually, a cash dividend is paid out of profits.

STOCK DIVIDENDS. A *stock dividend* normally is the capitalization of retained earnings through the issuance of shares of the company's own stock to existing stockholders in proportion to their current holdings in the company. A stock dividend may be paid in any class of the company's stock so long as it is not detrimental to any other class of the company's stockholders.

A stock dividend may be charged to retained earnings (which is usually done) or to any other account that is legally available for dividends. When the charge is to retained earnings, it results in the capitalization of past earnings and leaves the total equity unchanged.

It should be observed that a stock dividend must be paid with the paying corporation's own stock. A payment with stock of another corporation does not constitute a stock dividend; rather it is a dividend in kind (property).

Generally, stock dividends do not constitute income to the recipient either for accounting purposes or for tax purposes. The total cost of the recipient's investment has not changed. He merely has more units (shares) representing his holdings. For example, an investor who paid $10,000 for 100 shares of X Company stock before a 10 percent stock dividend would list an investment of $10,000 represented by 100 shares of stock at a cost of $100 per share. After the 10 percent stock dividend, he would list an investment of $10,000 represented by 110 shares at a cost of $90.909 per share.

In view of the fact that a stock dividend does not represent income to the recipient, why do corporations give them? Corporations give stock dividends for the following reasons:

1. When it is advantageous to reduce the (high) market value of its stock and thus make it more salable

2. When it is advantageous to give the stockholders something (psychologically speaking) because cash either is scarce or can be used advantageously within the corporation

3. When it is advantageous to the stockholders (as in a close corporation) not to receive taxable dividends

DIVIDENDS IN KIND (PROPERTY). Dividends payable only in assets other than cash are referred to as *dividends in kind* or *property dividends*. When the dividend recipients have the option of receiving their dividend payment either in cash or in other assets, the dividend is not considered a dividend in kind; rather, it is regarded as a cash dividend that is paid at a particular recipient's request with assets other than cash.

A dividend in kind may be declared and paid by a corporation when cash available for dividends is scarce or when it is mutually advantageous to both parties. The amount of corporate-dividend distribution usually is the net value of the property given up at the time of distribution.

LIQUIDATING DIVIDENDS. A *liquidating dividend* is a proportionate distribution of cash and/or other assets of a corporation as a result of a partial or complete liquidation of the firm (i.e., the partial or complete reduction of the paid-in capital of the firm). A distinction must be drawn between paid-in (contributed) capital and earned capital (retained earnings). That part of a dividend paid out of retained earnings represents income in the hands of the investor; whereas that part paid out of paid-in capital represents a return of capital (investment) to the investor.

A corporation should inform dividend recipients what portion, if any, of a dividend is a return of capital.

Liquidating dividends are especially common in corporations utilizing wasting assets such as mines, wells (e.g., oil or gas), and timber. A corporation engaged in exploiting a mine may plan on going out of business when that particular mine is exhausted. It is therefore justified in returning to the investors parts of their original investment from time to time as such funds are recovered through the sale of the natural resource. The revenue of such a firm, if profitable, is composed of two elements: the cost of the units of the wasting asset sold and the profit from operations. Generally, dividends are paid out of profits only, but under some special circumstances, it is quite proper to pay dividends out of recoveries of contributed capital.

For example, if the X Mining Company agrees to pay dividends of $12,000 ($6,000 from earnings and $6,000 from paid-in capital), the recipient of a dividend of $2,000 and a statement from the paying corporation that the dividend was composed of 50 percent profit and 50 percent paid-in capital would make the following entry:

Cash	$2,000	
Dividend income		$1,000
X Mining Company investment		1,000

In the event that liquidating dividends exceed the cost of the investment, the investor records a (capital) gain on the investment. If the investor has not recovered (past dividends out of profit being excluded) the cost of the investment by the time the liquidation is completed, a (capital) loss should be recorded.

SCRIPT DIVIDENDS. *Script dividends*, which are very rarely used, are dividends payable by notes referred to as *script*. These notes may or may not bear interest. They may mature at a single specified time or serially. They are almost always payable in cash but occasionally are payable in other assets. In effect, script dividends are deferred dividends on the part of the issuing corporation. However, the declaration of such a dividend creates a current liability for the corporation.

The dividend recipient, the investor, should recognize as income the fair market value of the note received at the time the dividend is received.

Stock Rights. For a discussion of stock rights from the point of view of the corporation, see Chapter 13. This chapter focuses on the point of view of the investor.

From the investor's viewpoint, the receipt of rights is very similar to stock dividends; the corporation has not distributed any assets, and the stockholder's equity has not changed at this point. However, the stockholder's investment is now evidenced by two items: the original stock and the rights to buy additional shares. The rights usually entitle the holder to buy shares at less than the market value, and thus they have value in themselves.

The recipient of stock rights has the following three options:

1. To exercise the rights by buying additional stock
2. To sell the rights
3. To permit them to lapse, at which time their allocated cost should be recognized as a loss

The cost of the original shares should be allocated between the shares of stock and the stock rights on the basis of market values.

The following formulas may be used in allocating the original cost of the shares to the stock and to the stock rights:

$$\text{Allocated cost of rights} = \frac{\text{market value of rights}}{\text{market value of stock ex-rights} + \text{market value of rights}} \times \text{original cost of stock}$$

$$\text{Allocated cost of stock} = \frac{\text{market value of stock ex-rights}}{\text{market value of stock ex-rights} + \text{market value of rights}} \times \text{original cost of stock}$$

For example, consider the case of an investor who bought 1,000 shares of stock for $60,000. At the time that the rights were issued, the rights had a market value of $4,000, and the stock had a market value of $76,000.

The $60,000 cost would be allocated as follows:

$$\text{Cost of rights} = \frac{\$4,000}{\$76,000 + \$4,000} \times \$60,000 = \$3,000$$

$$\text{Cost per right} = \$3,000 \div 1,000 = \$3$$

$$\text{Cost of stock} = \frac{\$76,000}{\$76,000 + \$4,000} \times \$60,000 = \$57,000$$

$$\text{Cost per share} = \$57,000 \div 1,000 = \$57$$

If the investor can buy one share for $35 and 5 rights, the following entry should be made to record the exercise of the 1,000 rights:

Investment in stock	$10,000	
Investment in stock rights		$3,000
Cash $\left(\dfrac{1,000}{5} \times 35\right)$		7,000

If instead of exercising the rights, the investor sells them for $4,000, the following entry should be made:

Cash	$4,000	
Gain on sale of stock rights		$1,000
Investment in stock rights		3,000

DEBT INSTRUMENTS: BONDS

Bonds differ from stocks in that they are certificates of indebtedness of the issuing company; whereas stocks represent ownership in the issuing corporation. From the point of view of the investor, two elements of a bond are important. (1) The debtor agrees to pay a stated amount of interest (except in the case of income bonds) to the bondholder on specified dates during the life of the bond. (2) The debtor agrees to pay the holder the principal or face amount of the bond at the maturity date of the bond.

Bonds are issued most frequently in denominations of $1,000, but sometimes, in order to attract small investors, they are issued in denominations of $500 or even $100. A bond with a face value of less than $1,000 is referred to as a *baby bond*. It should be observed that bond prices are quoted as a percent of their par or face value. For example, a $1,000 bond that is selling for $980 is quoted at 98. Also, a $100 bond selling for $98 is quoted at 98. A bond that sells for less than the par value is said to sell *at a discount;* a bond that sells for more than the par value is said to sell *at a premium.*

Bonds differ from notes in that a single bond represents only a part of the total debt. Bonds are issued under an *indenture,* which is, in effect, a master contract entered into by the issuers, the trustees for the bondholders, and indirectly, the bondholders. The indenture sets forth in detail the terms of the agreement.

The many types of bonds are discussed in Chapter 12.

The following definitions should prove helpful in understanding the discussion on bond investments:

Premium is that portion of the security purchase price in excess of its par, face, or principal value.

Discount is the excess of the face value of the security over the amount paid or received for it.

Nominal interest rate, also referred to as the *coupon* or *cash rate,* is the rate of interest named or stipulated in the instrument. This rate is applied to the par value of the security to determine the amount of interest due.

Effective interest rate, also referred to as the *market rate* or *yield,* is the actual rate of return on the securities based on the exchange price and the assumption that they will be held until maturity.

A bond sells at a premium or a discount because the effective interest rate required to attract investors is either lower or higher than the nominal rate on the particular bond. Thus, the amortization of premium or the accumulation of discount should be treated as an interest adjustment.

Valuation of Bonds. Bonds are long-term instruments and, therefore, should be carried on the books of the investor at book value; that is, cost plus amortized discount or cost less premium write-offs. Therefore, book value tends to equal par or principal value at the bond's maturity.

When bonds are purchased for cash, the cost can be determined rather easily and specifically. The total cost should include broker's commissions, fees, taxes, and any other costs directly identifiable with the acquisition of the bonds. When non-cash items, such as other assets or services, are exchanged for the bonds, either through a simple trade or through a reorganization or a merger, the true cost of the bonds may be difficult to establish. In such cases, the cost of the bonds should be recorded at the fair market value of the bonds received or that of the goods or services exchanged, whichever can be determined more accurately.

If the bond's current market value differs significantly from its book value, disclosure of the market value should be made in the firm's financial statements, either by a parenthetic statement or by a footnote.

In the event of a substantial and apparently permanent decline in the market value of the bonds because of financial or other difficulties of the issuer, the investment may be written down, and a loss may be recognized in the current period, rather than deferred until the bonds are realized.

PURCHASED AT INTEREST DATE. When bonds are bought at the interest date, there is no problem of allocating the cost between the investment (or bond) account and an accrued interest receivable account. The entire cost should be charged to the investment account.

PURCHASED BETWEEN INTEREST DATES. Interest on bonds in good standing is accrued. This is justified because the issuer of bonds has a legal liability to pay interest of a specified amount on the bonds at specified dates. Therefore, bonds are generally bought on a quoted price "and interest" basis. The buyer pays the seller the agreed price plus the interest earned since the last interest date. Such a pricing method is necessary because the issuer of the bonds will pay the entire amount of interest earned on the bonds during the interest period to holders of record (or holders of proper coupons) at each interest date.

For example, if a $1,000 6 percent bond with interest payable semiannually is bought at 104 plus interest three months after the last interest date, the purchase would be recorded as follows:

Investment in bonds	$1,040	
Bond interest receivable	15	
Cash		$1,055

The receipt of the interest three months hence would be entered as follows:

Cash	$30	
Bond interest receivable		$15
Bond interest income		15

It is evident from these entries that the investor made a capital investment of $1,040 for a bond and also bought accrued interest (an asset) of $15. Also, when the semiannual interest of $30 was collected, only $15 was recognized as income, and the $15 balance was applied to the elimination of the temporary asset (or deferred income).

An alternate method of recording these transactions is:

Investment in bonds	$1,040	
Interest income	15	
Cash		$1,055
Cash	30	
Interest income		30

The *net* interest income is $15. In these entries, no attempt has been made to reduce the original cost of the investment to current book value by the amortization of the $40 premium. Such an amortization of premium (or accumulation of discount) may be made each time interest is recorded as well as at the close of the accounting period or only at the end of the accounting period. It is simpler to record the amortization only at the end of the accounting period.

For example, assume that the bonds were bought forty months before maturity, that interest was payable on June 30 and December 31; that the investor closes his book on December 31; and that the bonds were bought on March 31. The $40 premium should be amortized over the remaining forty months of the bonds' life at $1 per month. The entry is as follows:

Interest income	$9	
Investment in bonds		$9

The reason the amortization should be charged against interest income is that the investor paid more than par value for the bond because the nominal interest rate, the rate which he would be paid, was higher than the rate which was required by him. (A detailed explanation of this is presented in the discussion of premium and bond discount amortization. See pages 163–165.)

PURCHASED WITH INTEREST IN DEFAULT. Bonds with interest in default and *income bonds* (bonds on which interest payments are contingent upon earnings) are priced without any accrued interest; that is, they are quoted *flat*. If an investor receives an interest payment that was in default at the time of purchase, it should be treated as a return of invested capital rather than as income. In fact, because of the uncertainty of ever receiving payments in excess of the purchase price, it may be appropriate to treat all payments received, whether purported by the bond issuer to be defaulted interest, current interest, or return of principal, as a reduction of the investment until the total amount of the investment has been recovered.

AMORTIZATION OF PREMIUM. When bonds are acquired as temporary investments, they should be carried at original cost during the entire holding period. Write-offs of premium or discount in the short run would not be significant in amount and might be more than offset by fluctuations in the market price. However, when bonds are acquired as long-term investments that quite likely will be held until maturity, the purchase price should be adjusted by systematic amortization of premium or accumulation of discount so that at maturity, the carrying value of the bonds will closely approximate the par value, the amount that the bond issuer will pay the investor for the matured bonds.

Bonds sell at a premium or a discount when the nominal rate differs from the market rate.

Two common methods (straight line and effective rate) of accounting for the amortization of bond premium are illustrated in the following example.

Assume that five-year 5 percent bonds, interest payable semiannually, with a face value of $100,000 are purchased at $104,491.30. This price will yield 4 percent.

Because the premium is the result of the excess of the nominal interest rate over the required effective rate, the amount of the premium that establishes the bond's price is determined by calculating the present value of the excess interest payments and adding that amount to the face value of the bond.

The amount of each interest payment at the nominal interest rate of 2½ percent (for one-half year) is $2,500. The amount of

PREMIUM AMORTIZATION: STRAIGHT-LINE METHOD

$100,000 FIVE-YEAR 5 PERCENT BONDS YIELDING 4 PERCENT

(A) Interest Periods	(B) Interest Received (2½% of Par)	(C) Premium Amortization (1/10 of $4,491.30)	(D) Effective Interest (B − C)	(E) Book Value
0				$104,491.30
1	$ 2,500.00	$ 449.13	$ 2,050.87	104,042.17
2	2,500.00	449.13	2,050.87	103,593.04
3	2,500.00	449.13	2,050.87	103,143.91
4	2,500.00	449.13	2,050.87	102,694.78
5	2,500.00	449.13	2,050.87	102,245.65
6	2,500.00	449.13	2,050.87	101,796.52
7	2,500.00	449.13	2,050.87	101,347.39
8	2,500.00	449.13	2,050.87	100,898.26
9	2,500.00	449.13	2,050.87	100,449.13
10	2,500.00	449.13	2,050.87	100,000.00
Total	$25,000.00	$4,491.30	$20,508.70	

interest at the required effective rate of 2 percent is $2,000. Thus, the purchaser of the bond during the next five years will receive ten payments of interest that are in excess of his (market) demands by $500 each. The problem is how much should an investor pay in advance for a $500 2 percent annuity for ten periods. The present value of an annuity of one at 2 percent for ten periods (as shown in actuarial tables) is $8.9826. Therefore, the present value of the excess interest payments is 8.9826 × $500 or $4,491.30.

Premium	$ 4,491.30
Par value	100,000.00
Price	$104,491.30

Each time the investor receives an interest payment, he would make the following entry:

Cash	$2,500.00	
Interest income		$2,050.87
Investment in bonds		449.13

The bond premium amortized in the preceding example by the straight-line method might have been amortized by the effective-interest-rate method. The schedule for the amortization by this method would be as follows:

PREMIUM AMORTIZATION: EFFECTIVE-INTEREST-RATE METHOD

$100,000 FIVE-YEAR BOND YIELDING 4 PERCENT

(A) Interest Periods	(B) Nominal Interest (2½% of Par)	(C) Effective Interest (2% of E)	(D) Premium Amortization (B − C)	(E) Carrying Value
0				$104,491.30
1	$ 2,500.00	$ 2,089.83	$ 410.17	104,081.13
2	2,500.00	2,081.62	418.38	103,662.75
3	2,500.00	2,073.26	426.74	103,236.01
4	2,500.00	2,064.72	435.28	102,800.73
5	2,500.00	2,056.01	443.99	102,356.74
6	2,500.00	2,047.13	452.87	101,903.87
7	2,500.00	2,038.08	461.92	101,441.95
8	2,500.00	2,028.84	471.16	100,970.79
9	2,500.00	2,019.41	480.59	100,490.20
10	2,500.00	2,009.80	490.20	100,000.00
Total	$25,000.00	$20,508.70	$4,491.30	

The entry to record the receipt of the first interest payment under this method would be as follows:

Cash	$2,500.00	
Interest income		$2,089.83
Investment in bonds		410.17

It should be observed that the total effective interest and the total amortization of premium reported during the ten periods is the same by either method but that the individual amounts differ.

Under the straight-line method, the same amounts are reported at the end of each period for premium amortization and effective interest; whereas under the effective-interest method, the amount of reported interest decreases with each succeeding period, and the amount of amortization increases.

Simplicity is the greatest advantage of the straight-line method. Accuracy is the greatest advantage of the effective-interest method. As shown in the example, the amount of effective interest decreased as the investment balance decreased.

AMORTIZATION (ACCUMULATION) OF DISCOUNT. The same principles that applied to the amortization of premium also apply to the accumulation of discount. In the interest of brevity, only the straight-line method will be illustrated here. Assume that the five-year 5 percent bonds, with interest payable semiannually, with a face value of $100,000 are purchased at $95,734.90, a price that will yield 6 percent.

DISCOUNT ACCUMULATION: STRAIGHT-LINE METHOD

$100,000 FIVE-YEAR 5 PERCENT BONDS YIELDING 6 PERCENT

(A) Interest Periods	(B) Nominal Interest (2½% of Par)	(C) Discount Accumulation (1/10 of $4,265.10)	(D) Effective Interest (B + C)	(E) Book Value
0				$ 95,734.90
1	$ 2,500.00	$ 426.51	$ 2,926.51	96,161.41
2	2,500.00	426.51	2,926.51	96,587.92
3	2,500.00	426.51	2,926.51	97,014.43
4	2,500.00	426.51	2,926.51	97,440.94
5	2,500.00	426.51	2,926.51	97,867.45
6	2,500.00	426.51	2,926.51	98,293.96
7	2,500.00	426.51	2,926.51	98,720.47
8	2,500.00	426.51	2,926.51	99,146.98
9	2,500.00	426.51	2,926.51	99,573.49
10	2,500.00	426.51	2,926.51	100,000.00
Total	$25,000.00	$4,265.10	$29,265.10	

The price of $95,734.90 is determined as follows:

Par value	$100,000.00
Less: Discount (500 × $8.5302[a])	4,265.10
Price	$ 95,734.90

[a] The present value of an annuity of 1 at 3 percent for ten periods.

The entry to record the receipt of an interest payment would be:

Cash	$2,500.00	
Investment in bonds	426.51	
Interest income		$2,926.51

DEBT INSTRUMENTS: MORTGAGES AND LONG-TERM NOTES

As will be explained in Chapter 12, bonds may or may not be secured by mortgages on assets. Likewise, long-term notes may or may not be secured by mortgages on assets. However, because of the great expense involved in floating a bond issue, it must involve for practical reasons a very large amount of money for a long period of time. Therefore, it is logical for a reader of financial data to assume, in the absence of specific information to the contrary, that bonds are long-term instruments, regardless of whether they are or are not secured by pledges of specific assets.

In the business community, the vast majority of short-term notes are not secured by any mortgages on specific assets; whereas long-term notes are frequently secured by mortgages on specific assets. Thus, an implied assumption has developed that in the absence of information to the contrary, a note is a short-term instrument and a mortgage is a long-term instrument.

Technically, even though it is almost universally done, it is incorrect to list a note secured by a mortgage as a "mortgage payable" or "mortgage receivable" because the note on which payment is given or received is usually a separate document from the mortgage. Payment is made on the note; the mortgage is merely a means of assuring the payment of the note. However, it is certainly correct to list "mortgage note payable" or "mortgage note receivable" because the adjective "mortgage" simply indicates the kind of note involved.

There is an important distinction between a note secured by a mortgage and bonds secured by a mortgage. In the case of the note, the mortgage provides security for a single claim, that of the holder of the note. In the case of bonds secured by a mortgage, that mortgage provides equal security for each bond in the group through the use of a mortgage trust indenture in the hands of a trustee.

NATURE OF TANGIBLE INVESTMENTS

Tangible investments are items having physical substance, the benefits of which are auxiliary to the primary functions of the firm. A building bought by a manufacturing firm and used for manufacturing purposes is not an investment in the restricted sense. But a building bought and held for possible future use or as a hedge against inflation is such an investment.

Fixed assets bought for present use in the regular operations of the business are noncurrent assets but not investments in the restricted sense.

Fixed assets bought, not for current use in the regular operations of the business, but for possible future use or for use ancillary to the main functions of the firm, are noncurrent assets and also investments.

It is important that both the tangible and intangible investments be separated from the operating assets so that certain analyses and ratios may be meaningful and not misleading. For example, if a firm has total assets of $200,000, broken down into $100,000 of operating assets and $100,000 of investments or non-operating assets, and an operating profit of $20,000, it would be misleading to divide operating income by total assets and state that there was only a 10 percent return on capital. It would be much more informative to divide operating income by operating assets and state that there was a 20 percent return on operating assets.

PART 2

Equities

In a generic sense, *equity* is any claim to assets. In this sense, it may be applied to both the claims of owners of assets and the claims of creditors against assets owned by others.

The AICPA has defined *liabilities* in essentially the same generic sense, as shown by the following quotation:

Something represented by a credit balance that is or would be carried forward upon a closing of the books of account according to the rules or principles of accounting, provided such credit balance is not in effect a negative balance applicable to an asset. Thus the word is used broadly to comprise not only items which constitute liabilities in the popular sense of debts or obligations (including provision for those that are unascertained), but also credit balances to be accounted for which do not involve the debtor and creditor relation. For example, capital stock and related or similar elements of proprietorship are balance-sheet liabilities in that they represent balances to be accounted for, though these are not liabilities in the ordinary sense of debts owed to legal creditors.[1]

In accounting, the term *equity* is frequently used in a restricted sense to apply only to the claims of owners of assets.

EQUITIES OF OUTSIDERS

It is sometimes suggested that the total value of a firm's assets is offset by an equal amount of claims against them: equities. These claims may be separated into two groups: The first group of claimants is the creditors, those to whom debts are owed, the outsiders; the second group is the owners of the firm (in the legal sense), the insiders.

This is illustrated by balance sheets that list all items owned by the firm on the left side under the general caption assets, and then on the right side under the generic caption equities list the liabilities and the ownership interests that must equal, in total,

1. *Accounting Research and Terminology Bulletins*, Final Edition, No. 1 (1961), pp. 13–14.

the amount of assets listed on the left side. In such cases, the creditors are referred to as the *outside* equity group. More frequently, the general heading of the right side of the balance sheet indicates the difference between the two groups of claims by using a heading such as liabilities and net worth.

Liabilities may be defined as obligations; that is, obligations to give assets or to provide services to another. Such obligations may have resulted from past or present transactions that are not yet settled. Settlement will require an additional act on the part of the obligor.

Liabilities will be discussed in Chapters 11 and 12.

EQUITIES OF INSIDERS

Equity has been defined as the net value of a firm or property established by deducting the total of all liens against the firm or property from its gross value. Thus, in corporate accounting, in a narrow sense, equity is total assets less liabilities; or assets minus claims of outsiders equals claims of insiders.

Insiders' claims, equities, will be discussed in Chapters 13, 14, and 15.

CHAPTER 11

Current Liabilities

All liabilities may be classified in one of two groups according to time of maturity. With few exceptions, those liabilities that mature or become due within a year or within the current operating cycle (whichever is longer) are classified as *current liabilities*. Those that do not become due until after the expiration of a year or the current operating cycle are classified as *noncurrent, fixed,* or *long-term liabilities*.

NATURE OF CURRENT LIABILITIES

Current liabilities are those liabilities that are payable

1. Within one year
2. Within the present operating cycle if longer than one year
3. Within a period longer than one year if it is general practice within the particular trade or industry to so classify them

The one-year rule is the criterion most commonly used for separating short-term liabilities from long-term liabilities. Liabilities that are going to be settled through the use of current assets or the creation of other current liabilities should be classified as current liabilities. For example, the currently maturing installment of a long-term loan should be classified as a current liability if it will be paid with cash from the general cash account or with other current assets; but it should continue to be classified as a long-term or fixed liability if payment will be made from assets (including cash funds) that are classified as long term or fixed. Current liabilities represent a claim against the current assets of the firm.

It is important to separate both assets and liabilities on a consistent basis into current groups and long-term groups so that both the *current ratio* and the (net) working-capital position will be meaningful.

VALUATION OF CURRENT LIABILITIES

From a theoretical point of view, current liabilities might be valued at the present value of the funds required to settle the claims at maturity. Since in the case of current liabilities, the time interval between the present date and the maturity date is short and, therefore, the difference between the present value and the maturity value is negligible, it is customary to value them at face or maturity value (explicit interest being accrued in a separate account).

DEFINITELY DETERMINABLE CURRENT LIABILITIES

Clear distinctions must be made between actual liabilities of definite amounts, actual liabilities of indefinite amounts, and uncertain (contingent) liabilities of indefinite amounts.

The *definitely determinable* current liabilities are obligations in actual existence for which both the maturity date and the amount of cash or cash equivalent required for settlement at maturity are exactly determined. Many current liabilities are of this type. Some of the more common ones are discussed in the paragraphs that follow.

Notes and Accounts Payable. Notes and accounts payable that are listed without any additional descriptive word or phrase are generally assumed to have arisen directly or indirectly from the purchase of goods or services in the regular course of business. These *trade payables* should thus be distinguished from accruals and other current liabilities not arising out of regular operations of the firm. Other payables should be listed in a way that will show their origin.

NOTES PAYABLE. A *note payable* is an unconditional promise in writing, signed by the maker, to pay a sum certain in money on demand or at a fixed or determinable future date to a designated person or bearer.

Theoretically, notes payable should be recorded at their discounted present value. Thus, a note bearing interest at the present going rate should be recorded at face value, and a non-interest-bearing note should be recorded at the face value, less discount at the going rate for the time intervening between the present date and the maturity date. However, for practical reasons, since the amount of discount would be relatively insignificant, it is frequently ignored.

For example, if a purchaser gives a supplier a $100 sixty-day non-interest-bearing note in exchange for merchandise, he will most likely record it as follows:

Merchandise (inventory)	$100	
Notes payable		$100

Preferably, if the going interest rate is 6 percent, it should be recorded as follows:

Merchandise (inventory)	$99	
Interest expense (prepaid interest)	1	
Notes payable		$100

ACCOUNTS PAYABLE. *Accounts payable* represent amounts owed to creditors, usually on open account. The liabilities are generally limited to unpaid balances for goods purchased and services received. These accounts should be distinguished from accruals and other current liabilities that result from irregular or unusual transactions.

Because there is often a delay in recognizing in the records the receipt of goods and the concomitant liability for the payment, and also because of the fact that title may pass, and thus the liability for paying for them may arise sometime in advance of the receipt of the goods, it is important that the accountant pay particular attention to the receipt of merchandise in order that the inventory and payables be correctly reported as of the end of each period.

Theoretically, accounts payable should be shown net of available cash discounts. However, the practical and acceptable method of listing the payables at the gross or invoice amount is often followed.

If one or more of the payable accounts have debit balances, they should not be offset against other payables with credit balances; both the total of debit balances and the total of credit balances should be reported on the balance sheet. A debit balance represents a receivable from, or an advance to, a supplier. Such a situation often results from a return of merchandise or an adjustment on it after payment for it had been made.

Dividends Payable. Cash dividends do not become liabilities until they are officially declared by the corporation's board of directors. The dividend declaration is the basis for recognizing the liability by debiting retained earnings (except in case of a liquidating dividend) and crediting (cash) dividends payable.

Cumulative preferred-stock dividends in arrears are not recognized as a legal liability because they have not been formally declared by the board of directors. When such dividends are declared by the board, they cease being in arrears and are then recorded as a current liability. However, the amount of such dividends in arrears should be shown on the balance sheet, either as a parenthetic expression in the capital stock section or as a footnote.

The declaration of stock dividends (those payable in shares of the corporation's stock) does not create a liability in the legal sense because the distribution of any cash or other assets or services to the stockholders is not required. The amount of such dividends is reported in the net worth section of the balance sheet because it represents retained earnings awaiting transfer to contributed capital.

Accrued Payroll. *Accrued payroll* represents the amount of wage and/or salary expense incurred by the firm but not yet paid. This situation results from the fact that employees are paid at preestablished times that do not correspond with the financial-statement dates. For example, the pay period may end on Wednesday, but the accounting period may end on Friday. Thus, appropriate expense accounts or production must be charged with the cost of the services provided by the firm's employees on Thursday and Friday. The credit would be to the accrued payroll account.

Unclaimed paychecks may be held for a short time, after which they should be redeposited in the bank and a special liability account, such as unclaimed wages, should be credited. The liability continues until either the employee claims the money, the statute of limitations eliminates the liability, or as is the case in many states, the money escheats to the state.

Accrued Payroll Taxes. These taxes are imposed on payrolls as a result of social legislation.

SOCIAL SECURITY TAXES. Old-age and survivors' benefits are provided for by the Federal Insurance Contributions Act (FICA). The act provides that each employer of covered employees shall withhold a stipulated percentage up to a specified amount from each employee's pay, that the employer shall match these amounts, and that at specific times the employer shall send the total amount to the proper federal agency. The employer is responsible for delivering to the government the proper amount of tax money due from both the employer and the employee. Thus, in the final analysis, the employer is liable for both amounts, and therefore, the two liabilities may be combined in one account.

Both the tax rate and the amount of earnings subject to tax have been changed frequently since the inception of the tax in 1937. Prior to 1972, the tax was applied only to the first $7,800 of an employee's earnings during the calendar year. In 1972, the tax base was increased to the first $9,000. In 1973 the tax base was increased to the first $10,800. During 1971–1972, the tax rate, including hospital insurance, was 5.2 percent. For the period 1973–1975, it has been raised to go to 5.85 percent.

FEDERAL UNEMPLOYMENT INSURANCE. In 1972, the tax base for a covered employee was increased from the first $3,000 earned per calendar year to $4,200. The tax rate remained unchanged at 3.2 percent. The employer may receive a credit against his federal tax for money paid to approved state tax plans, up to 90 percent of the federal tax if figured at the original 3 percent rate. Thus, if an employer pays to an approved state plan $4,200 × 2.7 percent, or $113.40 per employee, the federal government claims only ($4,200 × 0.5 percent), or $21 per employee.

STATE UNEMPLOYMENT INSURANCE. There is a close relationship between state and federal unemployment plans. In states having federally approved unemployment plans, the federal government will grant to the employers a credit on their federal unemployment tax. Most states had federally approved plans that called for a tax of at least 2.7 percent based on the first $3,000 of calendar-year earnings per employee, but in 1972, the base was increased to $4,200, in accordance with the change in the federal tax law.

In some states, it is possible for any employer to earn a merit-rating credit against his state tax because of good employment practices. In such a case, the federal government allows the employer a credit against his federal tax. This credit includes the amount paid to the state, plus the merit-rating credit granted by the state, except that in no case is the total credit for the state taxes allowed to exceed 90 percent of the federal tax figured at the old 3 percent rate.

Many states, following the lead of the federal government, tax only the employers; but a few states tax the employees, too. Also, some states use a rate higher than 2.7 percent and/or a base higher than $4,200. However, the credit granted by the federal government on the federal tax return may not exceed $4,200 × 2.7 percent, or $113.40 per covered employee. The unemployment tax charged against an employer is a labor-related expense, and the accrued amount should be reported as a current liability until paid. If withholdings are made from employees' pay, as is required under some state plans, these also should be reported as a current liability.

Income Taxes Withheld. It is important to maintain a difference between income taxes withheld and income taxes payable. *Income taxes withheld* are a current liability to the employer but came about by a withholding of a part of the earnings of the employees, rather than by a contribution of part of the firm's profits to the government. *Income taxes payable* are also a current liability but occur because of a required sharing of profits with the government.

Both are payables in the sense that they represent amounts that must be paid to outsiders, but their origins are significantly different and warrant showing the liabilities in separate accounts. Also, the amount deducted from the payroll is definitely determinable; whereas the firm's tax liability is only an estimate until the tax return is prepared.

Property Taxes Payable. Property taxes are based on the assessed value of property, both real and personal. Such taxes generally provide the major portion of revenue to local governmental units. The following tax-accrual dates are among those that have been suggested:

1. Dates of assessment
2. *Lien date* (date on which the tax becomes a lien on the property)

3. Date (or dates) on which the tax is payable
4. End of taxpayer's fiscal year
5. End of government unit's fiscal year

It is especially important to fix the tax liability when real estate is transferred in order to determine whether payment should be made by the buyer or the seller and to apportion the tax at the time of settlement.

The AICPA has expressed the following opinion: "Generally, the most acceptable basis of providing for property taxes is monthly accrual on the taxpayer's books during the fiscal period of the taxing authority for which the taxes are levied. The books will then show, at any closing date, the appropriate accrual or prepayment."[1]

Because property taxes are a cost of the right of ownership and thus a cost of the right of use, it is logical to charge such taxes against revenue during the fiscal year of the taxing authority.

Whether the amount of the accrued tax is definitely established or only estimated, it should be included in the current liabilities.

Sales and Use Taxes. *Sales* and *use taxes* are taxes levied by state or local governments on the sale or use of goods or services. Generally, such taxes are levied on goods and services only once, at a predetermined transfer level as they pass through a series of hands from their origin to their ultimate consumption, for example, from wholesaler to retailer or (more often) from the retailer to the consumer. Occasionally, the tax is assessed each time a transfer occurs. Such a tax is usually referred to as a *turnover tax* or *transaction tax.*

Such laws result in collections for a third party (a taxing authority). This in turn results in the creation of a current liability on the part of the vendor for the collected but unremitted taxes.

SALES TAXES MAY BE RECORDED WITH SALES. When this method is followed, it is necessary periodically to separate the total amount into sales (revenue) and sales taxes payable (a current liability).

SALES TAXES MAY BE RECORDED SEPARATELY. When this method is employed, the separation and tax recognition are made

1. *Accounting Research and Terminology Bulletins,* Final Edition (1961), pp. 83–84.

at the time of sale. For example, if a $100 item subject to a 6 percent tax is sold on account, the following entry would be made:

Accounts receivable	$106	
Sales		$100
Sales taxes payable		6

A few taxing authorities require that the tax be prepaid by requiring the vendor to buy stamps or tokens. Because such prepaid taxes result in an asset rather than a current liability, they do not fall within the scope of this chapter.

USE TAXES. The state or local taxing authority may assess a use tax when the sales tax does not apply. For example, a firm may be assessed a use tax on goods bought and used rather than resold. Also, the use tax may be assessed against a vendee within the jurisdiction of the taxing authority when the vendor is outside the jurisdiction of the particular taxing authority.

Vacation Pay. *Vacation pay* is pay for time not worked. It is one of an increasing number of fringe benefits provided to an employee by the employer.

Whether or not, from a legal point of view, the liability for vacation pay accrues may depend on the terms of employment or the union contract. In some cases, an individual must be employed by the firm at vacation time in order to receive vacation pay. In other cases, an employee may be paid for vacation time earned to the time of job termination.

However, under the going-concern concept, vacation pay should be accrued in order to allocate labor costs to products more precisely. For example, if a direct worker receives $5,200 per year ($100 per week for fifty-two weeks) but is on paid vacation for two of the fifty-two weeks, production should be charged with a labor cost of $104 for each of the fifty weeks worked.

The following entry should be made for each of the fifty weeks worked:

Work in process	$104	
Accrued vacation pay		$ 4
Accrued payroll (cash)		100

The following entry should be made to record the lump-sum payment of the two weeks of vacation pay:

Accrued vacation pay	$200	
Cash		$200

In the event vacation pay for direct workers is not accrued, the following entries would be in order:

Work in process	$100	
Accrued payroll (cash)		$100
Factory overhead	$200	
Accrued payroll (cash)		$200

By comparing these two methods, it may be observed that under the first (preferred) method, production is charged directly with the entire direct-labor cost of $5,200 but that under the second method, only $5,000 is charged directly to the product.

The accrual of vacation pay is appropriate in the case of all employees, both direct and indirect workers; but in the case of direct workers, it is especially important to improve product costing.

Bonus Pay. *Bonus pay* represents a reward to officers, managers, or employees for good or improved performance. In most cases, bonus payments are calculated on total period (usually one year) performance at the end of the period. They are frequently granted to indirect workers. Therefore, such bonuses are generally charged to overhead rather than to the product. However, a bonus may be charged to the product if it is granted for a special job to expedite filling a customer's order.

Bonuses may be calculated on such bases as sales or earnings. When earnings are the basis for bonus calculations, the appropriate method of calculation will depend on the earnings base. The earnings base is generally considered to be one of the following:

1. Net income before both income taxes and bonus
2. Net income before income taxes but after bonus
3. Net income before bonus but after income taxes
4. Net income after both income taxes and bonus

Each of these four methods will be illustrated here. The following assumed data will be used in each example: The divisional vice-presidents are to be allowed a bonus of 20 percent of earnings of over $100,000 by their respective divisions. Income taxes are 50 percent of net income. This particular division showed a profit of $400,000 before both income taxes and bonus. Let B = bonus, and T = taxes.

METHOD 1. BONUS BASED ON INCOME BEFORE BOTH INCOME TAXES AND BONUS

$$B = .20 \ (\$400,000 - \$100,000) = \$60,000$$

METHOD 2. BONUS BASED ON NET INCOME BEFORE INCOME TAXES BUT AFTER BONUS

$$B = .20 \ (\$400,000 - \$100,000 - B)$$
$$B = .20 \ (\$300,000 - B)$$
$$B = \$60,000 - .20B$$
$$1.20B = \$60,000$$
$$B = \$50,000$$

PROOF

Earnings	$400,000
Less: Exemptions	100,000
	$300,000
Less: Bonus	50,000
Earnings subject to bonus	$250,000
Bonus at 20% of $250,000	$ 50,000

METHOD 3. BONUS BASED ON NET INCOME BEFORE BONUS BUT AFTER INCOME TAXES

$$B = .20 \ (\$400,000 - \$100,000 - T)$$
$$T = .50 \ (\$400,000 - B)$$

Substitute for T in first equation, and solve for B.

$$B = .20 \ \{(\$400,000 - \$100,000) - [.50 \ (\$400,000 - B)]\}$$
$$B = .20 \ [(\$400,000 - \$100,000) - (\$200,000 - .50B)]$$
$$B = .20 \ (\$300,000 - \$200,000 + .50B)$$
$$B = \$60,000 - \$40,000 + .10B$$
$$.90B = \$20,000$$
$$B = \$22,222.22$$

Substitute for B in the second equation, and solve for T.

$T = .50 \ (\$400,000 - \$22,222.22)$

$T = .50 \times \$377,777.78$

$T = \$188,888.89$

PROOF

Gross earnings	$400,000.00
Less: Income taxes	188,888.89
	$211,111.11
Less: Earnings not subject to bonus	100,000.00
Earnings subject to bonus	$111,111.11
Bonus at 20% of $111,111.11	$ 22,222.22

METHOD 4. BONUS BASED ON NET INCOME AFTER BOTH INCOME TAXES AND BONUS

$B = .20 \ (\$400,000 - \$100,000 - B - T)$

$T = .50 \ (\$400,000 - B)$

Substitute for T in the first equation, and solve for B.

$B = .20 \ \{(\$400,000 - \$100,000) - B - [.50 \ (\$400,000 - B)]\}$

$B = .20 \ [(\$400,000 - \$100,000) - B - (\$200,000 - .50B)]$

$B = .20 \ (\$300,000 - B - \$200,000 + .50B)$

$B = \$60,000 - .20B - \$40,000 + .10B$

$1.10B = \$20,000$

$B = \$18,181.818$

PROOF

Gross earnings		$400,000.00
Less: Exemption	$100,000.00	
Bonus	18,181.82	
Taxes [.50 ($400,000 − $18,181.82)]	$190,909.09	
		309,090.91
		$ 90,909.09
Bonus (20% of $90,909.09)		$ 18,181.82

For income-tax purposes, a bonus is considered to be an expense, regardless of the manner in which it is calculated. After a bonus has been established, it should be shown as a current liability until paid.

Customer's Prepayments and Advances. *Customer's prepayments and advances* represent payments received by a seller for goods or services to be delivered to a buyer at some future time. Such prepayments and advances should be shown as liabilities on the books of the seller because they represent the value of goods or services for which the seller has accepted payment and has assumed the obligation for making delivery. In most instances, they are considered to be current liabilities because generally only a short time elapses between the prepayment or advance and the delivery of the agreed goods or services.

UNDETERMINED CURRENT LIABILITIES

In the preceding section, some typical current liabilities that can be definitely determined, with respect to both amount and due date, were discussed. In this section, some current liabilities that cannot be exactly determined with respect to either the amount or the due date or both will be discussed.

Estimated Liabilities. *Estimated liabilities* are claims against the firm that are known to exist at a given time but for which the final exact amount cannot be determined definitely at that time. The existence of a liability is established, but the amount of the liability is uncertain and subject to estimate. In the past, estimated liabilities were frequently referred to as *liability reserves*. However, the use of the term *reserves* in connection with liabilities has become archaic and should be discouraged. The term *reserves* should be restricted to capital or owners' equity accounts.

Although the amount of such liabilities is not exactly determinable, a reasonably approximate amount must be given recognition in the statements.

INCOME TAXES PAYABLE. Income taxes payable should be distinguished from income taxes withheld. Income taxes payable represent the liability of the taxpayer to pay the government a portion of his earnings or profit as a tax. This, of course, reduces the amount available for distribution to owners. Income taxes withheld (as explained previously) represents the amounts that are withheld from employees' pay by the employer and that the employer will transfer at the proper time to the government. Such payroll taxes do not affect the employer's profit except indirectly as they may result in the need to pay higher salaries and wages.

Both income taxes payable and income taxes withheld are liabilities in that during the period of accrual or withholding, they represent amounts that must be paid to the government. However, income taxes payable also represents an expense or a sharing of profits with the government; whereas income taxes withheld results in a reduction in the amount paid directly to the employees.

The amount of income taxes withheld is not subject to estimate but is definitely determined with the preparation of each payroll. The amount of the accruing income taxes payable can only be approximated during the fiscal year. The exact amount can be established only when the profit for the year is established.

LIABILITY FOR BONUS OR PROFIT-SHARING AGREEMENTS. If the bonus or profit-sharing period and the accounting period end at the same time, the amount of the bonus is definitely determinable (as discussed in the section "Bonus Pay"). However, if the bonus period extends beyond the end of the current accounting period, the amount accrued to the statement date can only be estimated. If the estimated amount is significant, it should be recognized in the statements.

LIABILITY FOR PENSION PLAN AGREEMENTS. A *pension plan* is a procedure adopted by an employer whereby payments of annuities or pensions will be systematically paid to retired employees. Pension plans are *funded* or *unfunded*. When an employer contributes money directly to the fund, the fund is said to be *self-administered* or *uninsured*. When the plan is entirely funded by an insurance company, the plan is said to be *insured*. In such insured plans, the premiums paid to the insurance company represent the total cost of the plan to the employer. Accrued premium costs represent a current liability.

If the employer, rather than making systematized payments to a fund or insurance company, makes payments as required directly to retired employees, an estimated liability should be recognized for the amount that is expected to be paid out as pension benefits during the next year or operating cycle.

LIABILITIES FOR GUARANTEES AND WARRANTIES. *Liabilities for guarantees and warranties* occur when a firm agrees as part of the sales contract to provide repair parts and/or service for a specified period of time.

In some cases, it is acceptable accounting practice to defer the recognition of the expense until the repair service or parts are provided. This is in accord with income-tax regulations, which do not allow a guarantee- or warranty-expense deduction until the expense has actually been incurred. However, because it provides a better matching of expenses and revenues, the preferred accounting practice is to recognize estimated future costs of parts and service provided under a guarantee or warranty as an expense of the period in which the sale is made.

Thus, if merchandise is sold at a price of $1,000 with a warranty that is expected to cost the seller $200 in future service and repair parts, the sale may be recorded as follows:

Cash (accounts receivable)	$1,000	
Guarantee or warranty expense	200	
Estimated liability under		
guarantees and warranties		$ 200
Sales		1,000

When service and/or parts are provided under the guarantee or warranty, an entry for the actual cost incurred is made as follows:

Estimated liabilities under guarantees		
and warranties	$50	
Parts inventory (or service costs)		$50

In some cases, a customer buys a warranty contract for a specified additional fee. The receipt of such fees should be recorded as follows:

Cash	$100	
Deferred warranty revenue		$100

As expenses under the warranty are incurred, the deferred warranty revenue account is charged with the actual expense incurred.

Contingent Liabilities. *Contingent liabilities* are possible (though improbable) future claims against the firm. A contingent liability exists when there is no current obligation or debt but when there is a possibility that a liability may develop. There is no legal obligation for a contingent liability; when the obligation becomes legal, the obligation is no longer contingent.

Contingent liabilities are not noted in the accounting records. However, they should be reported on the balance sheet. Depending on the nature of the contingent liability, it may be indicated (1) in a footnote, (2) in a contra-account, (3) in a parenthetic expression, or (4) it may be shown short in the liability section.

PENDING LAWSUITS. *Pending lawsuits* are a common type of contingent liability. If a firm is being sued or is likely to be sued, a contingent liability exists and should be mentioned in the financial statements. The outcome of such litigation cannot be determined in advance with respect to either the amount of the claim or the time of payment if a payment is required; and the publication of an amount by a defendant or potential defendant could have an adverse effect on the outcome of the litigation. Therefore, it is preferred practice to indicate the contingent liability by a footnote, without indicating a possible amount.

ENDORSEMENTS. *Endorsement* is the signing of one's name on the back of a negotiable instrument, with or without restrictive clauses. A *blank,* or *general,* endorsement is made by the signing of one's name on the back of the instrument without restrictive clauses. A blank endorsement is said to be *with recourse* because the endorser has not indicated his refusal to be held responsible for payment if payment is not made by the maker. Such an endorser becomes liable for the instrument in the event the maker fails to pay the amount due on the instrument at maturity. An endorser is assumed to have accepted liability for payment unless he has specifically indicated his refusal by resorting to a qualified endorsement, which is said to be *without recourse.* When an endorser gives an endorsement without recourse, he assigns whatever rights he has in the instrument but does not become liable for payment of the instrument in the event the maker fails to pay.

Discounted Notes Receivable. A note receivable that before maturity has been sold or transferred by endorsement to a third party is said to be *discounted.* Notes receivable may be discounted either with or without recourse. When they are discounted with a blank endorsement (i.e., with recourse), a holder in due course may hold the endorser liable in the event that the maker of the note fails to pay the note at maturity. In such cases, the discounter is contingently liable. Such a contingent liability should be reported on the balance sheet. This may be done in any of four accepted ways:

1. By use of a contra-account, such as notes receivable discounted (the preferred method)
2. By a parenthetic statement
3. By a footnote
4. By inclusion in a separate contingent liability section (the least-used method)

Very occasionally, a holder of a note receivable may get a third party to accept such a note endorsed in a way that frees the one transferring it of any liability for payment. To accomplish this, the transferrer must include as a distinct part of his endorsement the words *without recourse* or their equivalent. In such a transaction, the note has been collected on by the endorser, and there is no contingent liability. The note account is relieved of the value of the note; cash or another asset account is charged with the value received; and the difference is charged or credited either to an interest account or to a gain or loss account.

Accommodation Endorsements. An accommodation endorsement is an endorsement given without consideration (i.e., no value or benefit passing to the endorser) by one party on a note or other credit instrument for the benefit of another party. Such an endorsement is given to improve the credit of the other party. The accommodation endorser becomes liable for payment required by the instrument if the maker defaults. This contingent liability, if significant in amount, should be reported in a note on the endorser's balance sheet.

CHAPTER 12

Long-Term Liabilities

Long-term, or fixed, liabilities are obligations that will not become due within a year or within the current operating cycle, whichever is longer, and that will not be liquidated with company resources classified as current. Thus, a five-year note is reclassified in its fifth year as a current liability if it will be paid off during the year with money from the general cash fund, but if it is to be liquidated with fixed assets, as cash from a sinking fund, it should not be reclassified.

It is important that the distinction between short-term (current) liabilities and long-term liabilities be carefully maintained and that the two types be shown in separate sections of the balance sheet because the maturity dates of debts are of major importance to management, creditors, owners, and others interested in the financial condition of the firm.

The most common long-term liabilities are bonds, long-term notes, and advances from affiliated companies. Some less common long-term liabilities are pension and retirement plan obligations, deferred compensation, long-term product warranties, and long-term lease obligations.

BONDS PAYABLE

Bonds as an investment (specifically bonds receivable) were discussed in Chapter 10 (p. 158). Here, bonds are discussed from the opposite point of view, that is, as bonds payable. Bonds are long-term notes issued under formal legal procedures. Bonds represent fractional portions of a group contract in that all bonds of a given issue are covered by the same trust indenture.

The *trust indenture* lists the rights and obligations of the borrower, the lenders, and the trustee(s).

Types of Bonds. Bonds may be tailored to suit the needs of the borrower and at the same time make the issue attractive to the potential bond purchasers. A number of the more frequently used types of bonds are discussed in the paragraphs that follow.

MORTGAGE BONDS. *Mortgage bonds* are bonds on which payment is secured by a pledge of specified assets owned by the borrower, the mortgagor. The mortgagor retains legal title to the mortgaged assets, but if the mortgage terms are not met, the mortgagee, through recourse to the defeasance clause in the mortgage instrument, may "foreclose" or exclude all other interests and, upon obtaining a judgment, may have the property sold to satisfy the debt. A mortgage bond actually consists of two instruments: the bond and the mortgage.

DEBENTURE BONDS. *Debenture bonds,* often referred to as *debentures,* are bonds that are secured only by the general credit of the issuer; that is, no specific assets are pledged as security for the repayment of the bond. For this reason, such bonds are often called *unsecured.* Since investors recently have placed more reliance on the protective provisions of the bond indenture and the income-producing abilities of the firm and less reliance on specialized assets that might be pledged as security, debenture bonds have become more popular.

COLLATERAL TRUST BONDS. *Collateral trust bonds* are quite similar to mortgage bonds in that specific assets are pledged as security. They differ in that the assets pledged as security for mortgage bonds are tangible assets kept in the possession of the mortgagor; whereas in the case of collateral trust bonds, the pledged assets are intangibles, usually in the form of stocks or bonds that are transferred from the mortgagor to the trustee under the terms of the *collateral trust indenture.* The terms of the trust indenture empower the trustee in case of default by the mortgagor to sell the collateral and reimburse the bondholders.

REVENUE BONDS. *Revenue bonds* are bonds issued by a governmental unit or authority for the purpose of financing the purchase of construction of revenue-producing property. The payment of interest, as well as the repayment of the principal, is contingent upon the production of revenue by the acquired property.

Revenue bonds are issued by states, cities, port authoritie.,
state schools (for dormitories), toll-road authorities, and so
forth. One reason for the prevalence of revenue bonds is that
many governmental units have reached, or nearly reached, their
legal debt limits; and revenue bonds are generally held to be
excluded from the unit's indebtedness. Therefore, some states have
created a General State Authority as a means of financing many
state properties through the issuance of revenue bonds.

INCOME BONDS. *Income bonds* are bonds on which interest is
paid only if earned. Such bonds are also called *adjustment bonds*
because usually they are issued only in cases of reorganization as
a means of reducing the firm's fixed charges. The income feature
applies only to interest payments; the principal in the case of
corporate bonds is payable (without being contingent on earnings) just like that of other bonds. Income bonds may be secured
or unsecured with respect to principal. In the case of governmental income bonds (revenue bonds), both the payment of interest and the repayment of the principal are dependent upon
earnings.

GUARANTEED BONDS. *Guaranteed bonds* are bonds guaranteed
or warranted by a person, group, or firm other than the issuer.
Such a guarantee may take the form of an endorsement on each
bond, a contract with the issuer, or a contract with the issuer's
creditors. The purpose of the guarantee is to improve the investment quality of the bonds.

SERIAL BONDS. *Serial bonds* are bonds of a common issue that
mature in installments. Various bonds from the issue fall due on
different dates as determined by their respective serial numbers.
Serial bonds are usually quoted on a yield basis rather than on a
price basis.

TERM BONDS. *Term bonds* are bonds of a common issue that
have a common maturity date. Most bonds are term bonds.

SINKING-FUND BONDS. *Sinking-fund bonds* are bonds of any
issue that by terms of their indenture require the issuer periodically to set aside such funds which, with earnings, will be sufficient to redeem the bonds or a specified portion of them at
maturity. A sinking-fund approach may be taken for the provision of the retirement of term bonds even though the terms of
the indenture do not require the establishment of a sinking fund.

REGISTERED BONDS. *Registered bonds* are bonds the principal and sometimes the interest of which are payable only to parties whose names appear on the instrument and also on the books of the issuer or the trustee. Bonds are said to be *fully* registered when they are registered with respect to both principal and interest. When bonds are registered with respect to principal only, they are said to be only *partly* registered.

BEARER BONDS. *Bearer bonds,* sometimes referred to as *coupon bonds,* are negotiable by the bearer or holder without endorsement. The bearer, or coupon, bonds have attached to them dated or numbered coupons for each interest payment. These coupons are clipped by the holder at maturity and presented to the issuer or its agent in exchange for the interest payment. Because bearer bonds and/or their coupons can be negotiated without endorsement, title to lost or stolen bonds or coupons may pass to innocent purchasers for value.

As has been indicated, a bond may be registered with respect to principal but may be a bearer or coupon bond with respect to interest.

Valuation of Bonds. Bonds will sell at par or face value only when the nominal interest rate and the market interest rate are identical. If the nominal interest rate is higher than the market rate, the bonds will sell above par or at a premium. If the nominal rate is lower than market rate, the bonds will sell below par at a discount.

As was indicated in Chapter 10 (page 159), investors usually record a bond purchase at book value or cost, that is, par value adjusted directly for any premium or discount. However, the bond issuer usually records the bonds payable at face or maturity value with the premium or discount recorded in a separate adjunct account. Any such premium or discount should be systematically amortized (or in the case of discount, accumulated) over the life of the bonds. The cost of issuing the bonds may be added to the discount balance if the bonds are sold at a discount or deducted from the premium if the bonds are sold at a premium. Occasionally, an issuer prefers to use a separate adjunct account, such as bond issuance costs, for the recording of such costs.

When bonds are exchanged for noncash assets, the valuation

should be established at the cash value of bonds or the fair value of the assets received, whichever is more reliably determinable.

NOMINAL INTEREST VERSUS EFFECTIVE INTEREST. *Interest* is the service charge or rent charged for money or capital. It is usually expressed as a rate or percentage of the money involved.

The *nominal rate,* also referred to as a *named rate* or *contract rate,* is the rate stated on a bond. The amount of nominal interest is calculated by multiplying the face value of the bond by the nominal rate and that product by the time involved.

Often, the *market rate* for capital is not the same as the pre-established nominal rate printed on the bond. In order to sell a bond, the interest return on the investment must be adjusted to coincide with current market conditions. This is accomplished by selling the bond at a premium or a discount (i.e., above or below par value). When a bond is sold at a price other than par value, the effective yield or real interest rate differs from the nominal rate.

The nominal interest is based on the par value of the bond; the effective interest is based on the bond's carrying value. The true cost of borrowing money is represented by the effective interest. The approximate yield or effective annual interest rate is obtained by dividing the average carrying value of a bond by the annual nominal interest payments. A more exact effective rate may be obtained by recourse to bond tables.

AMORTIZATION OF BOND PREMIUM. It was explained in Chapter 10 (page 163) that an investor could use either the straight-line method or the effective-interest-rate method of amortizing premium or accumulating discount on bonds receivable. The same options are available to a bond issuer for the amortization of premium or the accumulation of discount.

Term Bonds. For example, assume that $100,000 worth of five-year 5 percent term bonds were issued at 4 percent, or $104,-491.30 (approximately $104.50) and that the issuer elects to amortize the premium by the straight-line method. Assume further that the issuer is on a calendar year and that the bonds were issued on March 1, with interest payable on March 1 and September 1 of each year.

The following entries based on the table on page 163 would be made during the first year of the bonds' existence:

March 1	Cash	$104,491.30	
	Premium on bonds		
	payable		$ 4,491.30
	Bonds payable		100,000.00
September 1	Interest expense	2,500.00	
	Cash		2,500.00
December 31	Interest expense	1,666.67	
	Interest payable		1,666.67
December 31	Premium	748.55	
	Interest expense		748.55
	$449.13 + (⅔ of $449.13)		

The premium might be amortized at each interest-payment date as well as at the end of the issuer's fiscal year. However, it saves time and effort to amortize the premium only at the end of the issuer's business year; and for reporting purposes, it is just as accurate.

The reader may adapt these entries to the effective-interest-rate method by referring to the table on page 164.

Serial Bonds. Amortization of premium on serial bonds is more involved than that of term bonds. The application of the straight-line method per se of premium amortization or of discount accumulation would result in substantial distortion in the periodic interest calculations during the life of the bond issue. Therefore, either the modified straight-line method (referred to as the *bonds-outstanding method*) or the effective-interest-rate method may be used.

The following example will be used to illustrate both methods: Serial 5 percent bonds with a par value of $100,000 are sold at a price to yield 4½ percent. At the end of each year, $20,000 worth of the bonds are to be redeemed.

The nominal interest on each installment ($20,000) is $1,000, but the desired interest is only $900. The bondholders will therefore receive an excess of $100 per year interest on each principal installment of $20,000. Of course, they will be required to pay the present value of the future excess receipts. By recourse to present-value tables, the present value of these annuities is determined to be $1,355.61; therefore, the total price of the bond issue would be $101,355.61.

Table 12.1 shows the amortization of the bonds by the bonds-

TABLE 12.1

AMORTIZATION OF SERIAL BONDS: BONDS-OUTSTANDING METHOD

(1) Year	(2) Bonds Outstanding During Year	(3) Portion Outstanding	(4) Premium Balance	(5) Premium Amortized[a]	(6) Nominal Interest, (5%)	(7) Effective Interest (6 − 5)[b]	(8) Principal Payment	(9) Net Decrease in Carrying Value (5 + 8)	(10) Year-End Carrying Value
0									$101,355.61
1	$100,000	10/30	$1,355.61	$451.87	$5,000	$4,548.13	$20,000	$20,451.87	80,903.74
2	80,000	8/30	903.74	361.50	4,000	3,638.50	20,000	20,361.50	60,542.24
3	60,000	6/30	542.24	271.12	3,000	2,728.88	20,000	20,271.12	40,271.12
4	40,000	4/30	271.12	180.74	2,000	1,819.26	20,000	20,180.74	20,090.38
5	20,000	2/30	90.38	90.38	1,000	909.62	20,000	20,090.38	0
	$300,000								

[a] Column 3 fraction × original premium of $1,355.61.
[b] Approximates 4½ percent of carrying value.

outstanding method. The annual premium amortization is determined by multiplying the original premium ($1,355.61) by a series of fractions whose denominators are always the original sum of the par value of the bonds outstanding ($300,000) and whose numerators are the par value of the bonds outstanding during each year ($100,000, $80,000, and so on).

The effective interest is the difference between the nominal interest calculated on the face value of the bonds outstanding during the year and the premium amortized. The effective interest calculated in this way should approximate the amount resulting from the multiplication of the current carrying value by the effective rate. Small differences may occur either because of rounding figures in either setting the bond price *or* in calculating the effective interest, as mentioned above. However, the effective interest must be of amounts that will permit the amortization of the total premium by deductions from the nominal interest during the life of the bonds.

Table 12.2 shows the amortization of the bonds by the effective-interest method. The nominal interest is calculated by multiplying the par value of the bonds outstanding by the nominal rate. The effective interest is determined by multiplying the carrying value by the effective rate. The excess of the nominal interest over the effective interest indicates the amount of premium to be amortized. On the final installment, there may be a small discrepancy between the premium amortization and the actual balance of the premium. Such discrepancies should be adjusted against the effective interest for the final period.

It should be observed that in the preceding explanations, it is assumed that all the bonds have the same interest rate. In many cases, each block or installment of a serial bond issue is sold at a different price and thus carries a different yield. In such cases, each block must be treated as a separate issue.

ACCUMULATION OF BOND DISCOUNT. The accumulation of bond discount may be handled by the same methods used for the amortization of premium. Therefore, only the effective-interest method will be illustrated here for both term and serial bonds.

Term Bonds. Assume that 4½ percent bonds with a par value of $100,000 and a five-year life are sold to yield 5 percent, that is, $97,835.26 as determined from bond tables. The discount accumulation could be scheduled as shown in Table 12.3.

TABLE 12.2

AMORTIZATION OF SERIAL BONDS: EFFECTIVE-INTEREST METHOD

(1) Year	(2) Par Value	(3) Nominal Rate × Par (5%)	(4) Effective Rate (4½%) × Carrying Value	(5) Premium Amortization (3 − 4)	(6) Principal Reduction	(7) Decrease in Carrying Value (5 + 6)	(8) Carrying Value
0	$100,000						$101,355.61
1	80,000	$5,000	$4,561.00	$439.00	$20,000	$20,439.00	80,916.61
2	60,000	4,000	3,641.25	358.75	20,000	20,358.75	60,557.86
3	40,000	3,000	2,725.10	274.90	20,000	20,274.90	40,282.96
4	20,000	2,000	1,812.73	187.27	20,000	20,187.27	20,095.69
5		1,000	904.31	95.69	20,000	20,095.69	0

TABLE 12.3

ACCUMULATION OF DISCOUNT: TERM BONDS

(1) Year	(2) Nominal Interest (Par × 4½%)	(3) Effective Interest (Carrying Value × 5%)	(4) Annual Accumulation (3 − 2)	(5) End of Year Balance
0				$ 97,835.26[a]
1	$4,500	$4,891.76	$391.76	98,227.02
2	4,500	4,911.35	411.35	98,638.37
3	4,500	4,931.92	431.92	99,070.29
4	4,500	4,953.52	453.52	99,523.81
5	4,500	4,976.19	476.19	100,000.00

[a] Present value of $100,000 discounted at 5%	$ 78,352.62
Present value of interest annuity discounted at 5%	19,482.64
Total	$ 97,835.26

Serial Bonds. Assume the same facts given in the term-bonds example except that $20,000 par value bonds will mature at the end of each of the five years. The discount accumulation could be scheduled as shown in Table 12.4.

Bond Retirement. *Reacquisition* and *retirement* of bonds payable complete the borrowing cycle. If there is a difference between the carrying value of the bonds at retirement and the redemption price, a gain or loss must be recognized at the time of redemption. Of course, the bond's carrying value and interest charges must be adjusted to the date of redemption before any gain or loss is computed.

TERM BONDS. Term bonds are payable at the end of a specified time period. If (as should be the case) the bond premium or discount and issuance costs have been properly amortized during the life of the bond, the carrying value and the retirement price should be the same, that is, face value.

At Maturity. When the carrying value has been adjusted to par value by the maturity date of the bonds, there is no recognizable gain or loss, and the retirement is recorded by a charge to bonds payable and a credit to cash or to sinking fund cash if such an account had been established. Any balance remaining in the sinking fund cash account after the retirement of the bonds should be transferred to the general cash account. The amount of any bonds not presented for payment at maturity should be

TABLE 12.4

ACCUMULATION OF DISCOUNT: SERIAL BONDS

(1) Year	(2) Par Value	(3) Nominal Interest Rate × Par (4½%)	(4) Effective Interest Rate (5%) × Carrying Value	(5) Discount Accumulation	(6) Principal Reduction	(7) Decrease in Carrying Value	(8) Carrying Value
0							$98,658.95[a]
1	$100,000	$4,500	$4,932.95	$432.95	$20,000	$19,567.05	79,091.90
2	80,000	3,600	3,954.60	354.60	20,000	19,645.40	59,446.50
3	60,000	2,700	2,972.32	272.32	20,000	19,727.68	39,718.82
4	40,000	1,800	1,985.94	185.94	20,000	19,814.06	19,904.76
5	20,000	900	995.24	95.24	20,000	19,904.76	0

[a] $P = (1+i)^{-n} + \dfrac{1 - (1+i)^{-n}}{i}$

Present value of 1 at compound interest $= V^n = (1+i)^{-n}$

Present value of annuity of 1 per period $= {}^a\overline{n}|_i = \dfrac{1 - (1+i)^{-n}}{i}$

Present value of interest bearing bond $= v^n + {}^a\overline{n}|_i$

$P_1 = \$20,000 \, (1.05)^{-1} + 900 \, {}^a1 \, 5\% = \$19,904.76$

$P_2 = 20,000 \, (1.05)^{-2} + 900 \, {}^a2 \, 5\% = 19,814.06$

$P_3 = 20,000 \, (1.05)^{-3} + 900 \, {}^a3 \, 5\% = 19,727.67$

$P_4 = 20,000 \, (1.05)^{-4} + 900 \, {}^a4 \, 5\% = 19,645.41$

$P_5 = 20,000 \, (1.05)^{-5} + 900 \, {}^a5 \, 5\% = 19,567.05$

Total	$98,658.95

segregated and placed in a special account, such as matured bonds payable. Matured but unredeemed bonds should be classified as current liabilities except in those cases where noncurrent assets, such as a sinking fund, are maintained for their redemption. It should be observed that interest does not accrue on matured bonds not in default.

Before Maturity. Bonds frequently are redeemed before maturity because of a call provision in the bond indenture, for sinking-fund purposes, or simply to reduce outstanding debt.

Bonds reacquired by the issuer before their maturity, depending on acquisition provisions, may be retired, held in a sinking fund, or held as treasury bonds for possible reissue in the future. When bonds are reacquired and canceled, the bonds payable account is charged with their face value; any unamortized premium or discount and issuance costs applicable to them are written off;

cash is credited for the retirement costs; and any resulting difference between debits and credits is recorded as a debit or credit to a loss or gain account in order to balance the entry. If reacquired bonds are to be held in the treasury or in a sinking fund, essentially the same entry would be made. In each of the three cases, there is either an actual or a potential permanent retirement of the bonds, and any gain or loss on them should be recognized at the time of reacquisition. The following entry is typical:

Bonds payable (treasury bonds)		
(sinking-fund bonds)	$50,000	
Discount on bonds payable		$ 500
Gain on bond redemption		500
Cash		49,000

On the balance sheet, it is customary to report bonds payable net of bonds held either in the treasury or in the sinking fund. The amount of bonds held in the treasury or the sinking fund may be indicated in a balance-sheet footnote.

SERIAL BONDS. Serial bonds have an advantage over term bonds in that certain groups or blocks of the bonds mature and are to be redeemed at the end of a number of specified periods; thus, the bond redemptions may be synchronized approximately with earnings generated from the use of the funds provided by the bond issue. The use of serial bonds reduces or eliminates the need for a bond sinking fund or the appropriation of retained earnings, as well as prematurity bond retirement.

The book, or carrying, value of a block of matured serial bonds should equal their par value; therefore, there would be no gain or loss to recognize at the time of their redemption. The redemption would be recorded by a charge to bonds payable for their face value and a credit to cash for a like amount.

If a block of serial bonds is retired before that particular block's maturity date, the transaction is quite similar to the transaction involving the early redemption of term bonds. In fact, each separate block of serial bonds may be treated as a separate issue of term bonds.

For example, assume that a block of bonds with a par value of $20,000 is redeemed at $102 and that the unamortized premium applicable to this block amounts to $150. The redemption would be recorded as follows:

Bonds payable	$20,000	
Premium on bonds payable	150	
Loss on bond redemption	250	
Cash		$20,400

Refunding Bonds. *Refunding bonds* are bonds issued for the purpose of retiring existing bonds. The new issue may be sold for cash and the proceeds used to retire the old bonds, or the new bonds may be exchanged for the old bonds.

When the refunding operation occurs at the maturity of the old issue, its carrying value and par value are equal. At maturity, there should be no unamortized premium or discount to reckon with, nor any gain or loss to recognize to cause problems. The bonds payable account would be charged with the carrying value, which by this time should also be the par value, and cash would be credited with the same par value amount.

If the refunding occurs before the maturity of the old issue, and if the issuing of the new bonds and the redemption of the old bonds are not considered to be two separate and distinct transactions, this refunding causes a split of opinion about how to account for gain or loss and any unamortized premium or discount applicable to the old issue, as well as any *call premium* (the amount above par required by the bond issuer as compensation for early retirement) required because of early redemption of the old bonds. Three different opinions are commonly recognized as ways of disposing of these items:

1. Charge them off immediately as realized loss on bond retirement.[1]

2. Charge them to a deferred account to be amortized over the remaining life of the old bonds.[2]

3. Charge them to a deferred account and expense them over the life of the new bonds.[3]

For example, assume that 6 percent bonds having a par value of $100,000 and a carrying value of $95,000, with a current call

1. *Accounting and Reporting Standards for Corporate Financial Statements and Preceding Statements* (Evanston, Ill.: American Accounting Association, 1957), p. 7.
2. *Accounting Research and Terminology Bulletins,* Final Edition (1961), pp. 130–132.
3. "Status of Accounting Research Bulletins," *Accounting Principles Board Opinion,* No. 6 (1965), p. 43.

price of $105, are being refunded ten years before maturity with the issue at par of $110,000 worth of 5 percent twenty-year bonds. The refunding transaction and the first year's interest charge are recorded below in accordance with each of the three opinions.

METHOD 1

Cash	$ 5,000	
Bonds payable (old)	100,000	
Loss on bond redemption	10,000	
Discount on bonds payable		$ 5,000
Bonds payable (new)		110,000
Interest expense	5,500	
Interest payable		5,500

METHOD 2

Cash	$ 5,000	
Bonds payable (old)	100,000	
Discount—new (refunding costs)	10,000	
Discount on bonds payable (old)		$ 5,000
Bonds payable (new)		110,000
Interest expense	6,500	
Discount—new (refunding costs)		1,000
Interest payable		5,500

METHOD 3

Cash	$ 5,000	
Bonds payable (old)	100,000	
Discount—new (refunding costs)	10,000	
Discount on bonds payable (old)		$ 5,000
Bonds payable (new)		110,000
Interest expense	6,000	
Discount—new (refunding costs)		500
Interest payable		5,500

Convertible Bonds. *Convertible bonds* are bonds that according to specific terms and limitations with respect to time, rate of exchange, and so on set forth in the bond indenture, may be exchanged at the option of the bondholder for other securities (frequently common stock) of the issuer.

Because the conversion privilege is exercisable at the option of the bondholder rather than the bond issuer, the issuer will be unable to predict when conversions will be made, and hence he should amortize bond premium and accumulate bond discount on the basis of the legal life of the bonds.

The major problem in accounting for conversions is the selection of a price for the securities being issued in exchange for the bonds. There are three possible bases that may be used in establishing an issuance price for the securities exchanged for the bonds:

1. The par value of the bonds being exchanged
2. The carrying value of the bonds being exchanged
3. The current market value of the bonds being turned in or of the securities being issued in the exchange, whichever is more reliably determinable

The first method is inferior because par is an arbitrary value that may bear little relationship to current values established in the market place.

The second method is the most widely used. Proponents argue that market prices should not be used because certain securities are being exchanged for others of like value.

The use of the third method is supported on the assumption that if a given security could be sold for a specific amount, it would only be exchanged for one of equal or greater value.

The following example will illustrate each of the three methods: Assume that bonds with a par value of $10,000 and a carrying value of $10,600 are exchanged for 100 shares of common stock with a par value of $100 but currently selling at $105.

METHOD 1

Bonds payable	$10,000	
Premium on bonds payable	600	
Gain on conversion of bonds		$ 600
Common stock		10,000

METHOD 2

Bonds payable	$10,000	
Premium on bonds payable	600	
Premium on common stock		
(contributed capital)		$ 600
Common stock		10,000

Method 3

Bonds payable	$10,000		
Premium on bonds payable	600		
Gain on conversion of bonds		$ 100	
Common stock		10,000	
Premium on common stock (contributed capital)		500	

MORTGAGE NOTES PAYABLE

Mortgage notes are notes secured by a lien on specific assets. Mortgage notes payable may be short-term or current liabilities. However, notes payable secured by a mortgage are generally long-term liabilities; that is, they do not generally mature within a year. Such liabilities are accounted for by charging an asset account(s) for the value received and crediting the liability account, mortgage notes payable, for the same amount.

LONG-TERM PURCHASE CONTRACTS

In many cases, possession and use of long-term assets are acquired before they are paid for in full. Such possession may be accomplished in either of two ways: (1) by giving the seller a mortgage on the purchased property for the unpaid balance of the purchase price of the assets involved or (2) by negotiating a purchase contract (conditional sales contract) for the property transferred.

In cases where assets are acquired in exchange for a down payment and a mortgage, no unusual accounting problems are encountered because the buyer has legal title to the property as well as possession and use of it. In the case of long-term purchase contracts, a peculiar accounting problem is created because by the normal terms of the sales contract, the buyer gets immediate possession and use of the assets, but legal title remains with the seller until the contract terms are fully complied with by the buyer. However, accountants are in general agreement that this technical difference should be overlooked in order that the unowned property and the unpaid balance may be reported on the balance sheet and the depreciation, if appropriate, may be reported as an expense on the income statement. For example, the purchase of a $50,000 machine with 10 percent cash paid down and the balance to be paid in four annual installments of $10,000 each plus interest of 6 percent would be recorded as follows:

Machinery	$50,000	
Cash		$10,000
Purchase contracts		40,000

Each year, the currently maturing installment should be reclassified from long-term liabilities to current liabilities, unless the payment will not be made from current assets.

Interest payments should not be capitalized but should be treated as an expense in the periods when paid. In some cases, the interest charges are not explicitly stated; however, if it appears that implicit interest is included in the purchase price, it should be excluded from the asset value and recorded as a deferred charge. For instance, if in the example just given, the $50,000 asset had been sold for $10,000 down and four annual payments of $10,000 each when money was worth 6 percent, the purchase would be recorded as follows:

Prepaid interest	$ 5,348.94	
Machinery	44,651.06	
Cash		$10,000
Purchase contracts		40,000

Present-value-of-annuity tables may be used in finding the present value of the $40,000 debt.

When both a cash price and a credit price are quoted, the cash price should be used in valuing the asset. The difference between the cash price and the credit price represents the interest charges.

LONG-TERM LEASES

A long-term lease represents an obligation on the part of the lessee to pay rent to the lessor over an extended period for the use of specified assets. Currently, the term may be applied not only to executory leases but also to sale-and-lease-back contracts and to contracts that are essentially installment-purchase contracts.

The APB in its opinions recognizes two methods of accounting for leases: the operating method and the financing method.

Operating Method.[4] The *operating method* is based on the assumption that the obligation due the lessor accrues with the passage of time as the asset is used. This is the method favored by lessees who desire to arrange "off balance sheet" financing. Under this method, the only entries made by the lessee are those recording the periodic rent payments and, of course, those recording operating and maintenance expenses incurred by the lessee.

Financing Method.[5] The *financing method* is applicable to some executory leases, but it is especially applicable to sale-and-lease-back leases and leases that resemble installment purchases. The financing method is based on the assumption that future obligations to the lessor represent a liability for deferred payments for property already received. Under such an arrangement, the lessor expects to receive the returns of his investment and interest on it while it is outstanding. It is assumed in this case that the property will be valueless at the expiration of the lease.

For example, consider the case in which a lessee leases a machine for $50,000 to be paid $10,000 at the time of signing the lease, $10,000 in twelve months, and a like sum at the beginning of each year thereafter for the next three years. The asset is expected to be worthless at the end of the fifth year. Money is currently worth 6 percent.

The value of the property in the hands of the lessee is, not $50,000, but the present value of the payments discounted at 6 percent, which is $44,651.06.

The lessee should record the acquisition of the machine as follows:

Leased machinery	$44,651.06	
Cash		$10,000.00
Lease payable		34,651.06

---

4. "Reporting of Leases in Financial Statements of Lessors," *Accounting Principles Board Opinion*, No. 7 (1966), p. 54.

5. "Accounting for Leases in Financial Statements of Lessors," *Accounting Principles Board Opinion*, No. 7 (1966), pp. 54–56.

At the end of the first year, the following entries would be made:

Depreciation—leased machine	$8,930.21	
Allowance for depreciation —leased machine (⅕ of $44,651.06)		$8,930.21
Interest expense	2,079.06	
Interest payable		2,079.06

At the beginning of the second year, the following entry should be made:

Interest payable	$2,079.06	
Lease payable	7,920.94	
Cash		$10,000.00

Under this method, the value of the asset is reported in a special noncurrent asset section of the lessee's balance sheet, and the present value of his future payments is listed among the liabilities. The installment due within a year should be classified as a current liability; the others should be listed as long-term liabilities.

CHAPTER 13

Contributed Capital: Capital Stock

Total stockholders' equity may be divided into two major classifications: contributed capital (discussed in this chapter and Chapter 14) and retained earnings (discussed in Chapter 15).

Contributed capital is payments of cash or other assets made to a corporation by its stockholders for stock, for an assessment on stock, or as a gift. As the term is currently used by accountants it is broad enough to include gifts from nonstockholders, such as donations from local governments.

That portion of the contributed, or paid-in, capital of a corporation that by law or by order of the board of directors becomes the par or stated value of the capital stock is referred to as *legal capital* or *stated capital*.

NATURE OF CAPITAL STOCK

Capital stock represents the ownership interest of a corporation. Capital stock represents the ownership per se of the corporation, not of the corporate assets. The corporate assets are owned by the corporation.

Capital stock is divided into identical units referred to as *shares of stock* or *shares*. Ownership of one or a group of shares is evidenced by a stock certificate.

Corporate capital stock may be separated into a variety of classes or types having various rights and preferences.

Rights of Stockholders. Certain basic rights are granted to stockholders regardless of the class of stock held unless they are specifically restricted or denied:

1. The right to have a voice in management and control through the right to vote for directors and on some major corporate policies

2. The right to maintain one's proportional interest in the corporation through the right to purchase proportional amounts of subsequent stock issues, known as the *preemptive right* (recently eliminated in some stock issues)

3. The right to share in distribution of corporate earnings

4. The right to share in distributions of assets in case of partial or total liquidation

Classes of Capital Stock. There are many classes of stock, and some have overlapping characteristics. For example, a common stock may have a par value and may also be callable.

COMMON STOCK. *Common stock* represents the residual ownership of a corporation. The common stockholders get nothing until prior claims, including those of preferred stockholders, if any, are settled. After all such claims have been satisfied, the balance is available to the holders of the common stock. Common stock bears the greatest loss risk, but it usually stands to be the most profitable if the corporation is successful. Normally, the management right rests with the holders of the common stock because even if there is preferred stock, its right to vote is usually denied or at least restricted. If only one class of stock is issued, it is, of course, common stock.

PREFERRED STOCK. *Preferred stock* is a class of stock that has been granted some type of preference over another class of stock. According to common law, all shares of stock are equal unless made different by specific stipulations in the articles of incorporation and/or by laws.

The most common preferences associated with preferred stock are:

1. Preference with respect to dividends

2. Preference in liquidation

3. Protection against dilution (provision that the corporation may not issue any stock with a claim prior to the preferred stock without the preferred stockholders' approval)

The most common restriction placed on preferred stock is that of voting. Holders of preferred stock are often denied any voting rights. In other cases, preferred stockholders may be permitted to vote only after they have not received dividends for a stipulated time.

PAR VALUE STOCK. *Par value* is face value, the value shown on the face of the stock. The par value of stock is also set forth in the corporate charter. In the case of stock having a par value, it is the amount that is recorded in the capital stock account when the stock is sold.

NO-PAR-VALUE STOCK. *No-par-value stock* (without a stated value) is capital stock that has no specified par, nominal, or stated value assigned to it. Under such circumstances, the entire amount paid to the corporation for the stock becomes legal capital.

Common stock is much more likely than preferred stock to be no-par. In cases where preferred stock is no-par, a specific liquidation value is usually assigned to it. This amount is deducted from total capital to establish the book value of the common stock.

STATED-VALUE STOCK. *Stated-value stock* is no-par-value stock to which the board of directors, or occasionally the stockholders, have assigned a specific value. It is this stated value that is recorded in the capital stock account as the stock is sold; any excess received is recorded in some other paid-in capital account, such as paid-in surplus or, more recently, additional contributed capital.

REDEEMABLE (CALLABLE) STOCK. *Redeemable,* or *callable, stock* is stock (usually preferred) that may by the terms of issue be called in for redemption and cancellation at the option of the issuing corporation. The call price that is set by the terms of the issue is usually established at a figure slightly higher than the original issue price. At the time of redemption, the investor should recognize the difference between the price paid for the stock and the amount received for it in redemption as a gain or loss.

The corporation's treatment of the difference between the issuing price and the redemption price depends upon which figure is larger, because a corporation is not permitted to recognize either a gain or a loss on transactions in its own stock, only net worth accounts may be involved. A gain should be credited to some paid-in capital account, and a loss should be charged to retained earnings.

CONVERTIBLE STOCK. *Convertible stock* is stock that may be exchanged at a stated ratio for another class of stock, according to the terms of the original issuance agreement. Such conversions should not increase retained earnings but may result in an increase in some form of contributed capital other than capital stock per se.

STOCK TRANSACTIONS

A corporation obtains its equity funds through the exchange of shares of stock for cash or other assets, services, or the reduction of liabilities. The issuing of stock requires a series of transactions. First, an authorization to issue the stock must be obtained from the state. The stock then can be offered for sale, and subscriptions can be taken. Later, the subscriptions may be collected, and the stock may be issued.

Stock Issued for Cash. Often cash is received at the time the sales agreement is entered into; thus, no subscription receivable account or capital stock subscribed account is needed. If the stock is sold at par or at a stated value, cash is charged with the money received, and the capital stock account is credited with the same amount.

Stock Issued for Assets Other than Cash. When stock is issued for assets other than cash, a problem of establishing values develops. It is generally agreed that in cases of this kind, the value should be determined by the fair market value of the property received or the fair market value of the stock transferred, whichever is more objectively determinable. If the stock currently is being actively traded, the cash market price is conceded to be the value to use.

In the absence of a reliable market price for the stock, the appraised value of the assets received may be used in valuing the transaction. The corporate board of directors is given broad discretionary powers in appraising such assets.

In no case should the par or stated value of the stock be used as the primary factor in the valuation procedure.

Stock Issued at a Premium. Par value stock is issued at a premium if the value of cash and/or other assets received in the exchange exceeds the par value of the stock exchanged. Thus, the receipt of $1,100 cash in exchange for 10 shares of $100 par value stock would be recorded as follows:

Cash	$1,100	
Premium on stock		$ 100
Capital stock		1,000

Stock Issued at a Discount. If par value stock is exchanged for assets of a lesser value than the par value of the stock given up, a discount should be recorded. For example, if stock with a par value of $1,000 is sold for $900, the transaction should be recorded as follows:

Cash	$900	
Discount on stock	100	
Capital stock		$1,000

Because a discount on stock represents a potential claim against the stockholder by creditors of the corporation in case of corporate insolvency, investors hesitate to purchase discounted stock. In fact, in many states, corporations are prohibited from issuing stock at a discount except under limited specified conditions.

Stock Issued at a Price in Excess of Stated Value. Stated-value stock may be issued above (or below) its stated value, just as par value stock may be issued above or below par value. The preferred practice in the case of stated-value stock is to credit or charge the excess or deficiency between the stated value and the value received to a paid-in capital account. However, some accountants record transactions in stated-value stock as though it were par value stock; that is, they credit premium on capital stock for any excess received over stated value and charge discount on capital stock with any deficiency in value received in relation to the stated value of the stock sold.

Stock Subscribed. When stock is subscribed to be paid for later, the corporation recognizes an asset subscriptions receivable at the time the stock is subscribed for. The receivable is canceled when the stock is paid for and the certificates are issued. It is general practice not to issue the stock (certificates) until the stock is fully paid for. This is true even though in many states, a subscriber for stock has the same rights, benefits, and obligations as a stockholder.

It should be observed that some accountants treat subscriptions receivable as a contra-account to capital stock, rather than as an asset.

SUBSCRIPTIONS PAID IN FULL. Subscriptions paid in full cause no problems. When payment in full is received, the asset or contra-account is canceled, and the stock is issued. For example, the following entry would be made upon the receipt of a subscription for 100 $10 par value shares at par:

Subscriptions receivable	$1,000	
Stock subscribed		$1,000

Later, when payment is received and the stock is issued, the following two entries should be made:

Cash	$1,000	
Subscriptions receivable		$1,000
Stock subscribed	1,000	
Capital stock		1,000

SUBSCRIPTIONS DEFAULTED. If a subscription call or a subscription installment is not paid when due, the subscription is said to be *in default*. There are several different ways of treating defaulted subscriptions, depending upon the laws of the state and the policy of the issuing corporation.

Because of the several alternate options, the defaulted subscriber may

1. Receive the number of shares that he has in effect paid for in full
2. Forfeit the entire amount that he has already paid
3. Be entitled to a refund
    a. Of the entire amount paid in
    b. Of the amount paid in, less the costs of resale and less any excess of the original price over the resale price

Each of these alternate treatments will be illustrated in the following examples. Assume that a subscriber subscribed for 100 shares of $100 par value stock at $105. After paying 50 percent of the subscription price ($5,250), the subscriber defaulted. The corporation was able to resell the stock at $101 after incurring selling expenses of $50.

The entries to record the original sale and the 50 percent payment would be the same, of course, regardless of the ultimate results:

Subscriptions receivable—stock	$10,500	
Premium on stock		$ 500
Stock subscribed		10,000
Cash	5,250	
Subscriptions receivable		5,250

METHOD 1

Stock subscribed	$10,000	
Premium on stock	250	
Subscriptions receivable—stock		$5,250
Capital Stock		5,000

METHOD 2

Stock subscribed	$10,000	
Premium on stock	500	
Subscriptions receivable—stock		$5,250
Contributed capital—forfeited subscriptions		5,250

METHOD 3a

Stock subscribed	$10,000	
Premium on stock	500	
Subscriptions receivable—stock		$5,250
Cash		5,250

METHOD 3b

Stock subscribed	$10,000	
Premium on stock	500	
Subscriptions receivable—stock		$ 5,250
Defaulted subscriber liability		5,250
Cash ($101 × 100 − $50)	10,050	
Defaulted subscriber liability	450	
Premium		500
Capital stock		10,000
Defaulted subscriber liability	4,800	
Cash		4,800

Watered Stock. *Watered stock* is any class of capital stock the book value of which is materially in excess of the amount of money that could be paid the holders of that class of stock if the corporation were to be liquidated. "Water" may be injected into stock by overvaluation of assets and occasionally by the **understatement** of liabilities.

The "water" can be eliminated by reducing the assets to a correct value (or by increasing understated liabilities) and debiting a net worth account. The debit may be to retained earnings or to a contributed capital account. A debit to a capital stock account may result in a reduction of the par or stated value of the stock.

Secret Reserves. *Secret reserves* are hidden reserves. They represent the amount by which net worth has been intentionally understated. Secret reserves are created by the intentional undervaluation, by omission of assets, or by overstatement of liabilities.

Obviously, there cannot be such an account per se in the accounting records.

DIVIDENDS ON STOCK

A *dividend* is a proportionate payment to the stockholders of a particular class of stock of a corporation, usually out of earnings. It is usually paid in cash.

Noncumulative Dividends. A *noncumulative dividend* is a dividend on preferred stock that, if passed over, does not have to be paid at a later date. If such a dividend is not declared and paid at preestablished times, it is forever lost to the preferred stockholders.

Cumulative Dividend. A *cumulative dividend* is a dividend on preferred stock that according to the terms of the issue is to be declared and payable at established rates at stipulated intervals. If for any reason it is not so paid, such arrearages are accumulated and along with the current dividend must be paid before any dividend can be paid on the common stock.

Most preferred stock carries the cumulative-dividend feature as one of the terms of issuance. In fact, if the corporate charter does not specify otherwise, most state laws regard the preferred stock as cumulative.

Nonparticipating Dividend. A *nonparticipating dividend* is a dividend on preferred stock that is limited to a predetermined amount.

Participating Dividend. A *participating dividend* is a dividend paid on preferred stock in excess of the specified minimum amount. The participation feature permits the preferred stockholders to share, up to a predetermined amount, in the profits that would otherwise be distributable exclusively to the common stockholders.

Participating preferred stockholders, after receiving the specified dividend, will receive nothing more until the holders of common stock have received an equal pro rata amount; thereafter, the two groups will share proportionately in any additional dividends to the extent of the preferred participation. If the preferred stock is fully participating, it will share proportionately with the common stock in all excess dividends.

However, the preferred stock may have limited participation rights. For example, 6 percent preferred may by the terms of issue participate to 10 percent. In such a case, the preferred would get 6 percent first; then the common would get 6 percent; next both the preferred and common would share equally in any additional distribution up to 4 percent (a total of 10 percent), after which any additional distribution would go only to the common stockholders.

STATED OR LEGAL CAPITAL

Stated, or *legal, capital* is that portion of a corporation's paid-in capital which either by law or by agreement becomes the par or stated value of the capital stock. It is the amount of the net assets that by law is restricted with respect to withdrawal.

BOOK VALUE

Book value is the net value assigned to an asset or equity on the books of account. As applied to capital stock, it is the book value of the net assets. Specifically, it is the book value of the corporate net assets available to the particular class of stock. This amount divided by the number of shares outstanding of the class yields the per-share book value.

Usually, the book value of a preferred share is the agreed liquidation value plus any accumulated dividends.

TREASURY STOCK

Treasury stock is fully paid and issued capital stock that is reacquired by the issuing corporation through either donation or purchase and held alive in the treasury for resale or for possible later cancellation. Once it is canceled, it can no longer be considered treasury stock. The term *treasury stock* is also not applicable to shares that have never been issued and to shares that are outstanding.

Treasury stock should be included as a separate item in the capital stock section of the balance sheet. Although there are several ways that treasury stock can be presented on the balance sheet, one of the more popular methods is to deduct the cost of the treasury stock from the combined paid-in capital and retained earnings. It may also be shown as a deduction from the capital stock balance. The SEC permits the treasury stock to be deducted at cost or par or stated value; however, most accountants prefer to use cost.

Acquisitions of treasury stock are limited by law. Generally, the total of dividend payments plus treasury stock purchased may not exceed the amount of retained earnings. In some states, the limit is controlled by the amount of retained earnings plus contributed capital in excess of par or stated value. Such a restriction protects corporate creditors by assuring the preservation of the corporation's legal capital.

Treasury-Stock Transactions on a Cost Basis. Treasury-stock transactions on a cost basis are considered a single combined transaction of a purchase and (later) a sale of shares of stock. Under this cost method, the treasury stock account assumes the characteristics of a capital suspense account. The recognition of any gain or loss resulting from the transaction, as well as any adjustment of the capital accounts, is deferred until the disposal of the stock by either resale or cancellation.

When the cost method, or basis, is used, the treasury stock account is charged with the value of the consideration given for the stock.

If the treasury stock is sold for more than its cost, the excess or gain is credited to some capital account such as contributed capital—treasury stock transactions.

If the treasury stock is sold for less than its cost, the disposal of the loss depends somewhat on the laws of the state of incorporation. Generally, such losses are charged first against contributed capital in excess of par or stated value in a ratio that the treasury stock bears to the previous total stock outstanding; any remaining losses are charged against retained earnings.

For example, a corporation with 100,000 shares of $100 par value stock issued at $110 and with a current balance in retained earnings of $20,000 purchased 1,000 shares at $105 and later sold them at $90.

Treasury stock	$105,000	
Cash		$105,000
Cash	90,000	
Contributed capital in excess of par	10,000	
Retained earnings	5,000	
Treasury stock		105,000

Treasury-Stock Transactions on a Noncost Basis. Treasury-stock transactions on a noncost basis (also referred to as the *par-value method* or the *retirement method*) presupposes separate and distinct transactions. The first transaction is the purchase of shares from a stockholder, and the second and unrelated transaction is the disposal of the treasury stock. Thus, a gain or loss should be recognized on each separate transaction.

Using the same example given for the cost basis, the following entries would be made for the purchase and sale of the treasury stock:

Treasury stock	$100,000	
Contributed capital in excess of par	10,000	
Contributed capital—treasury stock		
transactions		$ 5,000
Cash		105,000
Cash	90,000	
Contributed capital—treasury stock		
transactions	5,000	
Retained earnings	5,000	
Treasury stock		100,000

STOCK RETIREMENT

Stock retirement involves both the reacquisition by the issuing corporation of previously issued shares and the actual cancellation of them.

For example, if the stock in the preceding example were canceled rather than kept alive in the treasury and later reissued, the following entry would be in order:

Capital stock	$100,000	
Contributed capital in excess of par	10,000	
Contributed capital—stock retirement		$ 5,000
Cash		105,000

DONATED TREASURY STOCK

Donated treasury stock is stock that is given back to the issuing corporation.

Under the cost method of accounting for treasury stock, only a memorandum entry would be made at the time of the donation. At the time of resale, the proceeds would be credited to stock discount, if it exists, and then any balance would be credited to contributed capital in excess of par (or stated) value.

For example, assume that 1,000 shares of $100 par stock were issued at $97. (It is unusual and in some cases now illegal to issue stock at a discount.) Assume, also, the 1,000 shares were donated to the corporation and later sold at $95.

Using the cost basis, the following entries would be made:

Memo: 1,000 shares donated to the treasury.		
Cash	$95,000	
Discount on stock		$ 3,000
Contributed capital—donated stock		92,000

Using the par-value method, the following entries would be made:

Donated treasury stock	$100,000	
Discount on stock		$ 3,000
Contributed capital—donated stock		97,000
Cash	95,000	
Contributed capital—donated stock	5,000	
Donated treasury stock		100,000

INCORPORATION OF AN ALREADY-ESTABLISHED FIRM

Often a sole proprietorship or a partnership finds that it is advantageous to incorporate. Incorporation of an existing firm may be recorded by either of two general methods: (1) The books of the old firm may be continued in use and modified to fit the needs of the new corporation. (2) New books may be opened for the new corporation. Under either method, the book value as given in the old accounts is relatively insignificant. It is the current market value that is important. Therefore, all account balances should be reviewed and, where necessary, adjusted to current values. The amount of each adjustment may be recorded in an adjustment account, which will later be closed to the capital accounts; or if there are only a few adjustments, they may be recorded directly in the capital accounts.

If new books are to be used for the corporation, the accounts of the old firm are closed out (after adjustment), and entirely new books are prepared for the corporation.

If the corporation continues the use of the old books, the old capital accounts (after adjustment) are eliminated and replaced by new appropriate capital accounts. This method is illustrated by the following example.

John Black and Joe Brown have been operating a partnership in which they shared profits equally. On December 31, 1973, their balance sheet was as follows:

BLACK AND BROWN

BALANCE SHEET
DECEMBER 31, 1973

Cash		$ 1,000	Accounts payable		$5,000
Accounts receivable	$10,000		Black, capital	$21,000	
Less: Allowance for bad debts	1,000	9,000	Brown, capital	22,000	43,000
Inventories		8,000			
Equipment	$40,000				
Less: Allowance for depreciation	10,000	30,000			
Total assets		$48,000	Total equities		$48,000

Upon reviewing the accounts, the following current values were established:

1. It is expected that only $8,000 of the accounts receivable will be collected.
2. The market value of the inventories is $7,000.
3. The equipment has a market value of $36,000.

The following entries may be made:

Allowance for depreciation	$10,000	
Equipment		$ 4,000
Allowance for bad debts		1,000
Inventories		1,000
Black, capital		2,000
Brown, capital		2,000
Black, capital	23,000	
Brown, capital	24,000	
Capital stock		47,000

It should be observed that the contra-account is retained in the case of the receivables but eliminated in the case of the equipment.

STOCK WARRANTS AND RIGHTS

A *warrant* is a transferable certificate issued by a corporation evidencing the stock rights granted a stockholder. A *stock right* is the privilege granted a stockholder to subscribe to a proportionate number of shares of a new stock issue or occasionally other securities. Stock rights are frequently used for the following purposes:

1. To facilitate the sale of additional shares
2. In conjunction with issues of bonds or preferred stock to facilitate the sale of such securities
3. To provide special compensation to promoters, officers, or employees

Valuation of Rights. The corporation recognizes no revenue or expense on the issuance of the rights. Recognition of value or expense is deferred until the rights are exercised. Therefore, when rights are issued, only a memorandum entry is required, indicating the number of shares that should be reserved to satisfy the rights when they are exercised.

See Chapter 10 for valuation of rights from an investor's point of view.

Accounting for Rights. The amount of cash received when rights are exercised may be more than, equal to, or less than the par or stated value of the stock issued. Also, the stock may have neither a par nor a stated value. These conditions require slightly different accounting treatments:

1. When the cash received is more than the par or stated value of the stock issued, the excess should be credited to some other contributed capital account, such as premium on capital stock.

2. When the cash received is equal to the par or stated value of the stock issued (or in the case of stock with neither a par nor stated value), the entire amount is credited to the capital stock account.

3. When the cash received is less than the par or stated value of the stock issued, the deficit should be charged to retained earnings, thus permanently capitalizing the deficiency.

STOCK SPLITS AND REVERSE SPLITS

A *stock split* is a substantial and proportionate issue of additional shares to present stockholders without any change in the total capital. This may be accomplished either by simply issuing additional shares or by calling in all the shares of the particular class and issuing a greater number of new shares.

A *reverse stock split* is the calling-in of all the stock of a particular class in exchange for fewer shares.

Normally, the total amount in the capital stock account is not changed; only the number of shares and the par or stated value change. For example, if a corporation has 1,000 shares of $100 par value stock outstanding just prior to a two-for-one stock split, it would have 2,000 shares of $50 par value stock outstanding after the split.

Since a stock split or reverse split does not change the total capital of the corporation, the split or reverse split is made largely for the psychological effect it may have on current and potential stockholders. If the market price of a particular stock is very high, the public may believe that it is overpriced, and potential small investors may be discouraged because of the large size of the required investment. For example, if before a four-for-one split, a particular stock is selling for $400, theoretically, it should sell for $100 after the split. However, because of the psychological effect of a better price and the attraction of additional small investors, it may be expected to sell actually for slightly more than $100.

Conversely, if, for example, stock is selling for only $.10, investors may hesitate to buy it because they associate a very low market price with a poor investment. Therefore, after a ten-to-one reverse split, it is quite likely to sell for over $1.00 per share.

The change in the number of outstanding shares and the change in the par or stated value may be recorded by a memorandum entry only. However, it is better practice to close out the old capital stock account and open a new one.

CHAPTER 14

Contributed Capital: Other than Stock

Contributed capital is composed of the legal or stated capital plus additional contributed paid-in surplus. In order words, contributed capital is total stockholders' equity less retained earnings except in those rare instances in which a corporation has created appraisal surplus that may be treated either as a subdivision of contributed capital or as a third equity group between contributed capital and retained earnings.

EXCESS OVER PAR OR STATED VALUE RECEIVED FOR CAPITAL STOCK

That portion of contributed capital recognized as legal capital is recorded as capital stock, and the amount received in excess of that legal capital is recorded as some form of additional contributed capital or as some form of contributed surplus.

Paid-in Surplus. *Paid-in surplus* (also known as *capital surplus, contributed surplus,* or *additional contributed capital*), is a generic term applied to that part of contributed capital, regardless of source, not designated as legal capital, that is, capital stock. It may be created by the sale of par or stated-value stock at a price greater than the par or stated value, by the arbitrary assignment of part of the value received for true no-par stock (stock with neither par nor stated value), by dealings in the corporation's own stock, and by donations to the corporation.

The AICPA does not approve of the use of the term *surplus* because its accounting use is often misunderstood by laymen. Therefore, terms such as *paid-in surplus* are being replaced by terms such as *contributed capital in excess of par (or stated) value*.

Premium on Capital Stock. *Premium on capital stock* is a specific term encompassed by the generic term *paid-in surplus*. It is the excess over the par value paid for stock. Some accountants would suggest that it is the excess amount paid for stock over either the par value or the stated value of the stock. However, the preferred approach is to credit the amount paid in excess of the stated value of such stated-value stock to an account such as capital contributed in excess of stated value.

PAID-IN CAPITAL NOT DESIGNATED AS LEGAL CAPITAL

All capital that is contributed to the firm (other than earnings) and not credited to a capital stock account must be credited to some other capital account, such as those mentioned in the preceding section or those discussed in the following paragraphs.

Gain on the Reissue of Treasury Stock. Gain on the reissue of treasury stock should be credited to some capital account other than retained earnings. It is generally agreed that a corporation cannot generate income by buying and selling parts of itself.

Retirement of Stock at Less than Par or Stated Value. When stock is retired, the capital stock account and any adjunct accounts must be reduced proportionately, and any resulting gain should be credited to an appropriate contributed capital account.

Assume, for example, that a corporation had issued 1,000 shares of $100 par value stock at $110 and that this represented the firm's contributed capital at the time the company bought back 100 shares at $95 and canceled them.

The purchase would be journalized as follows:

Capital stock	$10,000	
Premium on stock	1,000	
Contributed capital—stock retirement		$1,500
Cash		9,500

Stock Assessments. *Stock assessments* are special levies on stockholders as a means of raising additional capital. Most stock may not now be levied against except on a voluntary basis. Under certain circumstances, stock issued at a discount may be subject to an involuntary assessment for the protection of creditors. Assume that a financially embarrassed corporation had issued 1,000 shares having a par value of $100 for $90,000, that no additional contributions had been made by the stockholders, and that the referee in bankruptcy was authorized to assess the stockholders for the amount of the discount.

The receipt of the assessment would be recorded as follows:

Cash	$10,000	
Discount on stock		$10,000

Donations of Cash or Other Property. Donations of cash or other property, if material, represent paid-in or contributed capital, rather than income to be credited to retained earnings. Municipalities frequently give land or other assets to corporations to induce them to locate in the area. Such a donation should be recorded by a charge to a land (or other appropriate asset) account for the reasonable value of the land or other asset and an offsetting credit to an account such as contributed (donated) capital—gift of land (or other asset). However, occasional gifts of insignificant value may be cleared through the income account.

APPRAISAL CAPITAL (SURPLUS): UNREALIZED INCREMENT

Appraisal capital results from increasing book values of fixed assets to current market or replacement values.

Nature of Appraisal Capital. Normally, the stockholders' equity section of a balance sheet is divided into two parts: the contributed capital section and the retained earnings section. Capital arising merely from an appraisal does not appropriately fit either category. Some accountants have placed such capital in the contributed group in order to avoid opening another section.

The majority of accountants, however, would create another section entitled appraisal capital. This they would place between the contributed capital section and the retained earnings section.

It is certainly agreed that the art of writing up the value of an asset does not immediately create income. However, some accounting authorities feel that by the time the asset is exhausted or consumed, it should have generated sufficient income to justify the increased valuation. Therefore, some accountants prefer to refer to this increase as an *unrealized increment*. This increment would then be realized through additional charges to depreciation or by a lump-sum transfer from the unrealized account to some realized account when the asset is retired.

Effect of APB Opinion No. 6. Appraisal write-ups have not been resorted to as frequently as they might have been because of the expressed position of the AICPA: "The board is of the opinion that property, plant and equipment should not be written up by an entity to reflect appraisal, market or current values which are above cost to the entity."[1]

1. "Status of Accounting Research Bulletins," *Accounting Principles Board Opinion,* No. 6 (1965), p. 42.

CHAPTER 15

Retained Earnings

Owners' equity of a corporation is divided into two broad categories: capital contributed by the owners or donated by others and accumulated (retained) earnings. Contributed capital was discussed in Chapters 13 and 14. Retained earnings are discussed in this chapter.

RETAINED EARNINGS

Retained earnings constitute that portion of a firm's net income which has not been distributed to the owners in the form of dividends or capitalized by transfers to some contributed capital account.

The term *retained earnings* has generally superseded the term *earned surplus*. To the layman, surplus commonly means excess, overplus, something not needed, or a residual quantity. This is at variance with the accountant's meaning; therefore, the AICPA first suggested in 1941 and reiterated in 1961

a general discontinuance of the use of the term *surplus* in corporate accounting, and a substitution therefore in the proprietorship section of the balance sheet of designations which would emphasize the distinction between (a) legal capital, (b) capital in excess of legal capital, and (c) undivided profits.[1]

Nature of Retained Earnings. In layman's terms, retained earnings represents profits plowed back into the business. Retained

---

1. *Accounting Research and Terminology Bulletins,* Final Edition, 1 (1961), p. 28.

earnings are increased by profits and decreased by losses and dividends distributed.

A debit balance in the retained earnings account is referred to as a *deficit*. In a quasi-reorganization, the deficit is eliminated, and a fresh start is given the retained earnings account and the corporation.

Current accounting practice dictates that gains or losses resulting from regular or ancillary business operations or any immaterial extraneous gains or losses should be cleared through the periodic income account rather than charged or credited directly to retained earnings. The APB states that

net income should reflect all items of profit and loss recognized during the period with the sole exception of the prior period adjustments. . . .
. . . Adjustments related to prior periods—and thus excluded in the determination of net income for the current period—are limited to those material adjustments which (a) can be specifically identified with and directly related to business activities of particular prior periods, and (b) are not attributable to economic events occurring subsequent to the date of the financial statements for the prior period, and (c) depend primarily on determinations by persons other than management and (d) were not susceptible of reasonable estimation prior to such determination.[2]

Source of Retained Earnings. Retained earnings may result from profitable operations. They represent the accumulated net income of the firm from its origin (or quasi-reorganization), less dividends and transfers to paid-in or contributed capital accounts.

CAPITALIZATION OF RETAINED EARNINGS

In balance-sheet presentation, it is important and informative to show the various amounts of equity capital according to sources. Such information is important to investors. Corporate growth may be developed by internal and/or external financing.

It should be observed, however, that equity classification by source loses meaning if transfers are made from retained earnings to contributed capital accounts by the transfer of earnings to either a capital stock account or some paid-in capital (or sur-

2. *Accounting Principles Board Opinion* 9 (1966), pp. 112–115.

plus) account. Also, quasi-reorganizations and some treasury-stock transactions will tend to nullify the value of classification of equity capital by source.

Presumably, the amount available for dividends is limited by the balance of the retained earnings. This amount may be further reduced by restrictions placed on (or appropriations of) retained earnings. The preceding general statement will be affected by the appropriate state laws concerning dividend payments.

SEC Regulation S–X, rule 5–02(39) requires that paid-in surplus, surplus arising from revaluation of assets, other capital surplus, unappropriated earned surplus, and appropriated earned surplus be listed separately on the balance sheet.

Retained earnings are said to be *capitalized* when transfers are made from retained earnings to a capital stock account. This may be accomplished either by a stock dividend or by an increase in the par or stated value of the stock.

Stock Dividend. A *stock dividend* is a distribution of additional shares of stock to existing stockholders in proportion to their current holdings. A stock dividend does not decrease the net assets of the corporation. Since the corporation has not parted with anything of value, the recipient of a stock dividend has not received anything of value and hence has received no income.

The recording of a stock dividend should result in the permanent capitalization of retained earnings equal to the fair market value of the additional shares issued. The value most frequently used is the market value at the time of the declaration of the dividend. The use of market value as the capitalization factor will often result in the capitalization of an amount in excess of the minimum legal requirements.

For example, if a corporation's common stock having a par value of $100 was selling at $112 when a stock dividend of 1,000 shares was declared, the dividend should be recorded as follows:

Retained earnings	$112,000	
Common stock		$100,000
Premium on common stock		12,000

Both the AICPA and the SEC recommend the use of fair market value as the basis for determining the amount of retained earnings to be capitalized.

A corporation may give stock dividends for the following reasons:

1. To retain funds permanently in the corporation, making them unavailable for cash dividends
2. To continue a policy of regular dividend payments, even when cash is not available for dividends because it is being used for expansion and so forth
3. To enhance the market position of the corporation's stock by increasing the number of shares available

Increased Par or Stated Value of Stock. Either increased par value, or increased stated value of stock has much the same effect as a stock dividend but lacks the psychological effect on the stockholder.

For example, if a firm has 1,000 shares outstanding with a stated value of $25 that are to be exchanged for 1,000 shares with a stated value of $30, the transaction should be recorded as follows:

Capital stock—stated value $25	$25,000	
Retained earnings	5,000	
Capital stock—stated value $30		$30,000

QUASI-REORGANIZATION

A *quasi-reorganization* is an informal accounting reorganization, as opposed to a formal legal reorganization. A quasi-reorganization is negotiated without court intervention or pressure from creditors. The primary purpose of such a reorganization is the elimination of a deficit; the secondary purpose is the elimination of the cause of the deficit, which may be, for example, excessive depreciation charges resulting from abnormally high asset valuation.

A quasi-reorganization should enable a firm to have a fresh start, free from the stigma of a large deficit and in such a condition that it may be expected to operate profitably in the future.

In a quasi-reorganization, the following steps should be taken:

1. All fixed assets should be valued at the lower of cost or current market. Any write-down should be charged to retained

earnings. (Just as with inventories, write-ups from cost to a higher market value are not generally approved.)

2. Any deficit in retained earnings after the asset write-downs should be charged against additional contributed capital accounts.

3. Any net deficit in the additional contributed capital accounts should be eliminated by a reduction in the par or stated value of the stock.

At the completion of the quasi-reorganization, the following conditions should prevail:

1. The balance of the retained earnings account should be zero.

2. There should be no deficit in any additional contributed capital (surplus) accounts.

3. The quasi-reorganization should have accomplished essentially the same ends as would have been accomplished by a legal reorganization, that is, the revaluation of assets and the restructuring of the owners' equity in a way that reduces the need for future reorganizations.

Because a quasi-reorganization has eliminated a deficit in the retained earnings account and probably has reduced the amount of future charges against income, the retained earnings should be dated as of the effective date of the fresh start. This date should be shown on subsequent balance sheets as long as the date bears significance.

SEC Regulation S–X, rule 5–02(39) requires that retained earnings should be dated for at least 10 years after the reorganization, and indicate for at least three years the amount of the deficit eliminated. The AICPA suggests that the dating of retained earnings would not be significant after ten years.[3]

RESTRICTIONS ON RETAINED EARNINGS

Free and unrestricted or unappropriated retained earnings may be permanently or temporarily reduced. Permanent reductions

3. *Accounting Research and Terminology Bulletins,* Final Edition, 46 (1961), p. 11.

of retained earnings may be effected by cash, property, or stock dividends; by recapitalizations; and by absorption of losses. Temporary reductions in unrestricted retained earnings do not affect total retained earnings. They may be occasioned by treasury-stock requirements and by various appropriations or reservations, such as those for plant expansion or possible future losses. It should be observed that appropriated, or reserved, restricted retained earnings is only a subdivision of retained earnings and is ultimately returned intact to (unrestricted) retained earnings. It is generally assumed that all amounts in any retained earnings account which does not include a restrictive word or phrase in its title are available for dividends.

Restrictions on the availability of retained earnings for dividends may arise because of any of the following three general reasons:

1. Law per se, for example, when the state laws stipulate that the total payments for treasury stock and dividends may not impair the legal capital

2. Contracts, for example, when the corporation agrees with the bondholders (through statements in the bond indenture) that certain limitations will be placed on the payment of dividends

3. Voluntary or discretionary, for example, when management decides that it would be more advantageous to finance a building program internally than to pay out all profits in dividends

With respect to retained earnings, the terms *reserve, appropriated,* and *restricted* may be considered synonyms. This is important because the AICPA takes the position that the term *reserve* should be used only to indicate an allocation of retained earnings.[4] Thus, such reservations, allocations, or restrictions would be restricted to the owner's equity section of the balance sheet. A separate reserve section on the balance sheet is not acceptable.

Treasury-Stock Requirements. As protection to creditors and minority stockholders, some state laws limit the purchase of treasury stock to an amount not in excess of the amount of retained earnings or earned surplus. Such laws have the effect of making an amount of retained earnings that is equal to the cost

4. *Accounting Research and Terminology Bulletins,* Final Edition (1961), p. 27.

of the treasury stock unavailable for distribution as dividends. This reduces the chances of capital impairment by restricting the total amount that may be disbursed for stock acquisition and for dividends to the balance of retained earnings.

In order to avoid an erroneous payment of dividends, a restriction equal to the purchase price should be placed on retained earnings at the time treasury stock is acquired. When the stock is resold, the restriction should be lifted.

Consider the following example: The Brown Corporation bought back 1,000 shares of $100 par value stock at par and later resold them at $110.

At the time of purchase, the following entries would be appropriate:

Treasury stock	$100,000	
Cash		$100,000
Retained earnings	100,000	
Retained earnings appropriated		
for treasury stock		100,000

When the stock is resold, the following entries would be appropriate:

Cash	$110,000	
Treasury stock		$100,000
Additional contributed capital		10,000
Retained earnings appropriated for		
treasury stock	100,000	
Retained earnings		100,000

Contractual Restrictions. Typical of contractual restrictions are contractual limitations on the payments of dividends included in some loan agreements or bond indentures. A bond indenture might stipulate that cash dividends would be paid only out of net earnings accumulated after a certain date or that specified amounts of earnings should be earmarked each year to enhance the assurance of the redemption of the bonds at maturity.

For example, consider the case of a $100,000 bond issue that required the appropriation of $10,000 of retained earnings at the end of each year during the ten-year life of the bonds.

An entry such as the following should be made at the end of each of the ten years:

Retained earnings	$10,000	
Retained earnings appropriated		
for bond redemption		$10,000

When the bonds are redeemed, the following entry should be made:

Retained earnings appropriated for		
bond redemption	$100,000	
Retained earnings		$100,000

The purpose of restrictions or limitations on cash dividends given in the loan agreement is to prevent the impairment of working capital to the detriment of the creditors. If adequate working capital is maintained, the ability of the firm to pay the loan at maturity is enhanced. Normally, only cash dividends are subject to control or restriction. Stock dividends, because they do not require disbursement of working capital, are usually not controlled.

The appropriation for bond retirement limits only the use of cash for dividends. This may not provide sufficient protection against working-capital impairment from other uses. In order to provide added protection to the bondholders, the indenture may require the establishment of a bond-redemption fund. Such a fund is an asset. It is established by periodic transfers of cash from the general cash account to a special-purpose cash account. This special account may be administered by the firm or by a trustee representing the bondholders.

Voluntary Restrictions. Voluntary restrictions include all restrictions placed on retained earnings by the discretionary actions of the board of directors.

The AICPA states its position in regard to contingency reserves, many of which are voluntary, as follows:

7. The committee is therefore of the opinion that reserves such as those created:
(a) for general undetermined contingencies, or
(b) for any indefinite possible future losses, such as, for example, losses on inventories not on hand or contracted for, or
(c) for the purpose of reducing inventories other than to a basis which is in accordance with generally accepted principles, or
(d) without regard to any specific loss reasonably related to the operations of the current period, or

(e) in amounts not determined on the basis of any reasonable esti-mates of costs or losses are of such a nature that charges or credits relating to such reserves should not enter into the determination of net income.

8. Accordingly it is the opinion of the committee that if a reserve of the type described in paragraph 7 is set up:

(a) it should be created by a segregation or appropriation of earned surplus,

(b) no costs or losses should be charged to it and no part of it should be transferred to income or in any way used to affect the determina-tion of net income for any year,

(c) it should be restored to earned surplus directly when such a re-serve or any part thereof is no longer considered necessary, and

(d) it should preferably be classified in the balance sheet as a part of shareholders' equity.[5]

APPROPRIATIONS FOR INVENTORY LOSSES. In accordance with the recommendations of the AICPA, current losses in inventory value should be charged directly or indirectly against income of the period, but reasonably expected future declines in the value of the inventory should be provided for temporarily by a restric-tion on retained earnings.

For example, consider a situation wherein at year-end the in-ventory is overvalued $1,000 and wherein it is reasonable to ex-pect that if expected economic conditions exist during the next year, the value of the inventory will decrease another $500. At the end of the first year, the following entries would be made:

Income and expense (or cost of goods sold)	$1,000	
Inventory		$1,000
Retained earnings	500	
Reserve for inventory loss (or retained earnings appropriated for inventory loss)		500

At the end of the second year, the second entry above should be reversed, as follows:

Reserve for inventory loss	$500	
Retained earnings		$500

This is true regardless of whether the anticipated loss did or did not occur; because by that time, the restriction placed on the

5. *Accounting Research and Terminology Bulletins,* Final Edition (1961), pp. 42–43.

availability of earnings for dividends would have served its purpose.

If an actual loss occurred during the second year, an entry similar to the first entry shown for the first year should be made for the actual amount of the loss.

The credit to the reserve account is still a part of retained earnings and should be listed in the net worth section of the balance sheet. It should not be listed as a contra-account to the asset account inventory in the current asset section, as has sometimes been done in the past.

APPROPRIATION (RESERVE) FOR PLANT EXPANSION. Corporations planning a major plant expansion that is to be financed entirely or to a great extent from within will find it expedient to restrict the payment of dividends. This may be accomplished by making periodic transfers from retained earnings to reserve for plant expansion or to retained earnings appropriated for plant expansion. Such a restriction on retained earnings will not guarantee the availability of funds for the payment for the plant because this restriction only prevents the disbursement of cash for dividends. (The cash could be spent for other purposes.)

After the expansion program has been completed, the accumulated credit balance in the reserve or appropriation account should be transferred back to the free or unappropriated retained earnings (or retained earnings) account.

It has been recommended (and logically so) by some that since the funds have in effect been capitalized into fixed assets, cash may not be available for dividends and that therefore the board of directors might capitalize the amount of the reserve through a stock dividend.

RESERVE FOR GENERAL CONTINGENCIES. The balance in the retained earnings account should act as a cushion to absorb possible future losses; however, some companies use general contingency reserves for this purpose. Occasionally, a firm's management will authorize an appropriation of retained earnings in an attempt to make assets available to absorb losses that may develop. But it is better practice to resort to appropriating retained earnings only in cases where it appears reasonable to expect a future loss due to a specific cause, such as a possible strike or loss of overseas investments because of the actions of foreign governments.

RESERVE FOR SELF-INSURANCE. *Self-insurance* occurs when management decides not to purchase insurance against a particular risk but, rather, to bear the risk of loss itself. Insurance is based on a philosophy of risk spreading, which firms with widely scattered holdings may decide they can do themselves.

A preferred method of treating self-insurance is to consider it for what it really is—no insurance—and give it no accounting recognition at all. However, there are those who recognize the fact that if they own a number of plants, they will from time to time suffer losses from fire, wind, and so forth. These people would like to (and some do) charge operations periodically with the estimated premium cost for insurance coverage and credit a like amount to reserve for self-insurance. If a loss should occur, it would be charged against the reserve account. It must be pointed out that this method is not generally accepted by accountants and theoretically is not justified.

There is a compromise between these approaches. Periodically, amounts may be transferred from retained earnings to reserve for self-insurance. When a loss occurs, it must be charged to expense, rather than to the reserve accounts. Such a procedure provides a measure of protection in that it prevents excessive dividend disbursements. It, too, is theoretically weak; but at least the reserve would be listed as a part of owner's equity, and losses would be charged to expense, rather than to the reserve.

RETAINED EARNINGS AVAILABLE FOR DIVIDENDS

Theoretically, any unrestricted, unappropriated, or unreserved retained earnings are available for dividends. However, it must be remembered that a balance in the retained earnings accounts, whether they be restricted or unrestricted, merely indicates the amount of past net earnings not distributed as dividends or formally capitalized. It does not indicate the amount of available cash because the cash may already be invested in other assets.

A restriction on retained earnings prevents the use of funds for one purpose only: the payment of dividends. By the same token, a balance in the free or unappropriated retained earnings account is no assurance that funds are available for dividends.

In a broad sense, management has more or less specific plans for the use of earnings retained in the firm, or it would distribute them in the form of dividends. Therefore, it is argued by many that since it is impractical to provide for all (some vague) planned uses of earnings, it is misleading to establish reserves for some of them because the readers of the statements may believe that under such circumstances all unrestricted retained earnings should be disbursed as dividends.

The AAA recommends that appropriation of retained income be disclosed by a footnote.[6] For example, such a footnote might state, "Ten thousand dollars of the retained earnings are appropriated for building expansion."

6. "Reserves and Retained Income Supplementary Statement No. 1," *Accounting Review* 26 (1951), p. 153.

PART 3

Financial
Statements
and Their
Analyses

A *financial statement* is the more or less formal presentation of financial data derived from accounting records. The primary purpose of financial statements is to provide interested readers with pertinent information so that they may make appropriate and knowledgeable decisions. The most common financial statements are income statements, balance sheets, retained-earnings statements, and funds-flow or cash-flow statements. These statements and statement analyses are discussed in the remaining chapters of this book.

NATURE AND OBJECTIVES OF FINANCIAL STATEMENTS

Collectively, the financial statements of a firm present a classified summary of the activity and financial position of that firm, based on its accounting records. All business transactions considered are placed on a common basis: money.

The Income Statement. The *income statement* is also referred to as a *profit and loss statement,* an *earnings statement,* a *statement of income and expense,* and an *operating statement.* Such a statement summarizes the revenues and expenses of the reporting firm or unit for a predetermined time period referred to as the *accounting period.* It shows the results of operations for the period.

Today the income statement is considered to be the most important financial statement.

The Balance Sheet. The *balance sheet* is also referred to as the *statement of financial position,* or the *statement of financial condition.* It presents in summary form the financial position of a firm or economic unit broken down into three categories: assets, liabilities, and owner(s)' equity.

Formerly, the balance sheet was considered the most important financial statement; but currently, it is considered second in importance to the income statement.

The Retained Earnings Statement. The *retained earnings statement* is sometimes referred to as a *statement of changes in capital*. It was formerly referred to as a *statement of earned surplus*. The primary function of this statement is to reconcile the beginning and ending balances reported in the retained earnings account.

This statement and the income statement are sometimes combined into a *statement of income and retained earnings*.

The Funds-Flow or Cash-Flow Statements. These statements trace inflows and outflows of funds or cash for the firm during the accounting period. In recent years, the importance accorded these statements has increased tremendously.

THE RELATIONSHIPS OF THE VARIOUS STATEMENTS

The income statement reflects the activity or the result of operations of a firm for a specified period of time; whereas the balance sheet indicates the firm's financial position at a specified moment of time. Neither statement alone yields a complete indication of a firm's progress and status. It is often said that two balance sheets are joined together by an income statement or that an income statement shows how a firm moved from its financial position at the beginning of the period to its financial position as of the end of the period.

The funds-flow statement, sometimes referred to as the *where got, where gone statement*, shows how funds were acquired and applied in the business during the period and how they affected the firm's financial position.

THE REPORTING PERIOD

The *reporting period* is the period of time covered by a financial report or statement. The following statements cover periods of time, rather than moments of time: income statements, retained earnings statements, and funds-flow statements. A balance sheet does not involve a time period, but only an instant of time.

For a long time now, a year has generally been accepted as the best time period to use for general reporting purposes. A shorter period is too short to provide a clear insight into the firm's activity; a period substantially longer than a year does not provide needed information quickly enough for efficient decision making.

The term *year* may be prefaced by three different modifiers: calendar, fiscal, and natural business. A *calendar year* is a twelve-month period ending on December 31. A *fiscal year* is any successive twelve months selected by a firm as its accounting period. A fiscal year may or may not correspond to a calendar year. A *natural business year* is a fiscal year that ends with the annual low point of the firm's activity, for example, at the close of a season or model year.

CHAPTER 16

The Financial Statements

The three main general-purpose financial statements are the income statement, the balance sheet, and the retained earnings statement. In this chapter, each is discussed.

THE INCOME STATEMENT

The *income statement* is the primary operating statement of a firm. It is carefully read by management, by current and potential investors and/or creditors, and by others as well.

Objectives of the Income Statement. A primary objective of the income statement is to measure and report periodic income or profit correctly on a consistent basis. In a broad sense, it reflects the results of operations. It presents in summary form all the information in the income and expense accounts. The income statement plays an important, although apparently indirect, role in the valuation of a firm's assets and the market value of a corporation's stock. An individual may purchase something for his personal satisfaction without giving any consideration to the rate of return on the investment. However, a knowledgeable investor will value a potential investment at an amount that may be expected to yield his desired rate of return on his investment. Thus, a second important objective of an income statement is to provide potential investors with a basis for valuing the assets or capital stock of the firm. This function of the income statement is given recognition by those corporations that list earnings per share at the bottom of the income statement.

Measurement of Periodic Income. Measurement of periodic income must be on a basis consistent with other periods, as well as in accordance with generally accepted accounting principles, if the information and the resulting analysis are to be meaningful. Periodic income can be measured and the income statement prepared only after the firm's books of accounts are completely posted as of the end of the period.

There are two basic philosophies applicable to the measurement of periodic income: the all-inclusive concept and the current-operating-performance concept.

The *all-inclusive method* of income measurement would include in income all transactions for the period tending to increase or decrease proprietory equity, including adjustments to prior years' profits and extraordinary and nonrecurring items except dividend and capital transactions.

The *current-operating-performance method* of income measurement would include in income only the income and expenses resulting from ordinary, normal, and recurring operations of the firm for the current period. Under this method, material gains or losses resulting from extraordinary or nonrecurring transactions or occurrences (such as corrections to prior years' net income) or casualty losses (such as losses caused by wind or fire) would be excluded.

The AICPA, through the APB, has finally taken a definitive position in regard to the treatment of extraordinary items and prior-period adjustments.

. . . net income should reflect all items of profit and loss recognized during the period with the sole exception of the prior period adjustments described below. *Extraordinary items* should, however, be segregated from the results of ordinary operations and shown separately in the income statement. . . .

. . . prior period adjustments, . . . those rare items which relate directly to the operations of a specific period or periods which are material and which qualify under the criteria described . . . should in single period statements be reflected as adjustments of the opening balance of retained earnings.[1]

In measuring and analyzing periodic income and expense, it is often helpful to classify the items according to source.

OPERATING REVENUES. *Operating revenue* is the income from the sale of goods or services in the regular course of business. In a sales organization, it is net sales. In a service organization, it is billed fees.

1. *Accounting Principles Board Opinion* 9 (1966), pp. 112–113.

It is generally assumed that income or revenue is realized when a sale is made under normal business conditions, even though cash may not yet have been collected.

COST OF GOODS SOLD. *Cost of goods sold,* sometimes referred to as *cost of sales,* is the total cost of goods sold during the accounting period under consideration. For a sales organization, this cost figure is determined by adding to the beginning inventory the cost of purchases made during the period, usually including some or all costs of acquisition (e.g., freight-in), and from this sum subtracting the value of the ending inventory. For a manufacturing firm, it is the production cost of the finished goods sold. This figure is established by adding to the beginning finished-goods inventory the production costs of material, labor, and factory overhead applicable to the finished goods completed during the period and then subtracting from this sum the value of the ending finished-goods inventory. On the income statement, this information may be shown in detail, or it may appear as only a summary figure that is detailed in a supporting schedule.

Cost of goods sold is also the title of the second major portion of a conventional multiple-step income statement.

Theoretically, the term should be *expense of goods sold,* rather than *cost of goods sold,* in keeping the current popular definition of expense as an expired cost. In the case of this expression, the fine distinction between *cost* and *expense* is observed more in the breach than in the keeping since cost of goods sold is almost universally used. In fact, the author has not seen and does not expect soon to see an income statement listing expense of goods sold.

OPERATING EXPENSES. *Operating expenses* are any of a varied group of expenses incurred in conducting the regular operations of a firm's business, excluding cost of goods sold and nonoperating or financial expenses.

A rather extensive classification of these operating expenses is essential for efficient management. The classification may appear on the income statement if the list is not too long. If the list is lengthy, it is appropriate to place it in a supporting schedule and to show only the total on the income statement.

Frequently, operating expenses are broken down into subgroups such as selling expenses and general and administrative expenses.

NONOPERATING INCOME AND EXPENSE. *Nonoperating income and expense* result from sources or activities other than the firm's regular activities, such as interest income or expense for a non-financial institution.

EXTRAORDINARY ITEMS. *Extraordinary items* are items of income or expense so unusual in either type and/or amount in relationship to the firm's regular activities that they require special separate treatment in the accounts and separate disclosure after income before extraordinary items in the income statement. For example, the sale of a significantly valuable asset bought for use, such as a major portion of a manufacturing plant, should be listed under extraordinary items. This would enable the reporting firm to clear all income and expense through the income account but still provide the reader of the statement with a readily available figure representing the income before extraordinary items, or income from regular operations.

Sample Statement Based on Conventional Cost Concept. There are two general formats that may be used in the preparation of income statements along conventional lines: the multiple-step form and the single-step form.

THE MULTIPLE-STEP FORM. In the *multiple-step form,* the various items are grouped according to functional cause, and a series of subtotals are developed. This method provides more information than the single-step method does. However, some accountants believe that listing a number of profits within the statement may cause confusion, especially if one of several profit figures is used out of context. It is also suggested by those who oppose the multiple-step statement that it appears to rank expenses, that is, to indicate that some expenses are more important than others, when actually all expenses are of equal importance.

This form gets its name from the fact that a number of distinct steps must be taken to arrive at net profit. These steps are:

1. Net sales − cost of goods sold = gross profit
2. Gross profit − operating expenses = operating profit
3. Operating profit ± nonoperating items = net income before taxes
4. Net income before taxes − income taxes = income before extraordinary items

5. Income before extraordinary items − (extraordinary items − applicable income tax) = net income

The multiple-step form is illustrated in Figure 16.1.

THE SINGLE-STEP FORM. The *single-step form* of income statement presents the data in more summarized form than the multiple-step statement does. The single-step statement has three parts joined together in one step. For example: Total revenue − total expenses = net profit. Advocates of this format believe that it is less confusing to the layman than the multiple-step statement is. The single-step form is illustrated in Figure 16.2.

Sample Statement Based on Marginal Cost Concept. Marginal costing, also referred to as *direct costing* or *variable costing,* is a practice by which all variable costs are classified as direct (or product) costs. The marginal cost concept is based on the premise that all costs result from two functions: production and the passage of time. *Marginal costs* (also referred to as *direct costs* or *variable costs*) are the costs added to the previous production cost by producing one additional unit. They are basically variable in nature.

Period costs are those costs that accrue as a result of the passage of time. They are costs that, within a relevant range, are not affected by production decisions; they are essentially fixed.

Under the marginal cost concept, the direct costs are charged to inventory and the period costs are charged directly to expense for the accounting period in which they are incurred; they never enter into or pass through the inventory account.

Under marginal costing, it is necessary to separate costs according to their characteristics of fixity and variability. Admittedly, in some cases the separation of costs according to their characteristics necessitates certain assumptions and in some cases may become rather arbitrary.

Marginal-costing data in many instances is a better management tool or aid than data provided on an absorption-costing basis. Marginal-costing data is useful in decision making in the short run. It is especially useful in decision making involving special production runs when there is idle capacity. It is also useful in short-run profit planning and in analyzing cost-volume-profit relationship.

Marginal costing is not generally accepted for reporting to the public. It is not accepted by the AICPA or the IRS. Therefore, most firms using marginal costing in reporting to management must adjust their reports to the absorption basis when preparing reports for tax purposes or for public dissemination.

The marginal-cost concept is used in the income statement in Figure 16.3.

The three income statements (Figures 16.1, 16.2, and 16.3) are grouped together for easy comparison.

A. B. HOWARD INCORPORATED

INCOME STATEMENT
FOR THE YEAR ENDED DECEMBER 31, 1973

Gross sales			$800,000
Less: Sales returns and allowances		$ 40,000	
Sales discounts		10,000	50,000
Net sales			$750,000
Cost of goods sold			
Raw-material inventory, January 1, 1973		$ 20,000	
Purchases	$300,000		
Less: Discounts	10,000		
Net cost of purchases	$290,000		
Add: Freight-in	12,000		
Delivered cost of purchases		302,000	
Material available for use		$322,000	
Less: Raw-material inventory, December 31, 1973		42,000	
Material used		$280,000	
Direct labor		100,000	
Factory overhead		100,000	
Total manufacturing cost		$480,000	
Add: Work in process inventory, January 1, 1973		20,000	$500,000
Less: Work in process inventory, December 31, 1973			40,000
Cost of production			$460,000
Add: Inventory finished goods, January 1, 1973			15,000
Goods available for sale			$475,000
Less: Inventory finished goods, December 31, 1973			55,000
Cost of goods sold[a]			$420,000
Gross profit			$330,000

Operating Expenses			
Selling expenses			
Sales salaries and commissions	$ 10,000		
Advertising	1,000		
Miscellaneous selling expenses	4,000		
Total selling expenses		$ 15,000	
General and administrative expenses			
Officers' salaries	$ 40,000		
Officers' bonuses	20,000		
Taxes	10,000		
Depreciation—office equipment	30,000		
Bad debts	10,000		
Total general and administrative expenses		110,000	
Total operating expenses			$125,000
Operating income			$205,000
Financial Items			
Interest expense	$ 5,000		
Interest income	3,000		
Net financial expense			2,000
Net income before income taxes			$203,000
Income taxes			43,000
Net income before extraordinary items			$160,000
Extraordinary items			
Gain on sale of building	$ 50,000		
Less: Applicable income tax	12,000		38,000
Net income			$198,000

[a] A supporting schedule cost of goods sold could have been used and would have shortened the income statement.

Figure 16.1. Multiple-Step income statement

THE BALANCE SHEET

As mentioned in the introduction to this section (page 240), the balance sheet is a statement of the financial position of an accounting entity. It is for this reason that the balance sheet is also referred to as a *statement of financial position* or a *statement of financial condition*.

The AICPA has defined a balance sheet as "a tabular statement or summary of balances (debit and credit) carried forward after an actual or constructive closing of books of account kept according to principles of accounting."[2]

2. *Accounting Research and Terminology Bulletins,* Final Edition (1961), p. 12.

A. B. HOWARD INCORPORATED

INCOME STATEMENT
FOR THE YEAR ENDED DECEMBER 31, 1973

Revenues		
Net sales		$750,000
Interest income		3,000
Gain on sale of building[a]		50,000
Total revenue		$803,000
Expenses		
Net material cost	$280,000	
Labor	100,000	
Factory overhead	100,000	
Increase in work in process	(20,000)	
Increase in finished goods	(40,000)	
Sales salaries and commissions	10,000	
Advertising	1,000	
Miscellaneous selling expenses	4,000	
Officers' salaries	40,000	
Officers' bonuses	20,000	
Taxes	10,000	
Depreciation—office equipment	30,000	
Bad debts	10,000	
Interest expense	5,000	
Income taxes	55,000	
Total expenses		605,000
Net income		$198,000

[a] In order to comply with the dictates of the APB, the gain on sale of building and the tax on it should be presented in a separate final section, but such a presentation would violate the single-step concept.

Figure 16.2. Single-Step income statement

The balance sheet involves all the real or permanent accounts; whereas the income statement involves all the nominal or temporary accounts.

On page 240, it was stated that the balance sheet had lost first place in importance to the income statement. However, the balance sheet is still recognized as a very important document and source of valuable information. It is considered the second-most-important general-purpose accounting statement.

A. B. HOWARD INCORPORATED

INCOME STATEMENT
FOR THE YEAR ENDED DECEMBER 31, 1973

Gross sales			$800,000
Less: Sales returns and allowances		$ 40,000	
Sales discounts		10,000	50,000
Net sales			$750,000
Marginal cost of goods sold			
Raw material inventory, January 1, 1973		$ 20,000	
Purchases	$300,000		
Less: Discounts	10,000		
Net cost of purchases	$290,000		
Add: Freight-in	12,000		
Delivered cost of purchases		302,000	
Material available for use		$322,000	
Less: Raw material inventory, December 31, 1973		42,000	
Material used		$280,000	
Labor		100,000	
Variable factory overhead		60,000	
Total marginal manufacturing costs		$440,000	
Add: Work in process inventory, January 1, 1973[a]		$ 17,000	
			$457,000
Less: Work in process inventory, December 31, 1973[a]			33,000
Marginal cost of production			$424,000
Add: Finished goods inventory, January 1, 1973[a]			12,500
Goods available for sale			$436,500
Less: Finished goods inventory, December 31, 1973[a]			45,000
Marginal cost of goods sold			$391,500
Manufacturing (gross) margin[b]			$358,500
Marginal (variable) operating expenses			
Sales commissions		$ 4,000	
Miscellaneous selling expenses		2,000	
Officers' bonuses		20,000	
Bad debts		10,000	
Total marginal operating expenses			$ 36,000

Operating margin		$322,500
Period costs		
Fixed factory overhead	$ 40,000	
Sales salaries	6,000	
Advertising	1,000	
Miscellaneous selling expenses	2,000	
Officers' salaries	40,000	
Taxes	10,000	
Depreciation—office equipment	30,000	
Total period costs		129,000
Operating profit		$193,500
Financial items		
Interest expense	$ 5,000	
Interest income	3,000	
Net financial expense		2,000
Net income before income taxes		$191,500
Income taxes		43,000
Net income before extraordinary items		$148,500
Extraordinary items		
Gain on sale of building	$ 50,000	
Less: Applicable income tax	12,000	38,000
Net income		$186,500

[a] Inventories at marginal cost.

[b] A distinction should be drawn between gross profit and gross margin. *Gross profit* is the difference between sales and total cost of goods sold; *gross margin* is the difference between sales and the marginal cost of goods sold.

Figure 16.3. Income statement based on marginal-cost concept

Objectives of the Balance Sheet. The objectives of the balance sheet are to indicate a firm's financial position as of a moment in time and to substantiate this position by showing the composition of, and the relationship between, the assets, the liabilities, and the owners' equity. Each balance sheet serves as a connecting link between two consecutive income statements.

The major objective of a balance sheet is to provide pertinent data, compiled according to generally accepted accounting principles, that may be used in making rational economic and managerial decisions.

ACCOUNTING ASSUMPTIONS. Accounting assumptions are necessary in the proper preparation and intelligent reading of a balance sheet. Some of the more fundamental ones are described in the following paragraphs.

Going-Concern Concept. It is assumed, in the absence of strong indications to the contrary, that a firm will continue to operate in the future, much as it has in the past; therefore, the firm's assets will be reported at book values, rather than at estimated realizable values as is done in statements of realization and liquidation for firms in receivership.

Economic- (Business-) Entity Concept. It is believed that in many cases, more effective reporting can be accomplished if the reports are based on an operating or business unit rather than on a legal-entity concept. Thus, the assumption is that the reports are prepared for the operating or business unit rather than for a legal unit, for example, a subsidiary or a holding company or for a division of a large company.

Stable-Money Assumption. Financial reports are prepared in monetary terms without giving effect to the changes in purchasing power of the monetary unit. For example, the cost of a plant purchased in the United States in 1930 is expressed in dollars of apparently the same value as dollars used in purchasing a plant in 1970. No adjustment is made for changes in the purchasing power of the dollar.

Cost Assumption. Accountants generally hold that cost is the most objective way of valuing assets (even if in some cases it is not the best) and should be used as a basis of valuation. In the case of fixed assets, value is cost less accumulated depreciation. In the case of inventories, the value is established at cost or sometimes modified to the lower of cost or market. In any event, cost is basic to the valuation procedures.

BALANCE-SHEET LIMITATIONS. A major limitation of the balance sheet is the close adherence in asset valuations to the cost principle rather than to market value or to the discounted-present-value-of-the-future-earnings method. A valuation developed by the discounted-present-value method is theoretically sound but practically very weak because it is extremely difficult to determine realistically the future actual earnings of an asset. Some valuable items of a firm are not reducible to dollar-and-cents accounting transactions and therefore are not included among the

A. B. HOWARD INCORPORATED

Balance Sheet
As of December 31, 1973

ASSETS

Current assets			
Cash		$ 10,000	
Marketable securities at cost (market value, $32,150)		30,000	
Accounts receivable	$ 40,000		
Less: Allowance for uncollectible accounts	1,000	39,000	
Notes receivable	$ 15,000		
Accrued interest on notes receivable	200	15,200	
Inventories—at lower of cost or market		100,000	
Prepaid insurance		1,500	
Supplies		300	
Total current assets		$ 196,000	
Long-term investments		50,000	
Miscellaneous stock at cost (market value $53,000)			

LIABILITIES AND STOCKHOLDERS' EQUITY

LIABILITIES

Current liabilities			
Accounts payable		$ 12,000	
Notes payable			$ 28,000
Accrued interest on notes payable		200	12,200
Current installment of mortgages payable			20,000
Estimated income taxes payable			10,000
Accrued salaries and wages			5,000
Total current liabilities			$ 75,200
Long-term liabilities			
Mortgage payable—less current installment		$200,000	
Bonds payable	$500,000		
Less: Unamortized discount	10,000	490,000	
Total long-term liabilities			690,000
Total liabilities			$ 765,200

Tangible noncurrent assets

Land		$ 60,000
Building	$600,000	
Less: Accumulated depreciation	50,000	550,000
Equipment	$800,000	
Less: Accumulated depreciation	75,000	725,000
Total tangible noncurrent assets		1,335,000

Intangible noncurrent assets

Goodwill at cost	$ 1,000	
Patents at amortized cost	15,250	
Total intangible noncurrent assets		16,250
Total assets		$1,597,250

STOCKHOLDERS' EQUITY

Contributed capital		
Common Stock		
Authorized 5,000 shares, par $100		
Issued 4,000 shares	$400,000	
Additional contributed capital		
Premium on common stock	40,000	
Total contributed capital		$440,000
Retained earnings		
Appropriated for plant expansion	$100,000	
Unappropriated	292,050	
Total retained earnings		392,050
Total stockholders' equity		832,050
Total liabilities and stockholders' equity		$1,597,250

Figure 16.4

valued assets reported on the balance sheet. Some examples are developed goodwill and momentum of start (the economic advantage that may accrue to the firm that first develops a new process or product) in a developing industry.

Therefore, many decisions must be based on estimates of future events and values.

Format of the Balance Sheet. Regardless of the overall structure of the balance sheet, the internal structure most often complies with the following formula:

$$\text{Assets} = \text{liabilities} + \text{owner(s)' equity}$$

Historically, the assets were listed on the left-hand side of the statement, and the liabilities plus the proprietary interest were listed on the right-hand side. The total amount listed on each side equaled that on the other; hence, the name *balance sheet*. This very popular type of balance sheet is illustrated in Figure 16.4. This left-side–right-side presentation is referred to as an *account form* because it resembles in form a ledger T account.

When the data are presented, not horizontally or side by side as in the T account, but vertically (i.e., the assets listed first and liabilities and owner(s)' equity listed below them), the resulting balance sheet is said to be in *report form*.

Because of the increasing emphasis on net working capital, some accounting experts have modified the accounting formula as follows:

$$\text{Current assets} - \text{current liabilities} + \text{other assets} - \text{long-term}$$
$$\text{liabilities} = \text{owner(s)' equity}$$

A report-form balance sheet, now more appropriately referred to as a *statement of financial position*, giving effect to this modification is shown in Figure 16.5.

Balance-Sheet Classifications. Regardless of the format used in the preparation of a balance sheet, appropriate and careful classification of assets, liabilities, and owner(s)' equity is necessary. For detailed discussions of the specific accounts, the reader should refer to the appropriate chapters of this text. It is sufficient here to list only the major groupings of the accounts.

BALANCE SHEET
As of December 31, 1973

INVESTMENT IN NET ASSETS

Current assets		
Cash		$ 10,000
Marketable securities at cost (market value $32,150)		30,000
Accounts receivable	$40,000	
Less: Allowance for uncollectable accounts	1,000	39,000
Notes receivable	$ 15,000	
Accrued interest on notes receivable	200	15,200
Inventories—at lower of cost or market		100,000
Prepaid insurance		1,500
Supplies		300
Total current assets		$ 196,000
Less: Current liabilities		
Accounts payable	$ 28,000	
Notes payable	$ 12,000	
Accrued interest on notes payable	200	12,200
Current installment of mortgage payable	20,000	
Estimated income taxes payable	10,000	
Accrued salaries and wages	5,000	
Total current liabilities		75,200
Net working capital		$ 120,800
Add: Other assets		
Miscellaneous stock at cost (market value $53,000)		50,000
Land		60,000
Buildings	$600,000	
Less: Accumulated depreciation	50,000	550,000
Equipment	$800,000	
Less: Accumulated depreciation	75,000	725,000
Goodwill at cost		1,000
Patents at amortized cost		15,250
Net working capital plus other assets		$1,522,050
Less: Long-term liabilities		
Mortgage payable—less current installment	$200,000	
Bonds payable	$500,000	
Less: Unamortized discount	10,000	490,000
Total long-term liabilities		690,000
Net capital invested		$ 832,050

EQUITY INVESTMENT

Contributed capital		
Common stock		
Authorized 5,000 shares, par $100		
Issued 4,000 shares		$ 400,000
Additional contributed capital		
Premium on common stock		40,000
Total contributed capital		$ 440,000
Retained earnings		
Appropriated for plant expansion	$100,000	
Unappropriated	292,050	
Total retained earnings		392,050
Total equity investment		$ 832,050

Figure 16.5. Report form balance sheet

The following grouping is typical.

Assets	*Liabilities*
Current assets	Current liabilities
Long-term investments	Long-term liabilities
Land	
Plant and equipment	*Stockholders' Equity*
Deferred charges	Capital stock
	Additional contributed capital
	Retained earnings
	Treasury stock (contra)

THE RETAINED EARNINGS STATEMENT

Retained earnings of a firm is that part of its accumulated net income that has been neither distributed to the owners nor capitalized. In a corporation, the distribution would be in the form of dividends, and the capitalization would result from a transfer from retained earnings to a capital stock account and/or to an additional contributed capital account. Such capitalizations usually result from stock dividends. The statement of retained earnings may be informally incorporated into the balance sheet as a part of the owner(s)' equity section or combined with the income statement as an addendum thereto, or it may take the form of a separate formal statement.

Objectives of the Retained Earnings Statement. The objectives of the retained earnings statement are to explain any changes in retained earnings during the period covered, normally a year, and to establish the ending balance of retained earnings.

Adjustments for Prior Periods. Adjustments for prior periods "which relate directly to the operations of a specific prior period or periods, which are material . . . should in single period statements be reflected as adjustments of the opening balance of retained earnings."[3]

Separate Retained Earnings Statement. A separate retained earnings statement may take the formalized format shown in Figure 16.6.

A. B. HOWARD INCORPORATED

RETAINED EARNINGS STATEMENT
FOR THE YEAR ENDED DECEMBER 31, 1973

	Appropriated for Building Expenses	Unappropriated	Total
Balance, January 1, 1973	$ 50,000	$194,050	$244,050
Less: Additional income tax for 1970		10,000	10,000
Adjusted balances	$ 50,000	$184,050	$234,050
Net income	50,000	148,000	198,000
Total	$100,000	$332,050	$432,050
Less: Dividends		40,000	40,000
Retained earnings, December 31, 1973	$100,000	$292,050	$392,050

Figure 16.6

Combined Statement of Income and Retained Earnings. A combined income and retained earnings statement is often employed when only a few changes are made in retained earnings during the year. Such a combined statement is also favored by those who believe that the retained earnings statement is not so frequently read as the income statement is and that therefore all equity changes should be shown on the income statement.

The statement shown in Figure 16.7 is a condensation of the

3. *Accounting Principles Board Opinion* No. 9 (1966), p. 113.

income statement in Figure 16.1 and the retained earnings statement in Figure 16.6:

A. B. HOWARD INCORPORATED

STATEMENT OF INCOME AND RETAINED EARNINGS
FOR THE YEAR ENDED DECEMBER 31, 1973

Net sales	$750,000
Cost of goods sold	420,000
Gross profit	$330,000
Operating expenses	125,000
Operating income	$205,000
Net financial expense	2,000
Net income before income taxes	$203,000
Income taxes	43,000
Net income before extraordinary items	$160,000
Gain from extraordinary items	38,000
Net income	$198,000
Retained earnings, January 1, 1973	$244,050
Less: Additional income taxes for 1970	10,000
Adjusted retained earnings	$234,050
Net income and adjusted retained earnings	$432,050
Less: Dividends	40,000
Total retained earnings, December 31, 1973	$392,050
Appropriated retained earnings, January 1, 1973	$ 50,000
Appropriated during 1973	50,000
Total appropriated retained earnings, December 31, 1973	$100,000
Balance: Unappropriated earnings	292,050
Total retained earnings, December 31, 1973	$392,050

Figure 16.7

CHAPTER 17

Statement of Changes in Financial Position

A statement of changes in financial position, also referred to as a *funds statement,* is an operative report of the inflows and outflows of funds for a specific firm for a given period of time.

This statement was formerly most commonly referred to as a *statement of source and application of funds,* but recently the AICPA has recommended that the title of such a statement be *statement of changes in financial position.*[1] Other names applied to such statements are *source and use of funds, source and disposition of working capital, changes in working capital, funds statement,* and in certain limited cases, *cash flows.*

NATURE AND PURPOSE OF FUNDS STATEMENTS

In accounting, primary emphasis has been placed on the measurement of economic data. But a very important function of accounting is the interpretation and communication of such data. When business units were smaller and less complex than they are today, and when the operative rules of the business sector were less involved, the income statement and the balance sheet were considered adequate for purposes of information. Today, however, many accountants believe that a funds statement is a necessary adjunct to the income statement and the balance sheet.

The purpose of a statement of changes in financial position is to provide an analysis and report of all funds received by the firm during the period, together with an analytical summarization of the use of such funds by the firm.

1. "Reporting Changes in Financial Position," *Opinion of the Accounting Principles Board,* No. 19 (1971), p. 374.

The information provided by such a funds statement is clearly divisible into the following four parts:

1. *Resources (funds) provided by operations.* Net profit is not the same as funds provided by operations because net profit is affected by various transactions, such as depreciation, that neither provide funds nor require the application of funds.

2. *Resources (funds) provided by other than operations.* Depreciation is a nonfund item in that no funds are currently required to offset the depreciation expense. However, when the amount of funds provided by operations are considered, depreciation must be regarded as an indirect source of funds because the net-income figure has been reduced by the recorded amount of depreciation.

Funds may also be provided by long-term borrowing, the sale of bonds (a form of borrowing), the receipt of equity capital, and the sale of noncurrent assets.

3. *Funds (used) applied.* Funds may be used to acquire noncurrent assets, to pay off noncurrent liabilities, to return funds to owners, or to increase net working capital.

4. *Effect of certain transactions on net working capital.* Net working capital may be increased either by increasing current assets or by decreasing current liabilities.

In transactions such as the following, net working capital will not change, and therefore funds will be neither provided nor applied:

a. A simultaneous equal increase or decrease in current assets and current liabilities will not affect net working capital. The payment of a current liability with cash is an example.

b. An increase in one current asset that is offset exactly by a decrease of the same amount in another current asset or an increase in a current liability that is offset exactly by a decrease in another current liability will not change net working capital. The giving of a note payable in payment of an account payable is an example.

A statement of changes in financial position is very adaptable. It is useful in planning and controlling operations, as well as in reporting to the public. As indicated in the next section, its predetermined primary use may have a bearing on which of several funds concepts will be applied in the preparation of the statement.

Four Types of Statements of Changes in Financial Position. The term *fund* is rather ambiguous because it means different things at different times or in different situations. According to a common definition, a fund is a sum of money or convertible wealth set aside or available for some particular use or purpose. Such a broad definition of funds makes it possible to prepare statements of changes in financial position based on any one of several funds concepts ranging from the very broad one that is general enough to include all assets as funds to the very narrow concept that limits funds to cash.

FUNDS DEFINED AS ALL (TOTAL) ASSETS. Under this concept, funds are considered to include both current and noncurrent assets. Therefore, this definition is also referred to as the *total-financial-resources concept*. This is the broadest-possible concept of funds.

FUNDS DEFINED AS NET CURRENT ASSETS. Under this concept, funds are considered to be current assets minus current liabilities. This has been one of the most frequently used concepts of funds.

FUNDS DEFINED AS NET QUICK ASSETS. When funds are considered to be *net quick assets*, they are defined as cash, receivables, and marketable securities, less current liabilities. This concept of funds is slightly broader than the cash concept.

FUNDS DEFINED AS CASH. When funds are considered to be cash, only inflows and outflows of cash and the resulting balance are included in the concept. This is the most limited concept of funds. When a funds statement is prepared according to this concept, it is appropriate to refer to it as a *cash-flow statement*.

Use of Statements of Changes in Financial Position. Such statements (by various names) have long been used by accountants as a means of providing useful information for both internal and external consumption. However, since the publication of APB Opinion No. 3 in 1963, the inclusion of some type of funds statement with the published conventional statements has greatly increased. Information about the source of funds generated by a firm, as well as information concerning the use made of such funds, may be very helpful in making both operating decisions and financial decisions.

USE OF THE FUNDS STATEMENT AS AN OPERATING STATEMENT. The funds statement is an operative report on the financial activities of the firm, just as the income statement is an operative report on the production or service activities of the firm. Funds statements are especially useful in establishing a relationship between changes in working capital and net income. When the statement includes all changes in financial position as recommended by APB Opinion No. 19, it provides evidence of how funds were acquired and how they were used. It reveals financial transactions not revealed by the income statement.

FUNDS-STATEMENT ANALYSIS FOR PLANNING AND DECISION MAKING. Funds statements are normally based on historical data. The analysis of these historical data is useful in developing an insight into possible current and future problems and their possible solutions. Many firms use the historical data as a basis for preparing projected future pro forma funds statements, which are used in forecasting the future needs for funds and the manner of their provision.

PREPARATION OF STATEMENTS OF CHANGES IN FINANCIAL POSITION

There is no standardized format for a funds statement. The material for funds statements is derived largely from comparative balance sheets, but it is also derived from the income statement and the retained earnings statement.

Cash-flow statements indicate cash provided and cash used. For other funds statements, the material, after some eliminations, combinations, and reclassifications of data, may be separated into two major groups and one minor group:

1. Sources (provision) of funds
2. Application (uses) of funds
3. Change (increase or decrease) in net working capital (or net quick assets)

Funds may be generated from five sources:

1. Sale of noncurrent assets
2. Incurrence of long-term debt
3. Increase in owner's equity by contributions
4. Income from operations
5. Figuratively, decrease in working capital

All fund applications may be classified in one of five categories:

1. Purchase of noncurrent assets
2. Decrease in long-term debt
3. Capital distributions
4. Loss from operations
5. Figuratively, increase in working capital

Funds Regarded as Total Assets. When the term *funds* is viewed as applicable to total (all) assets, consideration is given to all exchanges of assets, regardless of whether or not actual cash inflows or outflows occurred. Under this broadest definition of the term, if one asset is traded for another and no "boot" is given or received, it is viewed as an inflow of cash offset by an equal outflow of cash.

Work sheets are not necessary for the preparation of funds statements, but they may prove helpful in complicated cases. Therefore, a work sheet will be used only in the first of the following four examples. Each of the four solutions will be based on applicable data given in the first example.

As has been stated, the major source of information for the preparation of a funds statement is the comparative balance sheets (i.e., balance sheets as of the beginning and the end of the period involved), followed by an income statement and retained earnings statement for the period. In some cases, an analysis of certain ledger accounts might be helpful.

As a basis for the preparation of funds statements using each of the four methods, a comparative balance sheet (Figure 17.1) and a combined income statement and retained earning statement (Figure 17.2) for the Browning Company are illustrated. An analysis of various accounts provided the following data: Equipment that cost $10,000 but had a book value of $6,000 was sold for $7,000 cash. Additional equipment was bought for $40,000 cash. The $100,000 increase in land value resulted from

THE BROWNING

COMPARATIVE
AS OF DECEMBER

	December 31 1972	December 31 1973	Increase (Decrease)
ASSETS			
Current assets			
Cash	$ 80,000	$ 60,000	$(20,000)
Marketable securities	50,000	40,000	(10,000)
Accounts receivable	90,000	100,000	10,000
Inventories	150,000	200,000	50,000
Prepaid expenses	10,000	10,000	0
Total current assets	$380,000	$410,000	$ 30,000
Noncurrent assets			
Land	$100,000	$200,000	$100,000
Buildings	$200,000	$300,000	$100,000
Less: Accumulated depreciation	(50,000)	(70,000)	(20,000)
	$150,000	$230,000	$ 80,000
Equipment	$100,000	$130,000	$ 30,000
Less: Accumulated depreciation	(20,000)	(30,000)	(10,000)
	$ 80,000	$100,000	$ 20,000
Total noncurrent assets	$330,000	$530,000	$200,000
Total assets	$710,000	$940,000	$230,000

a cash payment of $50,000 and the issuance of $50,000 of stock.

This information served as the basis for the preparation of the working papers (Figure 17.3), which served in turn as the basis for the preparation of the statement of changes in financial position (Figure 17.4).

When working papers are prepared, the following steps should be taken:

1. The balances from the balance sheet as of the start of the period should be recorded in one column, followed in the next column to the right by the balances from the balance sheet as of the end of the period. For convenience, it is advisable to list all debit balances first and then to list all credit balances.

2. In the second pair of columns, the net change in each account should be recorded as a debit or credit, as appropriate.

COMPANY

BALANCE SHEET
31, 1972 AND 1973

| | | LIABILITIES AND OWNERS' EQUITY | | |
| | | LIABILITIES | | |
	December 31 1972	December 31 1973	Increase (Decrease)
Current liabilities			
Accounts payable	$ 70,000	$120,000	$ 50,000
Notes payable	60,000	50,000	(10,000)
Accrued expenses	10,000	20,000	10,000
Accrued income taxes	10,000	10,000	0
Total current liabilities	$150,000	$200,000	$ 50,000
Long-term liabilities			
Mortgage payable	$200,000	$300,000	$100,000
Total liabilities	$350,000	$500,000	$150,000
	OWNERS' EQUITY		
Common stock	$300,000	$350,000	$ 50,000[a]
Retained earnings	60,000	90,000	30,000
Total owners' equity	$360,000	$440,000	$ 80,000
Total liabilities and owners' equity	$710,000	$940,000	$230,000

[a] Land valued at $50,000 was acquired for stock with a par value of $50,000. The balance was purchased for cash.

Figure 17.1

3. The net change of each current asset account and each current liability account should be carried over without adjustment to the working capital columns.

4. The noncurrent accounts must be examined for possible elimination or adjustment before being extended to the funds columns. The account balances not needing adjustment may be carried over directly to the funds columns, or (as shown in Figure 17.3) eliminations of the balances may be made so that all funds balances are grouped together according to whether they are funds provided or funds applied.

5. Each of the last two pairs of columns should be balanced by adding to the appropriate column of each pair the change in working capital.

THE BROWNING COMPANY

STATEMENT OF INCOME AND RETAINED EARNINGS
FOR THE YEAR ENDED DECEMBER 31, 1973

Sales		$500,000
Cost of goods sold		315,000
Gross profit		$185,000
Operating expenses		
Selling expenses	$30,000	
General expenses	20,000	
Total operating expenses		50,000
Net operating profit		$135,000
Financial expenses		
Interest expense		16,000
Net profit before extraordinary profit		$119,000
Extraordinary profit		
Gain on sale of equipment		1,000
Net profit before income taxes		$120,000
Income taxes		60,000
Net profit after income taxes		$ 60,000
Retained earnings, January 1, 1973		60,000
Total		$120,000
Less: Dividends		30,000
Retained earnings, December 31, 1973		$ 90,000

Figure 17.2

The net-change amount of each account is accepted without adjustment unless a review of the ledger accounts indicates the need for adjustment. For example, in this case, additional data show the need for adjustments to the equipment and land accounts. The equipment account shows a net increase of $30,000; however, that net increase is the result of a decrease of $10,000 and an increase of $40,000. Also, there is a net increase in the allowance for depreciation of equipment of $10,000; but if there was a write-off of $4,000 when the old equipment was sold, there must have been a total increase for the year of $14,000, as well as a profit of $1,000 from the sale. (See adjustments *a, b,* and *e.*)

In the case of the land, the increase of $100,000 was the result of a cash payment of $50,000 and the issuance of $50,000 worth of stock. (See adjustments *c* and *d.*) Note that this results in showing a sale of stock of $50,000 and a land purchase of $100,000. Compare Figures 17.4 and 17.5 in this respect.

The remaining balances may now be transferred without further adjustment to funds provided or funds applied groups.

The amounts listed under funds provided are then extended to the funds provided column, and the amounts listed as funds applied are extended to the funds applied column.

Next the four columns at the right should be totaled. If the work sheet is correct to this point, the difference between the two funds columns and the difference between the two working capital columns will be equal in amount but opposite in character. This difference represents the change in working capital.

Once the work sheet (Figure 17.3) is completed, the statement of changes in financial position (Figure 17.4) may be prepared directly from the completed work sheet.

In Figure 17.4 the schedule of changes in working capital shows the beginning and ending balance in each current asset and each current liability account, as well as the increase or decrease in each account. Some accountants schedule only the increases or decreases of each account, which is adequate.

Funds Regarded as Net Working Capital. The essential difference between the total-assets concept applied in Figure 17.4 and the net-working-capital concept used in Figure 17.5 is the treatment accorded the $50,000 worth of stock exchanged for $50,000 worth of land. Under the total-assets concept, the fact that the stock was directly exchanged for the land is immaterial. It is, admittedly, a nonfund transaction (i.e., no actual cash was exchanged); however, under the total-assets concept, the transaction is treated as if the stock were sold for cash and then that cash used to buy the land. Because the working capital is not affected by such nonfund transactions, they are omitted from the statement. A work sheet similar to Figure 17.3 could have been prepared, but as mentioned on page 265, it was not necessary.

Funds Regarded as Net Quick Assets. The essential difference between the net-working-capital concept applied in Figure 17.5 and the net-quick-assets concept used in Figure 17.6 is the limitation on the number of accounts included in the "current schedule" under the net-quick-assets concept as compared with the number included under the net-working-capital concept.

Under the net-quick-assets concept, the changes in inventories

THE BROWNING COMPANY

Statement of Changes in Financial Position Working Papers
For the Year Ended December 31, 1973

	December 31, 1972	December 31, 1973	Net Change Dr.	Net Change Cr.	Adjustments and Eliminations Dr.	Adjustments and Eliminations Cr.	Funds Applied Dr.	Funds Provided Cr.	Working Capital Increase Dr.	Working Capital Decrease Cr.
DEBIT BALANCES										
Cash	$ 80,000	$ 60,000		$ 20,000						$20,000
Marketable securities	50,000	40,000		10,000						10,000
Accounts receivable	90,000	100,000	$ 10,000						$10,000	
Inventories	150,000	200,000	50,000						50,000	
Prepaid expenses	10,000	10,000								
Land	100,000	200,000	100,000			[c]$100,000				
Buildings	200,000	300,000	100,000			[h] 100,000				
Equipment	100,000	130,000	30,000		[a]$ 10,000	[b] 40,000				
	$780,000	$1,040,000								
CREDIT BALANCES										
Accumulated depreciation—building	$ 50,000	$ 70,000		20,000	[e] 20,000					
Accumulated depreciation—equipment	20,000	30,000		10,000	[e] 14,000	[a] 4,000				
Accounts payable	70,000	120,000		50,000						50,000
Notes payable	60,000	50,000	10,000						10,000	
Accrued expenses	10,000	20,000		10,000						10,000
Accrued income taxes	10,000	10,000								
Mortgage payable	200,000	300,000		100,000	[f] 100,000					
Common stock	300,000	350,000		50,000	[d] 50,000					
Retained earnings	60,000	90,000		30,000	[g] 60,000	[i] 30,000				
	$780,000	$1,040,000	$300,000	$300,000						

DEBIT BALANCES	December 31, 1972	December 31, 1973	Net Change Dr.	Net Change Cr.	Adjustments and Eliminations Dr.	Adjustments and Eliminations Cr.	Funds Applied Dr.	Funds Provided Cr.	Working Capital Increase Dr.	Working Capital Decrease Cr.
Funds provided										
Profit on operations from income statement						g $ 60,000		$ 60,000		
Depreciation						e 34,000		34,000		
Mortgage						f 100,000		100,000		
Sale of equipment						a 7,000		7,000		
Less: Gain on sale of equipment					a $ 1,000		$ 1,000			
Stock exchanged for land						d 50,000		50,000		
Funds applied										
Purchase of land—cash					c 50,000		50,000			
Purchase of land—stock					c 50,000		50,000			
Purchase of building					h 100,000		100,000			
Purchase of equipment					b 40,000		40,000			
Dividends					i 30,000		30,000			
Totals					$525,000	$525,000	$271,000	$251,000	$70,000	$90,000
Decrease in net working capital								20,000	20,000	
							$271,000	$271,000	$90,000	$90,000

Figure 17.3

THE BROWNING COMPANY

STATEMENT OF CHANGES IN FINANCIAL POSITION
FOR THE YEAR ENDED DECEMBER 31, 1973

Source of funds			
Mortgage borrowing			$100,000
Issuance of stock			50,000
Sale of equipment			7,000
			$157,000
Operations			
Profit per income statement	$60,000		
Less: Gain on equipment sale	1,000	$59,000	
Depreciation		34,000	93,000
			$250,000
Decrease in working capital (see Schedule A)			20,000
Total funds provided			$270,000
Application of funds			
Purchase of land—cash			$ 50,000
Purchase of land—stock			50,000
Purchase of building			100,000
Purchase of equipment			40,000
Dividends			30,000
Total funds applied			$270,000

SCHEDULE A

SCHEDULE OF CHANGES IN WORKING CAPITAL

	December 31, 1972	December 31, 1973	Changes Increase	Decrease
Current assets				
Cash	$ 80,000	$ 60,000		$20,000
Marketable securities	50,000	40,000		10,000
Accounts receivable	90,000	100,000	$10,000	
Inventories	150,000	200,000	50,000	
Prepaid expenses	10,000	10,000		
Total current assets	$380,000	$410,000		
Current liabilities				
Accounts payable	$ 70,000	$120,000		50,000
Notes payable	60,000	50,000	10,000	
Accrued expenses	10,000	20,000		10,000
Accrued income taxes	10,000	10,000		
Total current liabilities	$150,000	$200,000		
Net working capital	$230,000	$210,000		
			$70,000	$90,000
Decrease in net working capital		20,000	20,000	
	$230,000	$230,000	$90,000	$90,000

Figure 17.4. Funds regarded as total assets

THE BROWNING COMPANY

STATEMENT OF CHANGES IN FINANCIAL POSITION
FOR THE YEAR ENDED DECEMBER 31, 1973

Source of funds			
Mortgage borrowing		$100,000	
Sale of equipment		7,000	$107,000
Operations			
Profit per income statement	$60,000		
Less: Gain on sale of equipment	1,000	$ 59,000	
Depreciation		34,000	93,000
			$200,000
Application of funds			
Purchase land—cash		$ 50,000	
Purchase building		100,000	
Purchase equipment		40,000	
Dividends		30,000	220,000
Decrease in net working capital (see			
Schedule A)			$ 20,000

SCHEDULE A

SCHEDULE OF CHANGES IN WORKING CAPITAL

	December 31, 1972	December 31, 1973	Changes Increase	Changes Decrease
Current assets				
Cash	$ 80,000	$ 60,000		$20,000
Marketable securities	50,000	40,000		10,000
Accounts receivable	90,000	100,000	$10,000	
Inventories	150,000	200,000	50,000	
Prepaid expenses	10,000	10,000		
Total current assets	$380,000	$410,000		
Current liabilities				
Accounts payable	$ 70,000	$120,000		50,000
Notes payable	60,000	50,000	10,000	
Accrued expenses	10,000	20,000		10,000
Accrued income taxes	10,000	10,000		
Total current liabilities	$150,000	$200,000		
Net working capital	$230,000	$210,000		
			$70,000	$90,000
Decrease in net working capital		20,000	20,000	
	$230,000	$230,000	$90,000	$90,000

Figure 17.5. Funds regarded as net working capital

THE BROWNING COMPANY

STATEMENT OF CHANGES IN FINANCIAL POSITION
FOR THE YEAR ENDED DECEMBER 31, 1973

Quick assets were provided by			
Mortgage borrowing		$100,000	
Sale of equipment		7,000	$107,000
Operations			
Profit per income statement	$60,000		
Less: Gain on equipment sale	1,000	$ 59,000	
Depreciation		34,000	
		$ 93,000	
Deduct: Increase in inventories		50,000	43,000
			$150,000
Quick assets were applied to			
Purchase land		$ 50,000	
Purchase buildings		100,000	
Purchase equipment		40,000	
Dividends		30,000	220,000
Decrease in quick assets (see Schedule A)			$ 70,000

SCHEDULE A

SCHEDULE OF CHANGES OF QUICK ASSETS

Quick Assets	December 31, 1972	December 31, 1973	Changes	
			Increase	Decrease
Cash	$ 80,000	$ 60,000		$20,000
Marketable securities	50,000	40,000		10,000
Accounts receivable	90,000	100,000	$10,000	
Total quick assets	$220,000	$200,000		
Current liabilities				
Accounts payable	$ 70,000	$120,000		50,000
Notes payable	60,000	50,000	10,000	
Accrued expenses	10,000	20,000		10,000
Accrued income taxes	10,000	10,000		
Total current liabilities	$150,000	$200,000		
Net quick assets	$ 70,000	0		
			$20,000	$90,000
Decrease in quick assets			70,000	
			$90,000	$90,000

Figure 17.6. Funds regarded as net quick assets

THE BROWNING COMPANY

CASH FLOW STATEMENT
FOR THE YEAR ENDED DECEMBER 31, 1973

Cash was provided by			
Mortgage borrowing			$100,000
Sale of equipment			7,000
			$107,000
Operations			
Add: Net profit per income statement	$60,000		
Less: Profit on equipment sale	1,000	$ 59,000	
Depreciation		34,000	
Decrease in marketable securities		10,000	
Increase in accounts payable		50,000	
Increase in accrued expenses		10,000	
		$163,000	
Deduct:			
Increase in accounts receivable	$10,000		
Increase in inventories	50,000		
Decrease in notes payable	10,000	70,000	
			93,000
Total cash provided			$200,000
Cash was applied to			
Purchase land		$ 50,000	
Purchase building		100,000	
Purchase equipment		40,000	
Pay dividends		30,000	
Total cash spent			220,000
Decrease in cash			$ 20,000

Figure 17.7

are removed from the schedule of changes and included directly as a positive or negative source of funds.

Funds Regarded as Cash. When funds are considered to be cash (see Figure 17.7), there is reason for not including such a statement in the same category as the three statements just discussed. This statement is in effect an analysis of the cash account. In order to facilitate this analysis, the income account, as well as other revenue and expense accounts, may be reviewed.

COMPARISON OF THE FOUR TYPES OF STATEMENTS OF CHANGES IN FINANCIAL POSITION

The funds statement based on the total-assets concept is most informative in terms of the general financial health of the firm because all transactions of a financial nature, even the nonfund transactions, are included. The net-working-capital form of funds statement and the net-quick-assets type emphasize the importance of adequate currently available assets. In these types of statements, transactions not affecting working capital or quick assets are excluded. Statements prepared along these lines are especially useful to management in the short run.

The cash-flow type of funds statement is of limited value for general use either by management or by creditors and investors in the long run. This type of statement emphasizes the inflows and outflows of cash rather than inflows and outflows of working capital. However, a statement prepared along these lines does have value in evaluating short-run financial policies and results.

CHAPTER 18

Analysis of Financial Statements

The primary function of the analysis of financial statements is to increase the reliability of predictions about a firm's future and thus to provide a better basis for planning and decision making. Historically, the major users of such data were credit grantors and equity investors. Recently, many other groups, including management, labor, the public, trade associations, and regulatory and other government agencies, have come to use and rely on such data.

Analyses of financial statements provide only a part, although an important part, of the data used in making predictions about the future and plans of a firm.

The discussion in this chapter is limited to objectively determinable data developed from financial statements and related records. A more comprehensive study of a firm's position and its future could include evaluations of the general economy, the industry, the firm's relative position within the industry, and even a subjective evaluation of the firm's management.

SOURCE OF DATA

Management is in a position to generate internally data useful to planning and decision making. Outsiders must rely mainly on the published reports of the company, regulatory bodies, and financial advisory services.

Published Reports. Published annual reports are a requirement of publicly held corporations. Many corporations issue quarterly as well as annual statements to their stockholders. Such reports usually are made available to the public.

Securities and Exchange Commission (SEC). The SEC requires all corporations coming under its jurisdiction to file with it periodically financial statements prepared in accordance with SEC-prescribed rules and following a standardized format. Copies of such statements are available to the public at a nominal cost. Because of their standardization, they are especially useful for comparative analyses.

Credit and Investment Services. Credit and investment services provide valuable financial information about business and financial organizations. Among the most widely used of such services are Moody's various investment manuals and Standard and Poors *Corporation Records.* Dun and Bradstreet, Inc., and Robert Morris Associates provide valuable information especially on medium- and small-size firms.

Internally Generated Data. Not all internally generated data are available to the public. For example, data are not usually issued to the public more frequently than quarterly, even though management may get monthly, weekly, or even daily reports. Much detailed information given to, and needed by, management is never made available to the public. For example, management may develop an average inventory based on monthly figures; whereas the public probably will have only year-end inventory figures to use in computing an average inventory.

USERS OF DATA

Accountants' reports constitute the raw material from which an understanding of a firm's financial position, plans, and operations evolve. The statements per se provide much basic information, but additional valuable relationships and activities may be highlighted by analytical studies.

Various sectors of the business community have need for different special-purpose information. Therefore, before an analytical study is made, the sector to which it is aimed should be determined and the analysis tailored to that group's needs. For example, for general public use, a general-purpose analysis will be best; whereas for credit purposes, a special-purpose analysis is appropriate. The various groups discussed in the following paragraphs will, of course, have many interests in common with other groups, even though they may have certain special interests.

Management. Management in an unrestricted sense covers all activities of a firm. In order to be effective, management is divided into specialized areas with special interests and needs. For an example, the analysis needed by the production vice-president is quite different from the analysis needed by the marketing vice-president, and they both need much more detailed and frequent analyses than the public needs.

Creditors. Creditors are especially interested in an analysis that will indicate the debt-paying ability of the firm. Short-term creditors are especially interested in the current position of the firm as indicated by the current ratio and similar data. Long-term creditors are interested in the firm's long-run ability to pay, as may be indicated by such data as operating ratios.

Investors. Investors are interested in any analysis that will tend to indicate the profitableness or growth potential of the firm as indicated, for example, by earnings per share, dividends per share, and price-earnings ratio.

Employee Groups. Employee groups are interested in earnings indicators such as rate of return on total investment, price-earnings ratio, and earnings per employee.

ANALYTIC STATEMENTS

An *analytic statement* is any statement that either reduces the basic statement to a more understandable form or provides for logical comparisons of basic statement data.

Comparative Statements. *Comparative statements* are statements for two or more dates or periods or for two or more firms in which similar data are so arranged that comparisons may be drawn.

Financial data take on new significance when they are compared with like data for other dates, periods, or even when compared with those of other firms.

The AICPA for many years has recommended the use of comparative financial statements, and the majority of firms are now issuing them.

Comparative statements may be arranged for horizontal comparisons or analysis, or they may be arranged for vertical comparison or analysis.

HORIZONTAL ANALYSIS. *Horizontal analysis* is the more popular type of comparative analyses. Under horizontal analysis, each element of data is compared with a similar element for another date, period, or firm. The changes may be indicated in aggregate amounts or as proportions. If more than two sets of data are involved, either a fixed or a moving base may be used in establishing the change; that is, the base may be the data of the first statement of the series, or it may be the data of the statement just preceding the statement under analysis.

The comparative income statements shown in Figures 18.1 and 18.2 illustrate horizontal analysis. Figure 18.3 is a comparative income statement illustrating vertical analysis.

VERTICAL ANALYSIS. *Vertical analysis* is the establishment of relationships of various elements of the data of the statement with a base figure that is arbitrarily set at 100 percent.

In the case of the analysis of income statements, net sales universally becomes the base figure and is said to be 100 percent. A percentage relationship is then established between sales and every other amount on the income statement by dividing each amount by the sales amount (see Figure 18.3).

In the case of the vertical analysis of a balance sheet, the total assets figure usually becomes the base figure of 100 percent. The relative size or importance of each item on the balance sheet is then developed by dividing each item by the total assets.

Often when very large amounts are involved, a better insight into their significance can be obtained by considering their relative size, rather than the absolute amount (see Figure 18.4).

Common-Size Statements. *Common-size statements* are statements reduced to a standard size (i.e., data expressed in proportionate parts of 100 percent are substituted for dollar amounts). They are almost always comparative in form because their greatest value is for comparative analysis. If the dollar amounts were excluded from the statements in Figures 18.3 and 18.4, they would be strictly common-size statements. The income statements (Figure 18.3) for the three years are reduced to a common size in the percent columns, in that sales for each year, regardless

THE ALPHA CORPORATION

Comparative Income Statement
For Years Ended December 31, 1971, 1972, and 1973

	1971	1972	1973	Increase (Decrease) 1971–1972	Increase (Decrease) 1972–1973	Increase (Decrease) 1971–1972	Increase (Decrease) 1971–1973
Sales	$500,000	$600,000	$800,000	$100,000	$200,000	$100,000	$300,000
Cost of goods sold	300,000	350,000	400,000	50,000	50,000	50,000	100,000
Gross profit	$200,000	$250,000	$400,000	$ 50,000	$150,000	$ 50,000	$200,000
Selling expenses	$ 50,000	$ 75,000	$ 90,000	$ 25,000	$ 15,000	$ 25,000	$ 40,000
Administrative expenses	40,000	30,000	50,000	(10,000)	20,000	(10,000)	10,000
Total operating expenses	$ 90,000	$105,000	$140,000	$ 15,000	$ 35,000	$ 15,000	$ 50,000
Net operating income	$110,000	$145,000	$260,000	$ 35,000	$115,000	$ 35,000	$150,000
Other expenses	10,000	15,000	12,000	5,000	(3,000)	5,000	2,000
Net income before income taxes	$100,000	$130,000	$248,000	$ 30,000	$118,000	$ 30,000	$148,000
Income taxes	50,000	60,000	70,000	10,000	10,000	10,000	20,000
Net income after taxes	$ 50,000	$ 70,000	$178,000	$ 20,000	$108,000	$ 20,000	$128,000

Figure 18.1. A comparative income statement showing aggregate changes computed both on a moving base and on a fixed base. Ordinarily, only one method of computing changes would be used. Here both are used for illustrative purposes.

THE ALPHA CORPORATION

Comparative Income Statement
For Years Ended December 31, 1971, 1972, and 1973

	1971	1972	1973	Percent Increase (Decrease) 1971-72	Percent Increase (Decrease) 1972-73	Percent Increase (Decrease) 1971-72	Percent Increase (Decrease) 1971-73
Sales	$500,000	$600,000	$800,000	20	33	20	60
Cost of goods sold	300,000	350,000	400,000	17	14	17	33
Gross profit	$200,000	$250,000	$400,000	25	60	25	100
Selling expenses	$ 50,000	$ 75,000	$ 90,000	50	20	50	80
Administrative expenses	40,000	30,000	50,000	(25)	67	(25)	25
Total operating expenses	$ 90,000	$105,000	$140,000	17	33	17	55
Net operating expenses	$110,000	$145,000	$260,000	32	79	32	136
Other expenses	10,000	15,000	12,000	50	(20)	50	20
Net income before income taxes	$100,000	$130,000	$248,000	30	91	30	148
Income taxes	50,000	60,000	70,000	20	17	20	40
Net income	$ 50,000	$ 70,000	$178,000	40	154	40	256

Figure 18.2. A comparative income statement showing changes as a percentage of the base. Horizontal analysis.

THE ALPHA CORPORATION

COMPARATIVE INCOME STATEMENT
FOR YEARS ENDED DECEMBER 31, 1971, 1972, AND 1973

	1971		1972		1973	
	Amount	Percent[a]	Amount	Percent[a]	Amount	Percent[a]
Sales	$500,000	100	$600,000	100	$800,000	100
Cost of goods sold	300,000	60	350,000	58	400,000	50
Gross profit	$200,000	40	$250,000	42	$400,000	50
Selling expenses	$ 50,000	10	$ 75,000	13	$ 90,000	11
Administrative expenses	40,000	8	30,000	5	50,000	6
Total operating expenses	$ 90,000	18	$105,000	18	$140,000	17
Net operating income	$110,000	22	$145,000	24	$260,000	33
Other expenses	10,000	2	15,000	2	12,000	2
Net income before income taxes	$100,000	20	$130,000	22	$248,000	31
Income taxes	50,000	10	60,000	10	70,000	9
Net income after taxes	$ 50,000	10	$ 70,000	12	$178,000	22

[a] Rounded to two decimal places.

Figure 18.3. A comparative income statement. Vertical analysis

THE ALPHA CORPORATION

Comparative Balance Sheet
As of December 31, 1972 and 1973

Assets	1972 Amount	1972 Percent	1973 Amount	1973 Percent
Current assets				
Cash	$ 10,000	05	$ 30,000	10
Accounts receivable—net	12,000	06	54,000	18
Inventories	24,000	12	30,000	10
Prepaid items	4,000	02	6,000	02
Total current assets	$ 50,000	25	$120,000	40
Noncurrent assets				
Plant and equipment—net	$100,000	50	$135,000	45
Investments	40,000	20	36,000	12
Patents and copyrights	10,000	05	9,000	03
Total noncurrent assets	$150,000	75	$180,000	60
Total assets	$200,000	100	$300,000	100

Liabilities and Owners' Equity	1972 Amount	1972 Percent	1973 Amount	1973 Percent
Liabilities				
Current liabilities				
Accounts payable	$ 30,000	15	$ 45,000	15
Notes payable	10,000	05	15,000	05
Total current liabilities	$ 40,000	20	$ 60,000	20
Long-term liabilities				
Mortgage payable	0	00	$ 60,000	20
Total liabilities	$ 40,000	20	$120,000	40
Owners' Equity				
Capital stock	$100,000	50	$150,000	50
Retained earnings	60,000	30	30,000	10
Total owners' equity	$160,000	80	$180,000	60
Total liabilities and owners' equity	$200,000	100	$300,000	100

Figure 18.4

of dollar amounts, are set at 100 percent and all other amounts are expressed in relation to the common 100 percent.

In the case of the balance sheet (Figure 18.4), total assets represents 100 percent, and also total liabilities plus owners' equity represents 100 percent, regardless of dollar amounts involved, and all other amounts are expressed as proportionate parts of 100 percent.

Common-size statements are useful in the analysis of data pertaining to the same firm for a series of dates or periods or in the analysis of data for different firms for the same date or period.

BREAK-EVEN POINT

The *break-even point* is the level at which the firm operates without sustaining a loss or making a profit. It is the sales level at which revenues and expenses are equal.

Break-even analysis is useful in providing management with answers involving *cost-volume-profit* relationships at levels of operations other than the break-even point.

In break-even-point analysis, it is assumed that fixed expenses will remain constant through the relevant range of operations and that variable expenses will vary in direct proportion to changes in operations.

Break-even analysis is useful in providing answers to questions such as the following:

1. How much must sales be in order to provide a specified profit?
2. How much must sales increase to justify an additional investment in fixed assets?
3. What effect will a change in volume have on profits?
4. What effect will a change in unit price have on profits?

Similar questions, of course, could be applied to the required *profit point* (see p. 288) since firms are in business to make a profit, not just to break even.

Break-Even Determination by Graphs. The break-even point and, hence, the amounts of loss or profit at various levels within the relevant range can be determined graphically by break-even charts. Such charts indicate clearly and simply not only the level at which the firm must operate to break even but also the amount of profit or loss that may accrue to the firm at any level of operations. (See Figure 18.5.) A word of caution is in order regarding the meaning of the term *break-even point*. The use of the word *point* is unfortunate because it gives a false impression of exactness. Because it is impossible to classify all expenses as definitely fixed or exactly directly variable, it would be better to think of the results of the arbitrary classifications and assumptions regarding the nature of the expenses and revenues as providing a basis

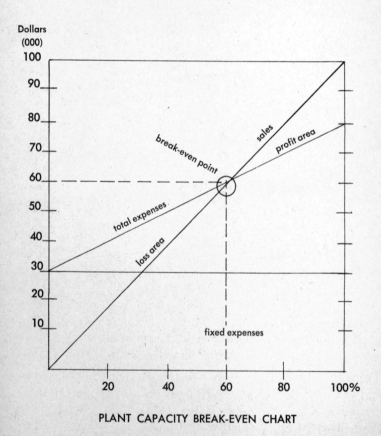

PLANT CAPACITY BREAK-EVEN CHART

Figure 18.5. Break-even chart

of establishing a break-even *area,* rather than a break-even point.

The break-even chart is prepared by using the first quadrant of an area graph, the lower left corner being zero. On the horizontal or *x* axis, plot the independent variable, the plant capacity. The capacity may be expressed as a percent of plant capacity (as in Figure 18.5) or in units of product. On the vertical or *y* axis, plot the dependent variable, both revenue and expenses, in dollars.

Any straight line may be extended in either direction if it is fitted to two points; however, the farther apart the points are, the smaller the error of fit in the plotted lines.

The sales line is plotted by drawing a line from the zero point to the point on the *y* axis corresponding to the total revenue at 100 percent of plant capacity. The fixed expenses are plotted as a horizontal line across the entire width of the graph at a level indicated by the amount of the fixed expenses ($30,000 in Figure 18.5). Variable expenses, of course, are zero at zero production. If they are equal to 50 percent of sales, then at $100,000 of sales, the variable expenses would amount to $50,000. Now if the variable costs are superimposed on the fixed costs, a total-cost line should be plotted from the $30,000 point at zero production to the $80,000 point at 100 percent of capacity production.

The break-even point or area is at the intersection of the sales line and the total-expense line. The vertical distance between these two lines at any place left of the break-even point represents the amount of loss; the vertical distance between these two lines to the right of the break-even point represents the amount of profit for that level of operations.

Break-Even-Point Determination by Formula. The break-even point can be calculated by the formula

$$B = \frac{F}{1 - (V/S)}$$

where B = break-even point

F = total fixed expenses

V = unit variable expenses

S = unit sales prices

Volume of Activity Required to Break Even. The volume of activity required to break even is that volume at which revenue from sales is exactly equal to the total of the variable expenses and the fixed expenses.

The sales dollar may be divided into two parts. The first part may be applied to the variable costs in making the dollar of sales. The second part is referred to as *marginal income*. Before the break-even point is reached, the marginal-income portion of the sales dollar is applied against the fixed expenses; and after the break-even point has been reached (the fixed costs covered), the marginal-income portion of each sales dollar is profit.

Consider the following example. Total fixed expenses of a plant with a capacity of 3,000 units amount to $4,000, and the unit variable expenses and unit sales price are $6 and $10, respectively.

$$B = \frac{\$4,000}{1 - \frac{6}{10}} = \frac{\$4,000}{\frac{4}{10}} = \$4,000 \times 1\frac{0}{4} = \$10,000$$

PROOF

Sales		$10,000
Cost of goods sold		
Fixed costs	$4,000	
Variable costs (60% of $10,000)	6,000	10,000
Profit		0

In this solution, the break-even point has been expressed in terms of dollars of sales. It may be converted into a break-even point in terms of units sold or percent of plant capacity required. The break-even point in terms of units of product is $10,000 ÷ $10, or 1,000 units. The break-even point in terms of percent of plant capacity is 1,000 ÷ 3,000, or 33⅓%.

In order for a break-even-point calculation to be meaningful, the physical quantity of production and sales must be essentially equal.

The denominator of the break-even point formula $[1 - (V/S)]$, when expressed as a ratio, becomes the *marginal-income ratio*, which is often referred to as the *profit-volume ratio* or *p/v ratio*.

VOLUME ACTIVITY REQUIRED TO PRODUCE A DESIRED PROFIT. The primary objective of the typical business firm is the making of a profit. The sales necessary to produce the desired profit can be calculated by recourse to a slightly modified break-even-point formula. For example:

$$R = \frac{F + P}{1 - (V/S)}$$

where R = required sales

F = total fixed expenses

V = unit variable expenses

S = unit sales prices

P = desired profit

Thus, if in this case a profit of $4,000 is desired, the required sales level would be calculated as follows:

$$R = \frac{\$4,000 + \$4,000}{1 - \%_{10}} = \frac{\$8,000}{\%_{10}} = \$8,000 \times 1\%_4 = \$20,000$$

PROOF

Sales		$20,000
Cost of sales		
Fixed costs	$ 4,000	
Variable costs (60% of 20,000)	12,000	16,000
Profit		$ 4,000

MARGIN OF SAFETY. *Margin of safety*, often referred to as the *M/S ratio*, is closely associated with break-even analysis. It is the relationship of sales above the break-even point to total sales. It indicates the amount or the percentage by which a firm's sales may decrease before a loss is sustained.

For example, if sales were $20,000 and the break-even point were $16,000, the *M/S* would be $4,000, or [($20,000 − $16,000) ÷ $20,000] 20%.

RATIO ANALYSIS

A *ratio* is the expressed quantitative relationship between two numbers or two similar quantities. It is the resulting quotient of one number divided by another number; in other words, it is the factor that when multiplied by one of the two numbers will produce the other number.

A ratio may be written as a fraction (¾), as an indicated division (3 ÷ 4), as a percentage (75%), or as an indicated relationship (3 : 4). The latter expression is frequently reduced so that the divisor is equal to one (.75 : 1). In fact, the unity of the divisor is implied when only the dividend is given as 75% or .75.

The relationship between two numbers must be significant if their ratio is to be significant. A ratio is more informative when compared with some standard or base, such as a firm or industry standard, previous-period ratios, or the ratios of another company.

In accounting, ratio analysis refers to the establishment of significant relationships between various items appearing in the financial statements or in similar reports.

Well-selected ratios will aid in determining the solvency, profitability, and managerial efficiency of a given firm. Also, ratios may be used as a common denominator in making comparisons of two or more firms.

Income-Statement Ratios. *Income-statement ratios* are so called because they establish a relationship between two numbers or groups of numbers appearing on the income statement. In the case of income-statement ratios, net sales are generally used as the divisor of the other income-statement number or group of numbers. As has been mentioned, in vertical analysis of an income statement (Figure 18.3), every other significant quantity on the statement may be divided by net sales, with net sales equal to 100 percent.

OPERATING RATIO. The *operating ratio* is the relationship of total operating expenses to net sales; written as a formula, it is:

$$\frac{\text{Total operating expenses}}{\text{Net sales}}$$

This ratio provides an indication of the operating efficiency of the firm.

The operating ratio should not be confused with the operating ratios, which are more specifically referred to as expense ratios or earning ratios.

EXPENSE RATIOS. *Expense ratios* often provide valuable information about the relationship between specific expenses and sales. Thus, the formula for the ratio of cost of goods sold to sales would be:

$$\frac{\text{Cost of goods sold}}{\text{Net sales}}$$

The ratio for depreciation would be:

$$\frac{\text{Depreciation}}{\text{Net sales}}$$

EARNING RATIO. The *earning ratio* gives an insight into the profitability of the firm. The earning ratio is complementary to the operating ratio. Written as a formula, it is:

$$\frac{\text{Net income}}{\text{Net sales}}$$

Balance-Sheet Ratios. *Balance-sheet ratios* take their generic name from the fact that in each case a relationship is established between two numbers or groups of numbers appearing on the balance sheet.

Whereas income-statement ratios are useful in evaluating a firm's operating efficiency and profitability, balance-sheet ratios are useful in evaluating a firm's liquidity and financial position.

There are many possible balance-sheet ratios. A few of the more significant ones are discussed in the paragraphs that follow.

CURRENT RATIO. The *current ratio,* also referred to as the *bankers' ratio,* is calculated by dividing the current assets by the current liabilities. The ratio of current assets to current liabilities is of great value to short-term creditors because it indicates the borrower's ability to pay his current obligations as they mature.

In the past, a rule of thumb held that a current ratio of 2 to 1 was ideal. It is now thought that such a generalization is inappropriate, that the current ratio should vary among industries and perhaps even among firms in the same industry.

QUICK RATIO. The *quick ratio,* often referred to as the *acid-test ratio,* is a refinement of the current ratio. It is calculated by dividing the sum of cash, accounts and notes receivable, and marketable securities by the total current liabilities. By excluding inventories and prepaid items from this ratio, the speedy generation of cash for quick payment of liabilities is stressed. Those who held that a current ratio of 2 to 1 was ideal generally held that a quick ratio of 1 to 1 was also ideal. Now it is believed that a satisfactory quick ratio may vary from industry to industry and from firm to firm. In fact, because of the seasonality of cash generation and cash needs, it may be expected to vary within the industry or firm from season to season.

NET WORKING CAPITAL. *Net working capital* is not a ratio in the true sense of the term because it is the *difference* between the current assets and the current liabilities, rather than the *relationship* that results from dividing current assets by current liabilities (which yields the current ratio). It is included in this discussion because of its close connection with both the current ratio and the quick ratio. The net-working-capital figure indicates the amount by which the current assets can shrink and still cover the current liabilities.

The net working capital is sometimes referred to as *working capital.* In any event, working capital should not be confused with the *working-capital ratio,* which is another name occasionally used for the current ratio.

DEBT TO TOTAL ASSETS. The relationship of *debt to total assets,* as the name implies, is established by dividing total debt by total assets.

OWNERS' EQUITY TO TOTAL ASSETS. The relationship of *owners' equity to total assets* is complementary to the debt-to-total-assets ratio. These two ratios show how the assets of the firm are financed. They indicate the relative strength of the firm.

FIXED ASSETS TO LONG-TERM DEBT. The relationship of *fixed assets (plant and equipment) to long-term debt* indicates the relative security provided long-term creditors when fixed assets are pledged as security for such obligations. If the ratio is high (i.e., the value of the assets is substantially greater than the obligations), it would indicate financial strength and a possible source of additional debt financing.

Mixed Ratios. *Mixed ratios,* sometimes referred to as *interstatement ratios,* are so called because each of the two numbers in the comparison are taken from different statements.

ACCOUNTS RECEIVABLE TURNOVER. *Accounts receivable turnover* is calculated by dividing credit sales for the period, usually the fiscal year, by the average trade receivables (accounts and notes). If possible, average receivables should be determined on a monthly basis because the amount of the receivables should be close to an annual low at the end of the fiscal year. If such were the case, and only year-end receivables were used in the calculation, it would yield an inflated turnover figure. This ratio indicates the speed with which the receivables are converted into cash. Some prefer to express this liquidity index as the *number of days sales in receivables*. This is easily accomplished by one additional step. If, for example, it is established that the receivables turn over ten times a year and that the year contains 300 selling days, then it can be said that there are 30 days' sales in the receivables ($300 \div 10$).

INVENTORY TURNOVER. *Inventory turnover* is calculated by dividing cost of goods sold by the average cost of inventory. Whenever possible, the average inventory developed on a monthly basis should be used in order to avoid a distortedly high turnover figure. In some cases, cost figures are not available; then net sales to average inventory at retail (selling price) may be used.

Such a turnover figure may give an indication of the amount of control over inventory and the effectiveness with which funds have been used for the inventory. If an inventory turns over slowly, it may indicate poor planning and control, as well as the inefficient use of funds. If an inventory turns over frequently, it tends to indicate good planning and control, as well as efficient use of funds. However, the most rapid turnover of merchandise would result from having practically no inventory at all, as a consequence of buying merchandise as orders are taken. The delays in filling orders, of course, could cause customer dissatisfaction and consequently a loss of potential sales.

The best inventory turnover is attained when the most profitable relationship is achieved between the costs of acquiring and carrying the inventory and the revenue resulting from the sales of that inventory. If the inventory and the inventory costs are too small, the loss of potential sales will be excessive. As the inventory is increased, it may be expected that revenue will increase more than expenses, *up to a point*. After that point has been reached, inventory expenses will increase more rapidly than revenue from sales.

SALES TO TOTAL PRODUCTIVE ASSETS. The relationship of sales to average total productive assets, sometimes referred to as *asset turnover*, is obtained by dividing sales (preferably *net* sales) by the total value of the assets used directly or indirectly in producing those sales. Assets held for possible future use or investments not related to the production of the sales should be excluded from the divisor. This ratio indicates the contribution made to sales by the utilization of the assets.

RATE EARNED ON TOTAL PRODUCTIVE ASSETS. This rate (ratio) is obtained by dividing net income (excluding extraordinary income or loss and income or loss from financial investments) by the average total productive assets. It indicates the profitability of the investment in assets used for production.

RATE EARNED ON STOCKHOLDERS' EQUITY. The *rate earned on the stockholders' equity* is calculated by dividing net income by the average stockholders' equity.

Entrepreneurial capital should always command some return commensurate with the risks involved and the value of goods or services provided. This rate will indicate the efficiency of management and the adequacy of the return with respect to alternative investments.

Rate Earned by Preferred Stock. The rate earned by preferred stock depends on the preferences and restrictions placed on the preferred stock. In general, the rate earned is the portion of net income available to the preferred stock divided by the value of the preferred stock. If the preferred stock is nonparticipating and noncumulative, the return on it could not be greater than the amount stipulated as the dividend amount, and even this is contingent upon its being earned and declared. If the preferred stock is fully participating and noncumulative, the earnings will be available proportionately to the preferred stock and the common stock.

Rate Earned by Common Stock. The rate earned by common stock is established by subtracting the amount of earnings allotted to preferred stock from total earnings and then dividing that amount by the common-stock equity.

TIMES INTEREST EARNED. *Times interest earned,* also referred to as *times fixed charges earned,* is a ratio arrived at by dividing net income before fixed charges and income taxes by the fixed charges. This ratio indicates the ability of the firm to pay the fixed charges. For creditors, this ratio indicates the safety of their investment.

Preferably, the ratio should be calculated before income taxes (as has been indicated); however, there are some accountants who calculate it on income after income taxes, with a resulting smaller number of times earned. Therefore, in judging the quality of the times-earned figure, it is necessary to determine if the ratio was calculated on income before or after income taxes.

Other Ratios. Some ratios depend for their calculation on data not necessarily provided entirely on the financial statements. Three significant ones are explained in the following paragraphs.

EARNINGS PER SHARE. The *earnings per share* are obtained by dividing the earnings available to the particular class of stock by the number of shares in the class.

PRICE-EARNINGS RATIO. The *price-earnings ratio* is established by dividing the market price of a given class of stock by its per-share earnings.

The price-earnings ratio and the earnings per share provide significant information to investors and financial analysts about the quality of the stock as an investment.

DIVIDENDS PER SHARE. *Dividends per share* represent the amount of money or other assets actually paid, or to be paid, to the stockholders on a per-share basis. There is a significant difference between earnings per share and dividends per share because a stockholder has no claim to the corporate earnings except as dividends are declared.

Problems

(Identified by the number of the chapter in which information related to the problem may be found.)

2.1 *Required:* A bank reconciliation statement.

The unadjusted cash balance of the Ray Lite Company as of December 31, 1973, was $8,820. Their bank statement of the same date showed a balance of $9,500. Additional pertinent data is as follows: On December 31, the company had issued four checks, for a total of $600, that did not clear the bank until in January. On the evening of December 31, the company had made a night deposit of $800 that was not recorded by the bank until January 2. Included in the canceled checks that the bank returned with the December statement was a Raymond Company check for $100 that the bank had charged to the Ray Lite account. The bank had collected a $1,000 draft for Ray Lite. Notification of the collection was included with the bank statement. A service charge of $20 was included on the bank statement.

2.2 *Required:* Calculate the loss on bad debts

(a) If the loss is calculated at ½ percent of sales
(b) If the loss is calculated by raising the balance in the allowance account of 2½ percent of the receivables balance

The James Company made sales of $100,000 during the year. At the end of the year, the accounts receivable balance was $20,000, and the allowance for loss on bad debts balance was $200.

3.1 *Required:* Calculate the inventory value by the gross-profit method.

The Alrite Company had a beginning inventory of $80,000 and purchases during the period of $450,000. During the same period, sales amounted to $800,000. The rate of gross profit is estimated at 40 percent.

3.2 *Required:* Calculate the inventory value at lower of cost or market by the retail-inventory method.

The Discount Sales Company made the following data available:

	Cost	Retail
Beginning inventory	$ 50,000	$ 80,000
Purchases	100,000	200,000
Freight-in	10,000	
Additional markups—net		40,000
Markdowns—net		20,000
Sales		200,000

4.1 *Required:* The value of the ending inventory

(a) If the periodic-inventory method is used, and
(b) If the perpetual-inventory method is used.

In each case, the inventory should be valued by (i) the FIFO method and (ii) the LIFO method.

The firm had a beginning balance of 200 units at a unit cost of $4. During the month, the purchases and issuances were as follows:

	Receipts	Issues
January 2	200 @ $5	
5	300 @ 6	
6		400
10	400 @ 7	
15		100
25	200 @ 8	
30		400

4.2 *Required:* The value of the inventories at the end of years 1, 2, 3, and 4 by the dollar-value LIFO method.

The X Company provided the following inventory data:

Year	Base Prices	Current Prices
0	$ 80,000	$ 80,000
1	100,000	120,000
2	120,000	156,000
3	130,000	182,000
4	100,000	120,000

4.3 *Required:* Calculate the optimum order size for part 12x.

The James Company expected to use 1,200 units of part 12x during the year. The costs of placing and receiving each order is estimated to be $6, and the cost of carrying a unit in stock is estimated at $1.

4.4 *Required:* Calculate the reorder point.

The cost accountant for the Johns Manufacturing Company developed the following data:

Optimum order size, 800 units
Usage during lead time, 400 units
Unit carrying cost, $2
Estimated annual unit stock-out cost, $30

5.1 *Required:* A journal entry to record the purchase of a temporary investment.

Assume the purchase of a $1,000, 6 percent bond at 102 plus two months' accrued interest.

5.2 *Required:* A journal entry to record the receipt of the semiannual interest on the bond purchased in problem 5.1.

6.1 *Required:* The cost of each lot by the basket-purchase method.

A developer paid $10,000 for a tract of land that he divided into six building lots. Before the lots could be sold, the developer would have to construct roads and sewers at an estimated cost of $20,000. The lots designated A, B, C, D, E, and F are expected to sell for the following respective prices: $5,000, $5,000, $6,000, $7,000, $8,000, and $9,000.

6.2 *Required:* Calculate the value at which the new machine should be recorded on

(a) The tax basis
(b) The replacement or accounting basis

The Exor Company traded an old truck for a new truck that is listed at $14,000. The old truck has a current book value of $4,000 and a trade-in value of $6,000. The truck dealer will accept the old truck and $8,000 for the new truck.

6.3 *Required:* Calculate the amount of the insurance claim.
The Imperial Box Company building, which was insured for $80,000, had a book value of $100,000. The building had a replacement value of $200,000. The building was 50 percent destroyed by fire. The insurance policy carried an 80 percent coinsurance clause.

7.1 *Required:* Calculate the first year's depreciation by each of the following methods:

(a) Straight line
(b) Units of output
(c) Sum of years' digits
(d) Double declining balance

The Omar Company purchased a machine for $15,000. It will have no salvage value at the end of its useful life, which may be estimated in either time or output. It is estimated that the machine will last for five years or for the production of 150,000 units of product. The first year, 40,000 units were produced.

7.2 *Required:* Calculate the depreciation to be recorded by

(a) The replacement method
(b) The retirement method

The Bangor Company replaced a machine that cost $5,000 with a machine that cost $6,000.

7.3 *Required:* Calculate the amount of unit depletion to be taken during the year.
The Apex Mining Company bought a tract of land for $800,000. It is estimated that the tract of land contains 50,000 tons of commercially recoverable ore. It is expected that after the mining

operation, it will cost $10,000 to restore the land according to legal requirements, at which time the land could be sold for $60,000. During the year, 12,000 tons of ore were extracted and sold.

8.1 *Required:* Journal entry to record the appraisal increase. The Millville Company purchased a building for $40,000 twenty years ago; it was expected to last for forty years. The building now has an appraised replacement cost new of $80,000 and an estimated remaining life of twenty years.

8.2 *Required:* Journal entry to record the annual building depreciation for problem 8.1

9.1 *Required:* Calculate the annual amortization for the patent.

The Baker Company incurred the following costs in developing and patenting a formula that is estimated to have commercial value for ten years:

Research	$300,000
Legal fees	50,000
Cost of winning an infringement suit	250,000

9.2 *Required:* Calculate the amount of goodwill based on

(a) Three year's excess earnings
(b) Capitalization of excess earnings

The Wayne Company, which is considering selling its entire operation to a New York syndicate, is concerned about the value of the goodwill that should be included in the selling price and has asked for two different calculations. The firm's net assets exclusive of goodwill are appraised at $1,000,000. The annual net income for the past five years has averaged $200,000, or 20 percent. The normal rate for this industry is only 10 percent.

10.1 *Required:* The cost allocated to

(a) Stock rights
(b) Stock

John Brown bought 1,000 shares of X Company stock for $90,000. The company issued rights at a time when a share of stock had a market value of $95 and a right had a market value of $5.

10.2 *Required:* Determine the amount of the cash disbursement required to purchase a $1,000 bond if

(a) The price is 98 "and interest"
(b) 98 "flat"

The Alpha Company is selling its 6 percent bonds two months after the last interest date at 98.

11.1 *Required:* Calculate the amount due the vice-president if the bonus is based on

(a) Income before both income taxes and bonus
(b) Income before income taxes but after bonus
(c) Income before bonus but after income taxes
(d) Income after both income taxes and bonus

The Doylestown Corporation pays its vice-president a bonus of 25 percent of annual earnings in excess of $200,000. The corporate income-tax rate is assumed to be 50 percent. The net profit before income taxes and bonus was established at $600,000.

11.2 *Required:* Calculate the amount that should be charged to work in process for the week as labor and labor-related costs

(a) If work in process is charged with the vacation costs as they accrue
(b) If factory overhead is charged with vacation costs when paid

The Allentown Corporation employs fifty direct workers at $4 per hour. The men work forty hours per week for fifty weeks a year. The plant is closed for two weeks each year for vacations, during which time each employee draws his normal weekly pay.

12.1 *Required:* Calculate

(a) The total annual interest expense
(b) The total annual cash disbursement

The Morgantown Company issued 100 $1,000 6 percent ten-year bonds at 95. The discount is being amortized on a straight-line basis.

12.2 *Required:* Calculate the total borrowing costs involved in the bond issue.

The Smithville Company issued 100 $1,000 6 percent ten-year bonds at 98. The bonds were retired at maturity.

13.1 *Required:* Journal entry to record the stock issue.

The Greene Corporation issued 1,000 shares of $100 par value stock at $98.

13.2 *Required:* Journal entry to record the purchase of treasury stock

(a) By cost method
(b) By the noncost method

The Browning Company had issued 1,000 shares of $100 par value stock at $105. The company has just purchased 100 of these shares for the treasury at $102.

14.1 *Required:* Journal entry to record stock retirement.

The Blackstone Corporation had issued 1,000 shares of $100 par value stock at par. The corporation has just bought 100 of these shares at $95 and retired them.

14.2 *Required:* Journal entry to record a stock assessment.

The Ardmore Corporation had issued 1,000 shares of no-par stock. Because of financial difficulties, a $5-per-share assessment had been agreed upon and paid by the stockholders.

15.1 *Required:* Determine the maximum amount that may be paid out in dividends.

In its treasury the Jewel Company has 100 shares of stock for which it paid $9,500. The company has total retained earnings of $15,000.

15.2 *Required:* Determine the amount available for dividends.

The net worth section of the Worthington Company shows the following balances:

Capital stock par $100	$100,000
Premium on capital stock	5,000
Retained earnings reserved for bond redemption per bond	
indenture	40,000
Retained earnings voluntarily reserved for plant expansion	50,000
Unappropriated retained earnings	20,000

16.1 *Required:* A multiple-step income statement for the High Street Company, showing, among other things

(a) Cost of goods sold
(b) Gross profit
(c) Operating income
(d) Net income after taxes

The High Street Company reported the following revenue and expense items for the calendar year 1974.

Inventory, January 1, 1974	$ 80,000
Inventory, December 31, 1974	90,000
Purchases	245,000
Purchase discounts	5,000
Freight-in	10,000
Gross sales	500,000
Sales discounts	10,000
Sales salaries	30,000
Officers salaries	40,000
Advertising	10,000
Taxes	50,000
Depreciation—office equipment	5,000
Depreciation—delivery equipment	5,000
Interest expense	6,000
Income taxes	54,000

16.2 *Required:* A balance sheet for the Broad Street Company for December 31, 1974, showing, among other things

(a) Total current assets
(b) Total current liabilities
(c) Net working capital
(d) Net capital invested
(e) Total equity investment

The company's real accounts showed the following balances:

Cash	$ 8,000
Accounts receivable	30,000
Notes receivable	20,000
Interest receivable	1,000
Inventory	80,000
Prepaid insurance	2,000
Allowance for bad debts	1,000
Accounts payable	20,000
Interest payable	1,000
Notes payable	10,000
Wages payable	9,000
Land	60,000
Buildings	500,000
Equipment	600,000
Accumulated depreciation—building	200,000
Accumulated depreciation—equipment	200,000
Bonds payable	300,000
Unamortized bond discount	10,000
Capital stock	500,000
Premium on capital stock	10,000
Retained earnings reserved for bond retirement	50,000
Retained earnings unappropriated	10,000

17.1 *Required:* A statement of changes in financial position when funds are regarded as total assets.

The Manion Company's comparative balance sheet is as follows:

THE MANION COMPANY

COMPARATIVE BALANCE SHEET
As of DECEMBER 31, 1973 AND DECEMBER 31, 1974

	December 31, 1973	December 31, 1974
ASSETS		
Current assets		
Cash	$ 60,000	$ 90,000
Receivables—net	40,000	70,000
Inventory	100,000	150,000
Total current assets	$200,000	$ 310,000

Noncurrent assets		
Land	$ 60,000	$ 80,000
Buildings	300,000	300,000
Less: Accumulated depreciation	(50,000)	(70,000)
Equipment	500,000	800,000
Less: Accumulated depreciation	(100,000)	(150,000)
Total noncurrent assets	$710,000	$ 960,000
Total assets	$910,000	$1,270,000

Liabilities and Owners' Equity

LIABILITIES

Current liabilities		
Accounts payable	$ 20,000	$ 30,000
Notes payable	10,000	15,000
Accrued expenses	10,000	5,000
Total current liabilities	$ 40,000	$ 50,000

OWNERS' EQUITY

Capital stock[a]	$820,000	$1,140,000
Retained earnings	50,000	80,000
Total owners' equity	$870,000	$1,220,000
Total liabilities and owners' equity	$910,000	$1,270,000

[a] The stock was issued in exchange for the additional land and equipment.

17.2 *Required:* A statement of changes in financial position for the Manion Company (problem 17.1) when funds are considered as net quick assets.

18.1 *Required:* Calculate the break-even point for the company expressed in terms of

(a) Money
(b) Volume (units)
(c) Percent of plant capacity

The Miller Company, with a plant capacity of 200,000 units and fixed expenses of $400,000, incurs $6 variable expenses per unit. Each unit sells for $10.

18.2 *Required:* Calculate the dollar sales that the company must have in order to make a profit of $40,000.

The Jones Company has fixed expenses of $20,000. The unit variable cost is $3, and the selling price is $5.

Answers

2.1 Corrected balance $9,800

2.2 (a) $500 (b) $300

3.1 $50,000

3.2 $50,000

4.1 (a) Periodic   (b) Perpetual
    (i) FIFO $1,600   (i) FIFO $1,600
   (ii) LIFO $1,000   (ii) LIFO $1,200

4.2

Years	Value
1	$104,000
2	130,000
3	144,000
4	104,000

4.3 120 units

4.4 350 units

5.1

Investment in bonds	$1,020	
Accrued interest receivable	10	
Cash		$1,030

5.2

Cash	$ 30	
Accrued interest receivable		$ 10
Interest income		20

6.1

A $3,750		D $5,250
B 3,750		E 6,000
C 4,500		F 6,750

6.2   (a) $12,000   (b) $14,000

6.3 $50,000

7.1   (a) $3,000   (b) $4,000   (c) $5,000   (d) $6,000

7.2   (a) $6,000   (b) $5,000

7.3 $180,000

8.1   Building—appraisal increase $40,000
           Accumulated depreciation—
                appraisal increase $20,000
           Appraisal capital   20,000

8.2   Depreciation $ 2,000
           Accumulated depreciation $ 1,000
           Accumulated depreciation—
                appraisal increase   1,000

9.1 $60,000

9.2   (a) $300,000   (b) $1,000,000

10.1   (a) $4,500   (b) $85,500

10.2   (a) $990   (b) $980

11.1   (a) $100,000   (b) $80,000   (c) $28,571.43
        (d) $22,222.22

11.2   (a) $8,320   (b) $8,000

12.1   (a) $6,500   (b) $6,000

12.2 $62,000

13.1   Cash $98,000
        Discount on capital stock   2,000
           Capital stock $100,000

13.2   (a) Treasury stock $10,200
               Cash $ 10,200

        (b) Treasury stock $10,000
            Premium on capital stock   500
               Contributed capital—
                    treasury stock $ 300
               Cash   10,200

14.1 Capital Stock $10,000
    Contributed capital—
      stock retirement $ 500
      Cash   9,500

14.2 Cash $ 5,000
    Contributed capital—
      stock assessment $ 5,000

15.1 $5,500

15.2 $20,000 (or $70,000 if board orders a release of the voluntary reservation)

16.1 (a) $240,000   (b) $250,000   (c) $110,000
    (d) $50,000

16.2 (a) $140,000   (b) $40,000   (c) $100,000
    (d) $570,000   (e) $570,000

17.1 Total source (and application) of funds $420,000

17.2 Quick assets provided $370,000
    Quick assets applied   320,000
      Increase in quick assets $ 50,000

18.1 (a) $1,000,000   (b) 100,000   (c) 50%

18.2 $150,000

Index

Variables
  price, 42
  quantity, 43
  rate, 43
  time, 43

Wasting assets, 85, 123
Watered stock, 213
Where got, where gone statement, 241

Working-capital ratio, 292
Work in process
  inventory, 33
  turnover, 73

Year
  calendar, 242
  fiscal, 242
  natural business, 242